THE KIERKEGAARD COLLECTION

SOREN KIERKEGAARD

Happy Hour Books

Published by:

HAPPY HOUR BOOKS

www.happyhoursbooks.com

email: happyhourbooks1@gmail.com

First published by Happy Hour Books 2023

Title : **The Kierkegaard Collection**

Paperback ISBN : 9789358480511

Hardback ISBN : 9789358480528

FEAR AND TREMBLING

INTRODUCTION II

Not only in the world of commerce but also in the world of ideas our age has arranged a regular clearance-sale. Everything may be had at such absurdly low prices that very soon the question will arise whether any one cares to bid. Every waiter with a speculative turn who carefully marks the significant progress of modern philosophy, every lecturer in philosophy, every tutor, student, every sticker-and-quitter of philosophy—they are not content with doubting everything, but "go right on." It might, possibly, be ill-timed and inopportune to ask them whither they are bound; but it is no doubt polite and modest to take it for granted that they have doubted everything—else it were a curious statement for them to make, that they were proceeding onward. So they have, all of them, completed that preliminary operation and, it would seem, with such ease that they do not think it necessary to waste a word about how they did it. The fact is, not even he who looked anxiously and with a troubled spirit for some little point of information, ever found one, nor any instruction, nor even any little dietetic prescription, as to how one is to accomplish this enormous task. "But did not Descartes proceed in this fashion?" Descartes, indeed! that venerable, humble, honest thinker whose writings surely no one can read without deep emotion—Descartes did what he said, and said what he did. Alas, alas! that is a mighty rare thing in our times! But Descartes, as he says frequently enough, never uttered doubts concerning his faith....

In our times, as was remarked, no one is content with faith, but "goes right on." The question as to whither they are proceeding may be a silly question; whereas it is a sign of urbanity and culture to assume that every one has faith, to begin with, for else it were a curious statement for them to make, that they are proceeding further. In the olden days it was different. Then, faith was a task for a whole life-time because it was held that proficiency in faith was not to be won within a few days or weeks. Hence, when the tried patriarch felt his end approaching, after having fought his battles and preserved his faith, he was still young enough at heart not to have forgotten the fear and trembling which disciplined his youth and which the mature man has under control, but which no one entirely outgrows—except insofar as he succeeds in "going on" as early as possible. The goal which those venerable men reached at last—at that spot every one starts, in our times, in order to "proceed further."...

PREPARATION

There lived a man who, when a child, had heard the beautiful Bible story of how God tempted Abraham and how he stood the test, how he maintained his faith and, against his expectations, received his son back again. As this man grew older he read this same story with ever greater admiration; for now life had separated what had been united in the reverent simplicity of the child. And the older he grew, the more frequently his thoughts reverted to that story. His enthusiasm waxed stronger and stronger, and yet the story grew less and less clear to him. Finally he forgot everything else in thinking about it, and his soul contained but one wish, which was, to behold Abraham: and but one longing, which was, to have been witness to that event. His desire was, not to see the beautiful lands of the Orient, and not the splendor of the Promised Land, and not the reverent couple whose old age the Lord had blessed with children, and not the venerable figure of the aged patriarch, and not the god-given vigorous youth of Isaac—it would have been the same to him if the event had come to pass on some barren heath. But his wish was, to have been with Abraham on the three days' journey, when he rode with sorrow before him and with Isaac at his side. His wish was, to have been present at the moment when Abraham lifted up his eyes and saw Mount Moriah afar off; to have been present at the moment when he left his asses behind and wended his way up to the mountain alone with Isaac. For the mind of this man was busy, not with the delicate conceits of the imagination, but rather with his shuddering thought.

The man we speak of was no thinker, he felt no desire to go beyond his faith: it seemed to him the most glorious fate to be remembered as the Father of Faith, and a most enviable lot to be possessed of that faith, even if no one knew it.

The man we speak of was no learned exegetist, he did not even understand Hebrew—who knows but a knowledge of Hebrew might have helped him to understand readily both the story and Abraham.

I

And God tempted Abraham and said unto him: take Isaac, thine only son, whom thou lovest and go to the land Moriah and sacrifice him there on a mountain which I shall show thee.[1]

It was in the early morning, Abraham arose betimes and had his asses saddled. He departed from his tent, and Isaac with him; but Sarah looked out of the window after them until they were out of sight. Silently they rode for three days; but on the fourth morning Abraham said not a word but lifted up his eyes and beheld Mount Moriah in the distance. He left his servants behind and, leading Isaac by the hand, he approached the mountain. But Abraham said to himself: "I shall surely conceal from Isaac whither he is going." He stood still, he laid his hand on Isaac's head to bless him, and Isaac bowed down to receive his blessing. And Abraham's aspect was fatherly, his glance was mild, his speech admonishing. But Isaac understood him not, his soul would not rise to him; he embraced Abraham's knees, he besought him at his feet, he begged for his young life, for his beautiful hopes, he recalled the joy in Abraham's house when he was born, he reminded him of the sorrow and the loneliness that would be after him. Then did Abraham raise up the youth and lead him by his hand, and his words were full of consolation and admonishment. But Isaac understood him not. He ascended Mount Moriah, but Isaac understood him not. Then Abraham averted his face for a moment; but when Isaac looked again, his father's countenance was changed, his glance wild, his aspect terrible, he seized Isaac and threw him to the ground and said: "Thou foolish lad, believest thou I am thy father? An idol-worshipper am I. Believest thou it is God's command? Nay, but my pleasure." Then Isaac trembled and cried out in his fear: "God in heaven, have pity on me, God of Abraham, show mercy to me, I have no father on earth, be thou then my father!" But Abraham said softly to himself: "Father in heaven, I thank thee. Better is it that he believes me inhuman than that he should lose his faith in thee."

When the child is to be weaned, his mother blackens her breast; for it were a pity if her breast should look sweet to him when he is not to have it. Then the child believes that her breast has changed; but his mother is ever the same, her glance is full of love and as tender as ever. Happy he who needed not worse means to wean his child!

II

It was in the early morning. Abraham arose betimes and embraced Sarah, the bride of his old age. And Sarah kissed Isaac who had taken the shame from her—Isaac, her pride, her hope for all coming generations. Then the twain rode silently along their way, and Abraham's glance was fastened on the ground before him; until on the fourth day, when he lifted up his eyes and beheld Mount Moriah in the distance; but then his eyes again sought the ground. Without a word he put the fagots in order and bound Isaac, and without a word he unsheathed his knife. Then he beheld the ram God had chosen, and sacrificed him, and wended his way home.... From that day on Abraham, grew old. He could not forget that God had required this of him. Isaac flourished as before; but Abraham's eye was darkened, he saw happiness no more.

When the child has grown and is to be weaned, his mother will in maidenly fashion conceal her breast. Then the child has a mother no longer. Happy the child who lost not his mother in any other sense!

III

It was in the early morning. Abraham arose betimes; he kissed Sarah, the young mother, and Sarah kissed Isaac, her joy, her delight for all times. And Abraham rode on his way, lost in thought—he was thinking of Hagar and her son whom he had driven out into the wilderness. He ascended Mount Moriah and he drew the knife.

It was a calm evening when Abraham rode out alone, and he rode to Mount Moriah. There he cast himself down on his face and prayed to God to forgive him his sin in that he had been about to sacrifice his son Isaac, and in that the father had forgotten his duty toward his son. And yet oftener he rode on his lonely way, but he found no rest. He could not grasp that it was a sin that he had wanted to sacrifice to God his most precious possession, him for whom he would most gladly have died many times. But, if it was a sin, if he had not loved Isaac thus, then could he not grasp the possibility that he could be forgiven: for what sin more terrible?

When the child is to be weaned, the mother is not without sorrow that she and her child are to be separated more and more, that the child who had first lain under her heart, and afterwards at any rate rested at her breast, is to be so near to her no more. So they sorrow together for that brief while. Happy he who kept his child so near to him and needed not to sorrow more!

IV

It was in the early morning. All was ready for the journey in the house of Abraham. He bade farewell to Sarah; and Eliezer, his faithful servant, accompanied him along the way for a little while. They rode together in peace, Abraham and Isaac, until they came to Mount Moriah. And Abraham prepared everything for the sacrifice, calmly and mildly; but when his father turned aside in order to unsheathe his knife, Isaac saw that Abraham's left hand was knit in despair and that a trembling shook his frame—but Abraham drew forth the knife.

Then they returned home again, and Sarah hastened to meet them; but Isaac had lost his faith. No one in all the world ever said a word about this, nor did Isaac speak to any man concerning what he had seen, and Abraham suspected not that any one had seen it.

When the child is to be weaned, his mother has the stronger food ready lest the child perish. Happy he who has in readiness this stronger food!

Thus, and in many similar ways, thought the man whom I have mentioned about this event. And every time he returned, after a pilgrimage to Mount Moriah, he sank down in weariness, folding his hands and saying: "No one, in truth, was great as was Abraham, and who can understand him?"

THE SICKNESS UNTO DEATH

Preface

To many the form of this "exposition" will perhaps seem strange; it will seem to them too strict to be edifying, and too edifying to be strictly scientific. As to this latter point I have no opinion. As to the first, however, this does not express my opinion of the matter; and if it were true that the form is too strict to be edifying, that, according to my conception, would be a fault. It is one question whether it cannot be edifying to everyone, seeing that not everyone possesses the capacity for following it; it is another question whether it possesses the specific character of the edifying. From the Christian point of view everything, absolutely everything should serve for edification. The sort of learning which is not in the last resort edifying is precisely for that reason unchristian. Everything that is Christian must bear some resemblance to the address which a physician makes beside the sick-bed: although it can be fully understood only by one who is versed in medicine, yet it must never be forgotten that it is pronounced beside the sick-bed. This relation of the Christian teaching to life (in contrast with a scientific aloofness from life), or this ethical side of Christianity, is essentially the edifying, and the form in which it is presented, however strict it may be, is altogether different, qualitatively different, from that sort of learning which is "indifferent," the lofty heroism of which is from a Christian point of view so far from being heroism that from a Christian point of view it is an inhuman sort of curiosity. The Christian heroism (and perhaps it is rarely to be seen) is to venture wholly to be oneself, as an individual man, this definite individual man, alone before the face of God, alone in this tremendous exertion and this tremendous responsibility; but it is not Christian heroism to be humbugged by the pure idea of humanity or to play the game of marveling at worldhistory. All Christian knowledge, however strict its form, ought to be anxiously concerned; but this concern is precisely the note of the edifying. Concern implies relationship to life, to the reality of personal existence, and thus in a Christian sense it is seriousness; the high aloofness of indifferent learning, is, from the Christian point of view, far from being seriousness, it is, from the Christian point of view, jest and vanity. But seriousness again is the edifying.

This little book therefore is in one sense composed in a way that a seminary student could write it; in another sense, however, in a way that perhaps not every professor could write it.

But the fact that the form in which this treatise is clothed is what it is, is at least the result of due reflection, and at all events it is certainly correct from a psychological point of view. There is a more solemn style which is so solemn that it does not signify much, and since one is too well accustomed to it, it easily becomes entirely meaningless.

Only one remark more, doubtless a superfluity, but for that I am willing to assume the blame: I would call attention once for all to the fact that in this whole book, as the title indeed says, despair is conceived as the sickness, not as the cure. So dialectical is despair. So also in the Christian terminology death is the expression for the greatest spiritual wretchedness, and yet the cure is simply to die, to "die from."

1848.

Introduction

"This sickness is not unto death" (John 11:4), and yet Lazarus died; for when the disciples misunderstood the words which Christ adjoined later, "Lazarus our friend is asleep, but I go to wake him out of his sleep" (11:11), He said plainly, "Lazarus is dead" (11:14). So then Lazarus is dead, and yet this sickness was not unto death; he was dead, and yet this sickness is not unto death. Now we know that Christ was thinking of the miracle which would permit the bystanders, "if they believed, to see the glory of God" (11:40), the miracle by which He awoke Lazarus from the dead, so that this sickness was not only not unto death, but, as Christ had foretold, "for the glory of God, that the Son of God might be glorified thereby" (11:4). Oh, but even if Christ had not awakened Lazarus from the dead, is it not true that this sickness, that death itself, was not a sickness unto death? When Christ comes to the grave and cries with a loud voice, "Lazarus, come forth" (11:43), it is evident enough that "this" sickness is not unto death. But even if Christ had not said these words -- merely the fact that He, who is "the resurrection and the life" (11:25), comes to the grave, is not this a sufficient sign that this sickness is not unto death, does not the fact that Christ exists mean that this sickness is not unto death? And what help would it have been to Lazarus to be awakened from the dead, if the thing must end after all with his dying -- how would that have helped Lazarus, if He did not live who is the resurrection and the life for everyone who believes in Him? No, it is not because Lazarus was awakened from the dead, not for this can one say that this sickness is not unto death; but because He lives, therefore this sickness is not unto death. For, humanly speaking, death is the last thing of all; and, humanly speaking, there is hope only so long as there is life. But Christianly understood death is by no means the last thing of all, hence it is only a little event within that which is all, an eternal life; and Christianly understood there is in death infinitely much more hope than merely humanly speaking there is when there not only is life but this life exhibits the fullest health and vigor.

So then in the Christian understanding of it not even death is the sickness unto death, still less everything which is called earthly and temporal suffering: want, sickness, wretchedness, affliction, adversities, torments, mental sufferings, sorrow, grief. And even if such things are so painful and hard to bear that we men say, or at all events the sufferer says, "This is worse than death" -- everything of the sort, which, if it is not a sickness, is comparable to a sickness, is nevertheless, in the Christian understanding of it, not the sickness unto death.

So it is that Christianity has taught the Christian to think dauntlessly of everything earthly and worldly, including death. It is almost as though the Christian must be puffed up because of this proud elevation above everything men commonly call misfortune, above that which men commonly call the greatest evil. But then in turn Christianity has discovered an evil which man as such does not know of; this misery is the sickness unto death. What the natural man considers horrible -- when he has in this wise enumerated everything and knows nothing more he can mention, this for the Christian is like a jest. Such is the relation between the natural man and the Christian; it is like the relation between a child and a man: what the child shudders at, the man regards as nothing. The child does not know what the dreadful is; this the man knows, and he shudders at it. The child's imperfection consists, first of all, in not knowing what the dreadful is; and then again, as an implication of this, in shuddering at that which is not dreadful. And so it is also with the natural man, he is ignorant of what the dreadful truly is, yet he is not thereby exempted from shuddering; no, he shudders at that which is not the dreadful: he does not know the true God, but this is not the whole of it, he worships an idol as God.

Only the Christian knows what is meant by the sickness unto death. He acquires as a Christian a courage which the natural man does not know -- this courage he acquires by learning fear for the still more dreadful. Such is the way a man always acquires courage; when one fears a greater danger, it is as though the other did not exist. But the dreadful thing the Christian learned to know is "the sickness unto death."

Part 1: The Sickness unto Death is Despair

Chapter 1: That Despair is the Sickness Unto Death

A. Despair is a Sickness in the Spirit, in the Self, and So It May Assume a Triple Form: in Despair at Not Being Conscious of Having a Self (Despair Improperly So Called); in Despair at Not Willing to Be Oneself; in Despair at Willing to Be Oneself.

Man is spirit. But what is spirit? Spirit is the self. But what is the self? The self is a relation which relates itself to its own self, or it is that in the relation [which accounts for it] that the relation relates itself to its own self; the self is not the relation but [consists in the fact] that the relation relates itself to its own self. Man is a synthesis of the infinite and the finite, of the temporal and the eternal, of freedom and necessity, in short it is a synthesis. A synthesis is a relation between two factors. So regarded, man is not yet a self.

In the relation between two, the relation is the third term as a negative unity, and the two relate themselves to the relation, and in the relation to the relation; such a relation is that between soul and body, when man is regarded as soul. If on the contrary the relation relates itself to its own self, the relation is then the positive third term, and this is the self.

Such a relation which relates itself to its own self (that is to say, a self) must either have constituted itself or have been constituted by another.

If this relation which relates itself to its own self is constituted by another, the relation doubtless is the third term, but this relation (the third term) is in turn a relation relating itself to that which constituted the whole relation.

Such a derived, constituted, relation is the human self, a relation which relates itself to its own self, and in relating itself to its own self relates itself to another. Hence it is that there can be two forms of despair properly so called. If the human self-had constituted itself, there could be a question only of one form, that of not willing to be one's own self, of willing to get rid of oneself, but there would be no question of despairingly willing to be oneself. This formula [i.e. that the self is constituted by another] is the expression for the total dependence of the relation (the self namely), the expression for the fact that the self cannot of itself attain and remain in equilibrium and rest by itself, but only by relating itself to that Power which constituted the whole relation. Indeed, so far is it from being true that this second form of despair (despair at willing to be one's own self) denotes only a particular kind of despair, that on the contrary all despair can in the last analysis be reduced to this. If a man in despair is as he thinks conscious of his despair, does not talk about it meaninglessly as of something which befell him (pretty much as when a man who suffers from vertigo talks with nervous self-deception about a weight upon his head or about its being like something falling upon him, etc., this weight and this pressure being in fact not something external but an inverse reflection from an inward experience), and if by himself and by himself only he would abolish the despair, then by all the labor he expends he is only laboring himself deeper into a deeper despair. The disrelationship of despair is not a simple disrelationship but a disrelationship in a relation which relates itself to its own self and is constituted by another, so that the disrelationship in that self-relation reflects itself infinitely in the relation to the Power which constituted it.

This then is the formula which describes the condition of the self when despair is completely eradicated: by relating itself to its own self and by willing to be itself the self is grounded transparently in the Power which posited it.

B. Possibility and Actuality of Despair

Is despair an advantage or a drawback? Regarded in a purely dialectical way it is both. If one were to stick to the abstract notion of despair, without thinking of any concrete despairer, one might say that it is an immense advantage. The possibility of this sickness is man's advantage over the beast, and this advantage distinguishes him far more essentially than the erect posture, for it implies the infinite erectness or loftiness of being spirit. The possibility of this sickness is man's advantage over the beast; to be sharply observant of this sickness constitutes the Christian's advantage over the natural man; to be healed of this sickness is the Christian's bliss.

So, then it is an infinite advantage to be able to despair; and yet it is not only the greatest misfortune and misery to be in despair; no, it is perdition. Ordinarily there is no such relation between possibility and actuality; if it is an advantage to be able to be this or that, it is a still greater advantage to be such a thing. That is to say, being is related to the ability to be as an ascent. In the case of despair, on the contrary, being is related to the ability to be as a fall. Infinite as is the advantage of the possibility, just so great is the measure of the fall. So, in the case of despair the ascent consists in not being in despair. Yet this statement is open to misunderstanding. The thing of not being in despair is not like not being lame, blind, etc. In case the not being in despair means neither more nor less than not being this, then it is precisely to be it. The thing of not being in despair must mean the annihilation of the possibility of being this; if it is to be true that a man is not in despair, one must annihilate the possibility every instant.

Such is not ordinarily the relation between possibility and actuality. Although thinkers say[2] that actuality is the annihilated possibility, yet this is not entirely true; it is the fulfilled, the effective possibility. Here, on the contrary, the actuality (not being in despair), which in its very form is a negation, is the impotent, annihilated possibility; ordinarily, actuality in comparison with possibility is a confirmation, here it is a negation.

Despair is the disrelationship in a relation which relates itself to itself. But the synthesis is not the disrelationship, it is merely the possibility, or, in the synthesis is latent the possibility of the disrelationship. If the synthesis were the disrelationship, there would be no such thing as despair, for despair would then be something inherent in human nature as such, that is, it would not be despair, it would be something that befell a man, something he suffered passively, like an illness into which a man falls, or like death which is the lot of all. No, this thing of despairing is inherent in man himself; but if he were not a synthesis, he could not despair, neither could he despair if the synthesis were not originally from God's hand in the right relationship.

Whence then comes despair? From the relation wherein the synthesis relates itself to itself, in that God who made man a relationship lets this go as it were out of His hand, that is, in the fact that the relation relates itself to itself. And herein, in the fact that the relation is spirit, is the self, consists the responsibility under which all despair lies, and so lies every instant it exists, however much and however ingeniously the despairer, deceiving himself and others, may talk of his despair as a misfortune which has befallen him, with a confusion of things different, as in the case of vertigo aforementioned, with which, though it is qualitatively different, despair has much in common, since vertigo is under the rubric soul what despair is under the rubric spirit, and is pregnant with analogies to despair.

So when the disrelationship -- that is, despair -- has set in, does it follow as a matter of course that it continues? No, it does not follow as a matter of course; if the disrelationship continues, it does not follow as a consequence of the disrelation but as a consequence of the relation which relates itself to itself. That is to say, every time the disrelation expresses itself, and every instant it exists, it is to the relation one must revert. Observe that we speak of a man contracting a disease, maybe through carelessness. Then the illness sets in, and from that instant it affirms itself and is now an actuality, the origin of which recedes more and more into the past. It would be cruel and inhuman if one were to continue to say incessantly, "This instant thou, the sick man, art contracting this disease"; that is, if every instant one was to resolve the actuality of the disease into its possibility. It is true that he did contract the disease, but this he did only once; the continuance of the disease is a simple consequence of the fact that he once contracted it, its progress is not to be referred every instant to him as the cause; he contracted it, but one cannot say that he is contracting it. Not so with despair: every actual instant of despair is to be referred to possibility, every instant the man in despair is contracting it, it is constantly in the present tense, nothing comes to pass here as a consequence of a bygone actuality superseded; at every actual instant of despair the despairer bears as his responsibility all the foregoing experience in possibility as a present. This comes from the fact that despair is a qualification of spirit, that it is related to the eternal in man. But the eternal he cannot get rid of, no, not to all eternity; he cannot cast it from him once for all, nothing is more impossible; every instant he does not possess it he must have cast it or be casting it from him -- but it comes back, every instant he is in despair he contracts despair. For despair is not a result of the disrelationship but of the relation which relates itself to itself. And the relation to himself a man cannot get rid of, any more than he can get rid of himself, which moreover is one and the same thing, since the self is the relationship to oneself.

C. Despair is "The Sickness unto Death."

The concept of the sickness unto death must be understood, however, in a peculiar sense. Literally it means a sickness the end and outcome of which is death. Thus one speaks of a mortal sickness as synonymous with a sickness unto death. In this sense despair cannot be called the sickness unto death. But in the Christian understanding of it death itself is a transition unto life In view of this, there is from the Christian standpoint no earthly, bodily sickness unto death. For death is doubtless the last phase of the sickness, but death is not the last thing. If in the strictest sense we are to speak of a sickness unto death, it must be one in which the last thing is death, and death the last thing. And this precisely is despair.

Yet in another and still more definite sense despair is the sickness unto death. It is indeed very far from being true that, literally understood, one dies of this sickness, or that this sickness ends with bodily death. On the contrary, the torment of despair is precisely this, not to be able to die So it has much in common with the situation of the moribund when he lies and struggles with death, and cannot die. So to be sick unto death is, not to be able to die -- yet not as though there were hope of life; no the hopelessness in this case is that even the last hope, death, is not available. When death is the greatest danger, one hopes for life; but when one becomes acquainted with an even more dreadful danger, one hopes for death. So when the danger is so great that death has become one's hope, despair is the disconsolateness of not being able to die.

It is in this last sense that despair is the sickness unto death, this agonizing contradiction, this sickness in the self, everlastingly to die, to die and yet not to die, to die the death. For dying means that it is all over, but dying the death means to live to experience death; and if for a single instant this experience is possible, it is tantamount to experiencing it forever. If one might die of despair as one dies of a sickness, then the eternal in him, the self, must be capable of dying in the same sense that the body dies of sickness. But this is an impossibility; the dying of despair transforms itself constantly into a living. The despairing man cannot die; no more than "the dagger can slay thoughts" can despair consume the eternal thing, the self, which is the ground of despair, whose worm dieth not, and whose fire is not quenched. Yet despair is precisely self-consuming, but it is an impotent self-consumption which is not able to do what it wills; and this impotence is a new form of self-consumption, in which again, however, the despairer is not able to do what he wills, namely, to consume himself. This is despair raised to a higher potency, or it is the law for the potentiation. This is the hot incitement, or the cold fire in despair, the gnawing canker whose movement is constantly inward, deeper and deeper, in impotent self-consumption. The fact that despair does not consume him is so far from being any comfort to the despairing man that it is precisely the opposite, this comfort is precisely the torment, it is precisely this that keeps the gnawing pain alive and keeps life in the pain. This precisely is the reason why he despairs -- not to say despaired -- because he cannot consume himself, cannot get rid of himself, cannot become nothing. This is the potentiated formula for despair, the rising of the fever in the sickness of the self.

A despairing man is in despair over something. So, it seems for an instant, but only for an instant; that same instant the true despair manifests itself, or despair manifests itself in its true character. For in the fact that he despaired of something, he really despaired of himself, and now would be rid of himself. Thus when the ambitious man whose watchword was "Either Caesar or nothing"[3] does not become Caesar, he is in despair thereat. But this signifies something else, namely, that precisely because he did not become Caesar he now cannot endure to be himself. So properly he is not in despair over the fact that he did not become Caesar, but he is in despair over himself for the fact that he did not become Caesar. This self which, had he become Caesar, would have been to him a sheer delight (though in another sense equally in despair), this self is now absolutely intolerable to him. In a profounder sense it is not the fact that he did not become Caesar which is intolerable to him, but the self which did not become Caesar is the thing that is intolerable; or, more correctly, what is intolerable to him is that he cannot get rid of himself. If he had become Caesar he would have been rid of himself in desperation, but now that he did not become Caesar he cannot in desperation get rid of himself. Essentially he is equally in despair in either case, for he does not possess himself, he is not himself. By becoming Caesar he would not after all have become himself but have got rid of himself, and by not becoming Caesar he falls into despair over the fact that he cannot get rid of himself. Hence it is a superficial view (which presumably has never seen a person in despair, not even one's own self) when it is said of a man in despair, "He is consuming himself." For precisely this it is he despairs of, and to his torment it is precisely this he cannot do, since by despair fire has entered into something that cannot burn, or cannot burn up, that is, into the self.

So, to despair over something is not yet properly despair. It is the beginning, or it is as when the physician says of a sickness that it has not yet declared itself. The next step is the declared despair, despair over oneself. A young girl is in despair over love, and so she despairs over her lover, because he died, or because he was unfaithful to her. This is not a declared despair; no, she is in despair over herself. This self of hers, which, if it had become "his" beloved, she would have been rid of in the most blissful way, or would have lost, this self is now a torment to her when it has to be a self without "him"; this self which would have been to her riches (though in another sense equally in despair) has now become to her a loathsome void, since "he" is dead, or it has become to her an abhorrence, since it reminds her of the fact that she was betrayed. Try it now, say to such a girl,

"Thou art consuming thyself," and thou shalt hear her reply, "Oh, no, the torment is precisely this, that I cannot do it."

To despair over oneself, in despair to will to be rid of oneself, is the formula for all despair, and hence the second form of despair (in despair at willing to be oneself) can be followed back to the first (in despair at not willing to be oneself), just as in the foregoing we resolved the first into the second (cf. I). A despairing man wants despairingly to be himself. But if he despairingly wants to be himself, he will not want to get rid of himself. Yes, so it seems; but if one inspects more closely, one perceives that after all the contradiction is the same. That self which he despairingly wills to be is a self which he is not (for to will to be that self which one truly is, is indeed the opposite of despair); what he really wills is to tear his self away from the Power which constituted it. But notwithstanding all his despair, this he is unable to do, notwithstanding all the efforts of despair, that Power is the stronger, and it compels him to be the self he does not will to be. But for all that he wills to be rid of himself, to be rid of the self which he is, in order to be the self he himself has changed to chose. To be self as he wills to be would be his delight (though in another sense it would be equally in despair), but to be compelled to be self as he does not will to be is his torment, namely, that he cannot get rid of himself.

Socrates proved the immortality of the soul from the fact that the sickness of the soul (sin) does not consume it as sickness of the body consumes the body. So also we can demonstrate the eternal in man from the fact that despair cannot consume his self, that this precisely is the torment of contradiction in despair. If there were nothing eternal in a man, he could not despair; but if despair could consume his self, there would still be no despair.

Thus it is that despair, this sickness in the self, is the sickness unto death. The despairing man is mortally ill. In an entirely different sense than can appropriately be said of any disease, we may say that the sickness has attacked the noblest part; and yet the man cannot die. Death is not the last phase of the sickness, but death is continually the last. To be delivered from this sickness by death is an impossibility, for the sickness and its torment . . . and death consist in not being able to die.

This is the situation in despair. And however thoroughly it eludes the attention of the despairer, and however thoroughly the despairer may succeed (as in the case of that kind of despair which is characterized by unawareness of being in despair) in losing himself entirely, and losing himself in such a way that it is not noticed in the least -- eternity nevertheless will make it manifest that his situation was despair, and it will so nail him to himself that the torment nevertheless remains that he cannot get rid of himself, and it becomes manifest that he was deluded in thinking that he succeeded. And thus it is eternity must act, because to have a self, to be a self, is the greatest concession made to man, but at the same time it is eternity's demand upon him.

Chapter 2: The Universality of This Sickness (Despair)

Just as the physician might say that there lives perhaps not one single man who is in perfect health, so one might say perhaps that there lives not one single man who after all is not to some extent in despair, in whose inmost parts there does not dwell a disquietude, a perturbation, a discord, an anxious dread of an unknown something, or of a something he does not even dare to make acquaintance with, dread of a possibility of life, or dread of himself, so that, after all, as physicians speak of a man going about with a disease in him, this man is going about and carrying a sickness of the spirit, which only rarely and in glimpses, by and with a dread which to him is inexplicable, gives evidence of its presence within. At any rate there has lived no one and there lives no one outside of Christendom who is not in despair, and no one in Christendom, unless he be a true Christian, and if he is not quite that, he is somewhat in despair after all.

This view will doubtless seem to many a paradox, an exaggeration, and a gloomy and depressing view at that. Yet it is nothing of the sort. It is not gloomy; on the contrary, it seeks to throw light upon a subject which ordinarily is left in obscurity. It is not depressing; on the contrary it is uplifting, since it views every man in the aspect of the highest demand made upon him, that he be spirit. Nor is it a paradox; on the contrary, it is a fundamental apprehension consistently carried through, and hence it is no exaggeration.

On the other hand, the ordinary view of despair remains content with appearances, and so it is a superficial view, that is, no view at all. It assumes that every man must know by himself better than anyone else whether he is in despair or not. So, whoever says that he is in despair is regarded as being in despair, but whoever thinks he is not in despair is not so regarded. Consequently, despair becomes a rather rare phenomenon, whereas in fact it is quite universal. It is not a rare exception that one is in despair; no, the rare, the very rare exception is that one is not in despair.

But the vulgar view has a very poor understanding of despair. Among other things (to mention only one which, if rightly understood, would bring thousands, yea, millions under this category), it completely overlooks the fact that one form of despair is precisely this of not being in despair, that is, not being aware of it. The vulgar view is exposed, though in a much deeper sense, to the same fallacy it sometimes falls into when it would determine whether a man is sick or not. In a much deeper sense, I say, for the vulgar view has a far more inadequate notion of spirit than of sickness and health -- and without understanding spirit it is impossible to understand despair. It is ordinarily assumed that a man is well when he does not himself say that he is sick, and still more confidently when he says that he is well. The physician on the other hand regards sickness differently. And why? Because he has a definite and well thought out conception of what it is to be in sound health, and by this he tests the man's condition. The physician knows that just as there is sickness which is only imaginary, so also there is such a thing as fictitious health. In the latter case, therefore, the physician first employs medicines to cause the disease to become manifest. Generally, the physician, just because he is a physician, i.e. the competent man, has no unconditional faith in a person's own assertion about the state of his health. If it were true that what every man says about the state of his health (as to whether he is sick or well, where he suffers, etc.) were absolutely to be relied upon, it would be an illusion to be a physician. For a physician does not merely have to prescribe medicines, but first and foremost he has to be acquainted with sickness, and so first and foremost to know whether a supposedly sick man really is sick, or whether a supposedly well man is not really sick. So, it is also with the physician of souls when dealing with despair. He knows what despair is, he is acquainted with it, and hence he is not satisfied with a man's assertion that he is in despair or that he is not. For it must be observed that in a certain sense not even all who say they are in despair always are so. One may affect despair, and one may make a mistake and confuse despair with all sorts of transitory dejection or grief which pass away without coming to the point of despair. However, the physician of souls does, it is true, regard these states also as forms of despair. He perceives very well that this is affectation -- but precisely this affectation is despair. He perceives very well that this dejection etc. does not mean much -- but precisely this fact, that it does not mean much, is despair.

Furthermore, the vulgar view overlooks the fact that, as compared with sickness, despair is much more dialectical than what is commonly called sickness, because it is a sickness of the spirit. And this dialectical quality, rightly understood, again brings thousands under the category of despair. For in case at a given moment a physician is convinced that this or that person is in good health and at a later moment becomes sick -- the physician may be right in affirming that the person was well then, and at a later moment became sick. With despair it is different.

As soon as despair manifests itself in a person, it is manifest that the person was in despair. For this reason, one cannot at a given moment decide anything about a person who is not saved by the fact that he has been in despair. For in case the condition comes about which brings him to despair, it is at that same moment manifest that he has been in despair throughout the whole of his previous life. On the other hand, one is by no means justified in saying, when a man has a fever, that he has had a fever throughout his whole life. But despair is a phenomenon of the spirit, is related to the eternal, and therefore has something of the eternal in its dialectic.

Not only is despair far more dialectical than an illness, but all its symptoms are dialectical, and for this reason the superficial view is so readily deceived in determining whether despair is present or not. For not to be in despair may mean to be in despair, and it may also mean to be delivered from being in despair. A sense of security and tranquility may mean that one is in despair, precisely this security, this tranquility, may be despair; and it may mean that one has overcome despair and gained peace. In this respect despair is unlike bodily sickness; for not to be sick cannot possibly mean to be sick; but not to be despairing may mean precisely to be despairing. It is not true of despair, as it is of bodily sickness, that the feeling of indisposition is the sickness. By no means. The feeling of indisposition is again dialectical. Never to have been sensible of this indisposition is precisely to be in despair.

This points to the fact, and has its ground therein, that man, regarded as spirit, is always in a critical condition -- and if one is to talk of despair, one must conceive of man as spirit. In relation to sickness, we talk of a crisis, but not in relation to health. And why not? Because bodily health is an "immediate" qualification, and only becomes dialectical in sickness, when one can speak of the crisis. But spiritually, or when man is regarded as spirit, both health and sickness are critical. There is no such thing as "immediate" health of the spirit.

So long as one does not regard man as spirit (in which case we cannot talk about despair) but only as a synthesis of soul and body, health is an "immediate" determinant, and only the sickness of soul or body is a dialectical determinant. But despair is expressed precisely by the fact that a person is unaware of being characterized as spirit. Even that which, humanly speaking, is the most beautiful and lovable thing of all, a feminine youthfulness which is sheer peace and harmony and joy -- even that is despair. For this indeed is happiness, but happiness is not a characteristic of spirit, and in the remote depths, in the most inward parts, in the hidden recesses of happiness, there dwells also the anxious dread which is despair; it would be only too glad to be allowed to remain therein, for the dearest and most attractive dwelling-place of despair is in the very heart of immediate happiness. All immediacy, in spite of its illusory peace and tranquillity, is dread, and hence, quite consistently, it is dread of nothing; one cannot make immediacy so anxious by the most horrifying description of the most dreadful something, as by a crafty, apparently casual half word about an unknown peril which is thrown out with the surely calculated aim of reflection; yea, one can put immediacy most in dread by slyly imputing to it knowledge of the matter referred to. For immediacy doubtless does not know; but never does reflection catch its prey so surely as when it makes its snare out of nothing, and never is reflection so thoroughly itself as when it is . . . nothing. There is need of an eminent reflection, or rather of a great faith, to support a reflection based upon nothing, i.e. an infinite reflection. So even the most beautiful and lovable thing of all, a feminine youthfulness which is sheer peace and harmony and joy, is nevertheless despair, is happiness. Hardly will one have the good hap to get through life on the strength of this immediacy. And if this happiness has the hap to get through, it would be of little help for it is despair. Despair, just because it is wholly dialectical, is in fact the sickness of which it holds that it is the greatest misfortune not to have had it -- the true good hap to get it, although it is the most dangerous sickness of all, if one does not wish to be healed of it. In other cases one can only speak of the good fortune of being healed of a sickness, sickness itself being misfortune.

Therefore it is as far as possible from being true that the vulgar view is right in assuming that despair is a rarity; on the contrary, it is quite universal. It is as far as possible from being true that the vulgar view is right in assuming that everyone who does not think or feel that he is in despair is not so at all, and that only he is in despair who says that he is. On the contrary, one who without affectation says that he is in despair is after all a little bit nearer, a dialectical step nearer to being cured than all those who are not regarded and do not regard themselves as being in despair. But precisely this is the common situation (as the physician of souls will doubtless concede), that the majority of men live without being thoroughly conscious that they are spiritual beings -- and to this is referable all the security, contentment with life, etc., etc., which precisely is despair. Those, on the other hand, who say that they are in despair are generally such as have a nature so much more profound that they must become conscious of themselves as spirit, or such as by the hard vicissitudes of life and its dreadful decisions have been helped to become conscious of themselves as spirit -- either one or the other, for rare is the man who truly is free from despair.

Ah, so much is said about human want and misery -- I seek to understand it, I have also had some acquaintance with it at close range; so much is said about wasted lives -- but only that man's life is wasted who lived on, so deceived by the joys of life or by its sorrows that he never became eternally and decisively conscious of himself as spirit, as self, or (what is the same thing) never became aware and in the deepest sense received an impression of the fact that there is a God, and that he, he himself, his self, exists before this God, which gain of infinity is never attained except through despair. And, oh, this misery, that so many live on and are defrauded of this most blessed of all thoughts; this misery, that people employ themselves about everything else, or, as for the masses of men, that people employ them about everything else, utilize them to generate the power for the theater of life, but never remind them of their blessedness; that they heap them in a mass and defraud them, instead of splitting them apart so that they might gain the highest thing, the only thing worth living for, and enough to live in for an eternity -- it seems to me that I could weep for an eternity over the fact that such misery exists! And, oh, to my thinking this is one expression the more of the dreadfulness of this most dreadful sickness and misery, namely, its hiddenness -- not only that he who suffers from it may wish to hide it and may be able to do so, to the effect that it can so dwell in a man that no one, no one whatever discovers it; no, rather that it can be so hidden in a man that he himself does not know it! And, oh, when the hour-glass has run out, the hourglass of time, when the noise of worldliness is silenced, and the restless or the ineffectual busyness comes to an end, when everything is still about thee as it is in eternity -- whether thou wast man or woman, rich or poor, dependent or independent, fortunate or unfortunate, whether thou didst bear the splendor of the crown in a lofty station, or didst bear only the labor and heat of the day in an inconspicuous lot; whether thy name shall be remembered as long as the world stands (and so was remembered as long as the world stood), or without a name thou didst cohere as nameless with the countless multitude; whether the glory which surrounded thee surpassed all human description, or the judgment passed upon thee was the most severe and dishonoring human judgement can pass -- eternity asks of thee and of every individual among these million millions only one question, whether thou hast lived in despair or not, whether thou wast in despair in such a way that thou didst not know thou wast in despair, or in such a way that thou didst hiddenly carry this sickness in thine inward parts as thy gnawing secret, carry it under thy heart as the fruit of a sinful love, or in such a way that thou, a horror to others, didst rave in despair. And if so, if thou hast lived in despair (whether for the rest thou didst win or lose), then for thee all is lost, eternity knows thee not, it never knew thee, or (even more dreadful) it knows thee as thou art known, it puts thee under arrest by thyself in despair.

Chapter 3 The Forms of This Sickness, i.e., of Despair

The forms of despair must be discoverable abstractly by reflecting upon the factors which compose the self as a synthesis. The self is composed of infinity and finiteness. But the synthesis is a relationship, and it is a relationship which, though it is derived, relates itself to itself, which means freedom. The self is freedom. But freedom is the dialectical element in the term's possibility and necessity.

Principally, however, despair must be viewed under the category of consciousness: the question whether despair is conscious or not, determines the qualitative difference between despair and despair. In its concept all despair is doubtless conscious; but from this it does not follow that he in whom it exists, he to whom it can rightly be attributed in conformity with the concept, is himself conscious of it. It is in this sense that consciousness is decisive. Generally speaking, consciousness, i.e. consciousness of self, is the decisive criterion of the self. The more consciousness, the more self; the more consciousness, the more will, and the more will the more self. A man who has no will at all is no self; the more will he has, the more consciousness of self he has also.

A. Despair Regarded in Such a Way That One Does Not Reflect Whether It Is Conscious or Not, So That One Reflects Only upon the Factors of the Synthesis.

(a). Despair viewed under the aspects of Finitude/Infinitude.

The self is the conscious synthesis of infinitude and finitude which relates itself to itself, whose task is to become itself, a task which can be performed only by means of a relationship to God. But to become oneself is to become concrete. But to become concrete means neither to become finite nor infinite, for that which is to become concrete is a synthesis. Accordingly, the development consists in moving away from oneself infinitely by the process of infinitizing oneself, and in returning to oneself infinitely by the process of finitizing. If on the contrary the self does not become itself, it is in despair, whether it knows it or not. However, a self, every instant it exists, is in process of becoming, for the self [potentially] does not actually exist, it is only that which it is to become. In so far as the self does not become itself, it is not its own self; but not to be one's own self is despair.

(1). The Despair Of Infinitude Is Due To The Lack Of Finitude.

The truth of this is inherent in the dialectical fact that the self is a synthesis [of two factors], the one of which is constantly the opposite of the other. No kind of despair can be defined directly (i.e.

undialectically), but only by reflecting upon the opposite factor. The despairing person's condition of despair can be directly described, as the poet does in fact by attributing to him the appropriate lines. But to describe despair is possible only by its opposite; and if the lines are to have poetic value, they must contain in their coloring a reflection of the dialectical opposite. So then every human existence which supposedly has become or merely wills to become infinite is despair. For the self is a synthesis in which the finite is the limiting factor, and the infinite is the expanding factor. Infinitude's despair is therefore the fantastical, the limitless. The self is in sound health and free from despair only when, precisely by having been in despair, it is grounded transparently in God.

The fantastical is doubtless most closely related to fantasy, imagination, but imagination in turn is related to feeling, knowledge, and will, so that a person may have a fantastic feeling, or knowledge, or will. Generally speaking, imagination is the medium of the process of infinitizing; it is not one faculty on a par with others, but, if one would so speak, it is the faculty instar omnium [for all faculties). What feeling, knowledge, or will a man has, depends in the last resort upon what imagination he has, that is to say, upon how these things are reflected, i.e. it depends upon imagination. Imagination is the reflection of the process of infinitizing, and hence the elder Fichte quite rightly assumed, even in relation to knowledge, that imagination is the origin of the categories. The self is reflection, and imagination is reflection, it is the counterfeit presentment of the self, which is the possibility of the self. Imagination is the possibility of all reflection, and the intensity of this medium is the possibility of the intensity of the self.

Generally the fantastical is that which so carries a man out into the infinite that it merely carries him away from himself and therewith prevents him from returning to himself.

So when feeling becomes fantastic, the self is simply volatilized more and more, at last becoming a sort of abstract sentimentality which is so inhuman that it does not apply to any person, but inhumanly participates feelingly, so to speak, in the fate of one or another abstraction, e.g. that of mankind in abstracto. As the sufferer from rheumatism is unable to master his physical feelings which are under the sway of wind and weather, with the result that he is involuntarily aware of a change in the air etc., so it is with him whose feeling has become fantastic; he becomes in a way infinitized, but not in such a way that he becomes more and more himself, for he loses himself more and more.

So it is with knowledge when it becomes fantastic. The law for the development of the self with respect to knowledge, in so far as it is true that the self becomes itself, is this, that the increasing degree of knowledge corresponds with the degree of self-knowledge, that the more the self knows, the more it knows itself. If this does not occur, then the more knowledge increases, the more it becomes a kind of inhuman knowing for the production of which man's self is squandered, pretty much as men were squandered for the building of the Pyramids, or as men were squandered in the Russian horn-bands to produce one note, neither more nor less.

When the will becomes fantastic, the self likewise is volatilized more and more. In this case the will does not constantly become concrete in the same degree that it is abstract, in such a way that the more it is infinitized in purpose and resolution, the more present and contemporaneous with itself does it become in the small part of the task which can be realized at once, so that in being infinitized it returns in the strictest sense to its self, so that what is farthest from itself (when it is most infinitized in purpose and resolution) is in the same instant nearest to itself in accomplishing the infinitely small part of the task which can be done even today, even at this hour, even at this instant.

And when feeling, or knowledge, or will have thus become fantastic, the entire self may at last become so, whether in a more active form, as when a man runs headlong into the fantastic, or in a more passive form, when he is carried away, but in either case with moral responsibility. The self thus leads a fantastic existence in abstract endeavor after infinity, or in abstract isolation, constantly lacking itself, from which it merely gets further and further away. So, for example, in the religious sphere. The God-relationship infinitizes; but this may so carry a man away that it becomes an inebriation, it may seem to a man as though it were unendurable to exist before God -- for the reason that a man cannot return to himself, cannot become himself. Such a fantastic religious individual would say (to characterize him by putting into his mouth these lines), "That a sparrow can live is comprehensible; it does not know anything about existing before God. But to know that one exists before God -- and then not to go crazy or be brought to naught!"

But in spite of the fact that a man has become fantastic in this fashion, he may nevertheless (although most commonly it becomes manifest) be perfectly well able to live on, to be a man, as it seems, to occupy himself with temporal things, get married, beget children, win honor and esteem -- and perhaps no one notices that in a deeper sense he lacks a self. About such a thing as that not much fuss is made in the world; for a self is the thing the world is least apt to inquire about, and the thing of all things the most dangerous for a man to let people notice that he has it. The greatest danger, that of losing one's own self, may pass off as quietly as if it were nothing; every other loss, that of an arm, a leg, five dollars, a wife, etc., is sure to be noticed.

(2). The Despair of Finitude is Due to the Lack of Infinitude.

The truth of this (as was shown under 1) is inherent in the dialectical fact that the self is a synthesis [of two factors], one of which is the opposite of the other.

The lack of infinitude means to be desperately narrow-minded and mean-spirited. Here of course it is only a question of ethical meanness and narrowness. The world really never talks of any narrowness but intellectual or aesthetic narrowness -- or about the indifferent, which is always the principal subject of the world's talk; for worldliness means precisely attributing infinite value to the indifferent. The worldly view always clings fast to the difference between man and man, and naturally it has no understanding of the one thing needful (for to have that is spirituality), and therefore no understanding of the narrowness and meanness of mind which is exemplified in having lost one's self -- not by evaporation in the infinite, but by being entirely finitized, by having become, instead of a self, a number, just one man more, one more repetition of this everlasting Einerlei.

Despairing narrowness consists in the lack of primitiveness, or of the fact one has deprived oneself of one's primitiveness; it consists in having emasculated oneself, in a spiritual sense. For every man is primitively planned to be a self, appointed to become oneself; and while it is true that every self as such is angular, the logical consequence of this merely is that it has to be polished, not that it has to be ground smooth, not that for fear of men it has to give up entirely being itself, nor even that for fear of men it dare not be itself in its essential accidentality (which precisely is what should not be ground away), by which in fine it is itself. But while one sort of despair plunges wildly into the infinite and loses itself, a second sort permits itself as it were to be defrauded by "the others." By seeing the multitude of men about it, by getting engaged in all sorts of worldly affairs, by becoming wise about how things go in this world, such a man forgets himself, forgets what his name is (in the divine understanding of it), does not dare to believe in himself, finds it too venturesome a thing to be himself, far easier and safer to be like the others, to become an imitation, a number, a cipher in the crowd.

This form of despair is hardly ever noticed in the world. Such a man, precisely by losing his self in this way, has gained perfectibility in adjusting himself to business, yea, in making a success in the world. Here there is no hindrance, no difficulty, occasioned by his self and his infinitization, he is ground smooth as a pebble, courant as a well-used coin. So far from being considered in despair, he is just what a man ought to be. In general the world has of course no understanding of what is truly dreadful. The despair which not only occasions no embarrassment but makes one's life easy and comfortable is naturally not regarded as despair. That this is the view of the world can also be seen in almost all the proverbs, which are merely rules for shrewd behavior. It is said, for example, that a man ten times regrets having spoken, for the once he regrets his silence. And why? Because the fact of having spoken is an external fact, which may involve one in annoyances, since it is an actuality. But the fact of having kept silent! Yet this is the most dangerous thing of all. For by keeping silent one is relegated solely to oneself, no actuality comes to a man's aid by punishing him, by bringing down upon him the consequences of his speech. No, in this respect, to be silent is the easy way. But he who knows what the dreadful is, must for this very reason be most fearful of every fault, of every sin, which takes an inward direction and leaves no outward trace. So it is too that in the eyes of the world it is dangerous to venture. And why? Because one may lose. But not to venture is shrewd. And yet, by not venturing, it is so dreadfully easy to lose that which it would be difficult to lose in even the most venturesome venture, and in any case never so easily, so completely as if it were nothing . . . one's self. For if I have ventured amiss -- very well, then life helps me by its punishment. But if I have not ventured at all -- who then helps me? And, moreover, if by not venturing at all in the highest sense (and to venture in the highest sense is precisely to become conscious of oneself) I have gained all earthly advantages . . . and lose my self! What of that?

And thus, it is precisely with the despair of finitude. In spite of the fact that a man is in despair he can perfectly well live on in the temporal, in fact all the better for it; he may be praised by men, be honored and esteemed, and pursue all the aims of temporal life. What is called worldliness is made up of just such men, who (if one may use the expression) pawn themselves to the world. They use their talents, accumulate money, carry on worldly affairs, calculate shrewdly, etc., etc., are perhaps mentioned in history, but themselves they are not; spiritually understood, they have no self, no self for whose sake they could venture everything, no self before God -- however selfish they may be for all that.

(b). Despair Viewed Under the Aspects of Possibility/Necessity.

For the purpose of becoming (and it is the task of the self freely to become itself) possibility and necessity are equally essential. Just as infinitude and finitude ( ) [The limitless/the finite -- important terms in Plato's philosophy, especially in his Philebus, 30.] both belong to the self, so also do possibility and necessity. A self which has no possibility is in despair, and so in turn is the self which has no necessity.

(1). The Despair of Possibility is Due to the Lack Of Necessity.

The truth of this proposition, as was shown, is inherent in the dialectical situation.

Just as finitude is the limiting factor in relation to infinitude, so in relation to possibility it is necessity which serves as a check. When the self as a synthesis of finitude and infinitude is once constituted, when already it is then in order to become it reflects itself in the medium of imagination, and with that the infinite possibility comes into view. The self is just as possible as it is necessary; for though it is itself, it has to become itself. Inasmuch as it is itself, it is the necessary, and inasmuch as it has to become itself, it is a possibility.

Now if possibility outruns necessity, the self runs away from itself, so that it has no necessity whereto it is bound to return -- then this is the despair of possibility. The self becomes an abstract possibility which tries itself out with floundering in the possible, but does not budge from the spot, nor get to any spot, for precisely the necessary is the spot; to become oneself is precisely a movement at the spot. To become is a movement from the spot, but to become oneself is a movement at the spot.

Possibility then appears to the self ever greater and greater, more and more things become possible, because nothing becomes actual. At last it is as if everything were possible -- but this is precisely when the abyss has swallowed up the self. Every little possibility even would require some time to become actuality. But finally the time which should be available for actuality becomes shorter and shorter, everything becomes more and more instantaneous. Possibility becomes more and more intense -- but only in the sense of possibility, not in the sense of actuality; for in the sense of actuality the meaning of intensity is that at least something of that which is possible becomes actual. At the instant something appears possible, and then a new possibility makes its appearance, at last this phantasmagoria moves so rapidly that it is as if everything were possible -- and this is precisely the last moment, when the individual becomes for himself a mirage.

What the self now lacks is surely reality -- so one would commonly say, as one says of a man that he has become unreal. But upon closer inspection it is really necessity the man lacks. For it is not true, as the philosophers explain, that necessity is a unity of possibility and actuality; no, actuality is a unity of possibility and necessity. Nor is it merely due to lack of strength when the soul goes astray in possibility -- at least this is not to be understood as people commonly understand it. What really is lacking is the power to obey, to submit to the necessary in oneself, to what may be called one's limit. Therefore the misfortune does not consist in the fact that such a self did not amount to anything in the world; no, the misfortune is that the man did not become aware of himself, aware that the self he is, is a perfectly definite something, and so is the necessary. On the contrary, he lost himself, owing to the fact that this self was seen fantastically reflected in the possible. Even in looking at one's self in a minor it is requisite to know oneself; for, if not, one does not behold one's self but merely a man. But the mirror of possibility is not an ordinary mirror, it must be used with the utmost precaution. For of this minor it is true in the highest sense that it is a false mirror. That the self looks so and so in the possibility of itself is only half truth; for in the possibility of itself the self is still far from itself, or only half itself. So the question is how the necessity of the self determines it more precisely. A case analogous to possibility is when a child is invited to participate in some pleasure or another: the child is at once willing, but now it is a question whether the parents will permit it -- and as with the parents, so it is with necessity.

In possibility, however, everything is possible. Hence in possibility one can go astray in all possible ways, but essentially in two. One form is the wishful, yearning form, the other is the melancholy fantastic -- on the one hand hope; on the other, fear or anguished dread. Fairy-tales and legends so often relate that a knight suddenly perceived a rare bird, which he continues to run after, since at the beginning it seemed as if it were so very near -- but then it flies off again, until at last night falls, and he has become separated from his companions, being unable to find his way in the wilderness where he now is. So it is with the possibility of the wish. Instead of summoning back possibility into necessity, the man pursues the possibility -- and at last he cannot find his way back to himself. -- In the melancholy form the opposite result is reached in the same way. The individual pursues with melancholy love a possibility of agonizing dread, which at last leads him away from himself, so that he perishes in the dread, or perishes in that in which he was in dread of perishing.

(2). The Despair of Necessity is Due to the Lack of Possibility.

If one will compare the tendency to run wild in possibility with the efforts of a child to enunciate words, the lack of possibility is like being dumb. Necessity is like a sequence of consonants only, but in order to utter them there must in addition be possibility. When this is lacking, when a human existence is brought to the pass that it lacks possibility, it is in despair, and every instant it lacks possibility it is in despair.

One commonly thinks that there is a certain age which is especially rich in hope, or one talks about being or having been at a certain period or a particular moment of one's Life so rich in hope and possibility. All this is merely human talk, which never reaches the truth. All this hoping and all this despairing is not yet the true hope and the true despair.

The decisive thing is, that for God all things are possible. This is eternally true, and true therefore every instant. This is commonly enough recognized in a way, and in a way it is commonly affirmed; but the decisive affirmation comes only when a man is brought to the utmost extremity, so that humanly speaking no possibility exists. Then the question is whether he will believe that for God all things are possible -- that is to say, whether he will believe. But this is completely the formula for losing one's mind or understanding; to believe is precisely to lose one's understanding in order to win God. Suppose it occurs as follows. Picture a man who with all the shuddering revolt of a terrified imagination has represented to himself some horror as a thing absolutely not to be endured. Now it befalls him, precisely this horror befalls him. Humanly speaking his destruction is the most certain of all things -- and the despair in his soul fights desperately to get leave to despair, to get, if you will, repose for despair, the consent of his whole personality to despair, so that he would curse nothing and nobody more fiercely than him who attempted (Or it may be the attempt) to prevent him from despairing, as the poet's poet so capitally, so incomparably expresses it in Richard II, Act 3, Scene Z:

> Beshrew thee, cousin, which didst lead me forth Of that sweet way I was in to despair.

So then, salvation is humanly speaking the most impossible thing of all; but for God all things are possible! This is the fight of faith, which fights madly (if one would so express it) for possibility. For possibility is the only power to save. When one swoons people shout for water, Eaude-Cologne, Hoffman's Drops; but when one is about to despair the cry is, Procure me possibility, procure possibility! Possibility is the only saving remedy; given a possibility, and with that the desperate man breathes once more, he revives again; for without possibility a man cannot, as if were, draw breath. Sometimes the inventiveness of a human imagination suffices to procure possibility, but in the last resort, that is, when the point is to believe, the only help is this, that for God all things are possible.

Thus is the fight carried on. Whether he who is engaged in this fight will be defeated, depends solely and alone upon whether he has the will to procure for himself possibility, that is to say, whether he will believe. And yet he understands that humanly speaking his destruction is the most certain thing of all. This is the dialectical character of faith. For the most part a man knows no more than that this or that, as he has reason to hope, as seems probable, etc., will not befall him. If it befalls him, then he succumbs. The foolhardy man plunges into a danger involving this or that possibility; if it befalls him, he despairs and succumbs. The believer perceives, and understands, humanly speaking, his destruction (in what has befallen him and in what he has ventured), but he believes. Therefore he does not succumb. He leaves it wholly to God how he is to be helped, but he believes that for God all things are possible. To believe in his own destruction is impossible. To understand that, humanly, it is his own destruction, and then nevertheless to believe in the possibility, is what is meant by faith. So then God helps him -- perhaps by letting him escape the terror, perhaps by means of the terror -- in the fact that here, unexpectedly, miraculously, divinely, help appears. Miraculously -- for it is a strange pedantry to assume that only eighteen hundred years ago it could occur that a man was helped miraculously. Whether a man has been helped by a miracle depends essentially upon the degree of intellectual passion he has employed to understand that help was impossible, and next upon how honest he is toward the Power which helped him nevertheless. But usually, it is neither the one thing nor the other: men cry that there is no help, without having strained the understanding to find help, and afterwards they lie ungratefully.

The believer possesses the eternally certain antidote to despair, viz, possibility; for with God all things are possible every instant. This is the sound health of faith which resolves contradictions. The contradiction in this case is that, humanly speaking, destruction is certain, and that nevertheless there is possibility. Health consists essentially in being able to resolve contradictions. So it is bodily or physically: a draft is indifferently cold and warm, disparate qualities undialectically combined; but a healthy body resolves this contradiction and does not notice the draft. So, it is also with faith.

The loss of possibility signifies: either that everything has become necessary to a man/or that everything has become trivial.

The determinist or the fatalist is in despair, and in despair he has lost his self, because for him everything is necessary. He is like that king who died of hunger because all his food was transformed into gold. Personality is a synthesis of possibility and necessity. The condition of its survival is therefore analogous to breathing (respiration), which is an in- and an a-spiration. The self of the determinist cannot breathe, for it is impossible to breathe necessity alone, which taken pure and simple suffocates the human self.

The fatalist is in despair -- he has lost God, and therefore himself as well; for if he has no God, neither has he a self. But the fatalist has no God -- or, what is the same thing, his god is necessity. Inasmuch as for God all things are possible, it may be said that this is what God is, viz, one for whom all things are possible. The worship of the fatalist is therefore at its maximum an exclamation, and essentially it is dumbness, dumb submission, he is unable to pray. So to pray is to breathe, and possibility is for the self what oxygen is for breathing. But for possibility alone or for necessity alone to supply the conditions for the breathing of prayer is no more possible than it is for a man to breathe oxygen alone or nitrogen alone. For in order to pray there must be a God, there must be a self plus possibility, or a self and possibility in the pregnant sense; for God is that all things are possible, and that all things are possible is God; and only the man whose being has been so shaken that he became spirit by understanding that all things are possible, only he has had dealings with God. The fact that God's will is the possible makes it possible for me to pray; if God's will is only the necessary, man is essentially as speechless as the brutes.

In the case of philistinism or triviality, which also lacks possibility, the situation is somewhat different. Philistinism is spiritlessness, in the literal sense of the word; determinism and fatalism are spiritual despair; but such spiritlessness is also despair. Philistinism lacks every determinant of spirit and terminates in probability, within which the possible finds its insignificant place. Thus it lacks sufficient possibility to take notice of God. Devoid of imagination, as the Philistine always is, he lives in a certain trivial province of experience as to how things go, what is possible, what usually occurs. Thus the Philistine has lost his self and God. For in order to be aware of oneself and God imagination must enable a man to soar higher than the misty precinct of the probable, it must wrench one out of this and, by making possible that which transcends the quantum satis of every experience, it must teach him to hope and fear, or to fear and hope. But imagination the Philistine does not possess, he does not want to have it, he abhors it. So here there is no help. And if sometimes reality helps by tenors which transcend the parrot-wisdom of trivial experience, then philistinism despairs -- that is, it becomes manifest that it was in despair. It lacks the possibility of faith in order by God's help to be able to deliver itself from certain destruction.

Fatalism and determinism, however, have enough imagination to despair of possibility, and have possibility enough to discover impossibility. Philistinism tranquilizes itself in the trivial, being equally in despair whether things go well or ill. Fatalism or determinism lacks the possibility of relaxing and soothing, of tempering necessity, and so it lacks possibility as assuagement. Philistinism lacks possibility as revival from spiritlessness. For philistinism thinks it is in control of possibility, it thinks that when it has decoyed this prodigious elasticity into the field of probability or into the mad-house it holds it a prisoner; it carries possibility around like a prisoner in the cage of the probable, shows it off, imagines itself to be the master, does not take note that precisely thereby it has taken itself captive to be the slave of spiritlessness and to be the most pitiful of all things. For with the audacity of despair that man soared aloft who ran wild in possibility; but crushed down by despair that man strains himself against existence to whom everything has become necessary. But philistinism spiritlessly celebrates its triumph.

B. Despair Viewed Under the Aspect of Consciousness.

With every increase in the degree of consciousness, and in proportion to that increase, the intensity of despair increases: the more consciousness, the more intense the despair. This is everywhere to be seen, most clearly in the maximum and minimum of despair. The devil's despair is the most intense despair, for the devil is sheer spirit, and therefore absolute consciousness and transparency; in the devil there is no obscurity which might serve as a mitigating excuse, his despair is therefore absolute defiance. This is the maximum of despair. The minimum of despair is a state which (as one might humanly be tempted to express it) by reason of a sort of innocence does not even know that there is such a thing as despair. So when consciousness is at its minimum the despair is least; it is almost as if it were a dialectical problem whether one is justified in calling such a state despair.

(a). The Despair which is Unconscious that it is Despair, or the Despairing Unconsciousness of having a Self and an Eternal Self.

That this condition is nevertheless despair and is rightly so denominated may be taken as an expression for a trait which we may call, in a good sense, the opinionativeness of truth. Veritas est index sui et falsi. But this opinionativeness of truth is, to be sure, held in

scant honor, as also it is far from being the case that men in general regard relationship to the truth, the fact of standing in relationship to the truth, as the highest good, and it is very far from being the case that they, Socratically, regard being under a delusion as the greatest misfortune; their sensuous nature is generally predominant over their intellectuality. So when a man is supposed to be happy, he imagines that he is happy (whereas viewed in the light of the truth he is unhappy), and in this case he is generally very far from wishing to be torn away from that delusion. On the contrary, he becomes furious, he regards the man who does this as his most spiteful enemy, he considers it an insult, something near to murder, in the sense that one speaks of killing joy. What is the reason of this? The reason is that the sensuous nature and the psycho-sensuous completely dominate him; the reason is that he lives in the sensuous categories agreeable/disagreeable, and says goodbye to truth etc.; the reason is that he is too sensuous to have the courage to venture to be spirit or to endure it. However vain and conceited men may be, they have nevertheless for the most part a very lowly conception of themselves, that is to say, they have no conception of being spirit, the absolute of all that a man can be -- but vain and conceited they are . . . by way of comparison. In case one were to think of a house, consisting of cellar, ground-floor and premier étage, so tenanted, or rather so arranged, that it was planned for a distinction of rank between the dwellers on the several floors; and in case one were to make a comparison between such a house and what it is to be a man -- then unfortunately this is the sorry and ludicrous condition of the majority of men, that in their own house they prefer to live in the cellar. The soulish-bodily synthesis in every man is planned with a view to being spirit, such is the building; but the man prefers to dwell in the cellar, that is, in the determinants of sensuousness. And not only does he prefer to dwell in the cellar; no, he loves that to such a degree that he becomes furious if anyone would propose to him to occupy the bel étage which stands empty at his disposition -- for in fact he is dwelling in his own house.

No, to be in error or delusion is (quite un-Socratically) the thing they fear the least. One may behold amazing examples which illustrate this fact on a prodigious scale. A thinker erects an immense building, a system, a system which embraces the whole of existence and worldhistory etc. -- and if we contemplate his personal life, we discover to our astonishment this terrible and ludicrous fact, that he himself personally does not live in this immense high-vaulted palace, but in a barn alongside of it, or in a dog kennel, or at the most in the porter's lodge. If one were to take the liberty of calling his attention to this by a single word, he would be offended. For he has no fear of being under a delusion, if only he can get the system completed . . . by means of the delusion.

So then, the fact that the man in despair is unaware that his condition is despair, has nothing to do with the case, he is in despair all the same. If despair is bewilderment (Forvildelse), then the fact that one is unconscious of it is the additional aggravation of being at the same time under a delusion (Vildfarelse). Unconsciousness of despair is like unconsciousness of dread (cf. The Concept of Dread by Vigilius Haufniensis): the dread characteristic of spiritlessness is recognizable precisely by the spiritless sense of security; but nevertheless, dread is at the bottom of it, and when the enchantment of illusion is broken, when existence begins to totter, then too does despair manifest itself as that which was at the bottom.

The despairing man who is unconscious of being in despair is, in comparison with him who is conscious of it, merely a negative step further from the truth and from salvation. Despair itself is a negativity, unconsciousness of it is a new negativity. But to reach truth one must pierce through every negativity. For here applies what the fairy-tale recounts about a certain enchantment: the piece of music must be played through backwards; otherwise, the enchantment is not broken. However, it is only in one sense, in a purely dialectical sense, that he who is unconscious of despair is further away from truth and salvation than the man who is conscious of his despair and yet remains in it. For in another sense, an ethical-dialectic sense, the despairing man who consciously remains in despair is further from salvation, since his despair is more intense. But unawareness is so far from removing despair, or of transforming despair into non-despair, that, on the contrary, it may be the most dangerous form of despair. By unconsciousness the despairing man is in a way secured (but to his own destruction) against becoming aware -- that is, he is securely in the power of despair.

In unconsciousness of being in despair a man is furthest from being conscious of himself as spirit. But precisely the thing of not being conscious of oneself as spirit is despair, which is spiritlessness -- whether the condition be that of complete deadness, a merely vegetative life, or a life of higher potency the secret of which is nevertheless despair. In the latter instance the man is like the sufferer from consumption: he feels well, considers himself in the best of health, seems perhaps to others to be in florid health, precisely when the sickness is most dangerous.

This form of despair (i.e. unconsciousness of it) is the commonest in the world -- yes, in what people call the world, or, to define it more exactly, what Christianity calls "the world," i.e. paganism, and the natural man in Christendom. Paganism as it historically was and is, and paganism within Christendom, is precisely this sort of despair, it is despair but does not know it. It is true that a distinction is made also in paganism, as well as by the natural man, between being in despair and not being in despair; that is to say, people talk of despair as if only certain particular individuals were in despair. But this distinction is just as deceitful as that which paganism and the natural man make between love and self-love, as though all this love were not essentially self-love. Further, however, than this deceitful distinction it was impossible for paganism, including the natural man, to go; for the specific character of despair is precisely this: it is unconscious of being despair.

From this we can easily perceive that the aesthetic concept of spiritlessness by no means furnishes the scale for judging what is despair and what is not -- which moreover is a matter of course; for since it is unable to define what spirit truly is, how could the aesthetical make answer to a question which does not exist for it at all? It would also be a prodigious stupidity to deny that pagan nations en masse, as well as individual pagans, have performed amazing exploits which have prompted and will prompt the enthusiasm of poets; to deny that paganism exhibits examples of achievement which aesthetically cannot be sufficiently admired. It would also be foolish to deny that in paganism lives have been led which were rich in aesthetic enjoyment, and that the natural man can lead such a life, utilizing every advantage offered with the most perfect good taste, even letting art and learning enhance, embellish, ennoble the enjoyment. No, it is not the aesthetic definition of spiritlessness which furnishes the scale for judging what is despair and what is not; the definition which must be used is the ethico-religious: either spirit/or the negative lack of spirit, spiritlessness. Every human existence which is not conscious of itself as spirit, or conscious of itself before God as spirit, every human existence which is not thus grounded transparently in God but obscurely reposes or terminates in some abstract universality (state, nation, etc.), or in obscurity about itself takes its faculties merely as active powers, without in a deeper sense being conscious whence it has them, which regards itself as an inexplicable something which is to be understood from without -- every such existence, whatever it accomplishes, though it be the most amazing exploit, whatever it explains, though it were the whole of existence, however intensely it enjoys life aesthetically -- every such existence is after all despair. It was this the old theologians meant when they talked about the virtues of the pagans being splendid vices. They meant that the most inward experience of the pagan was despair, that the pagan was not conscious of himself before God as spirit. Hence it came about (to cite here an example which has at the same time a deeper relation to the whole study) that the pagans judged self-slaughter so lightly, yea, even praised it, notwithstanding that for the spirit it is the most decisive sin, that to break out of existence in this way is rebellion against God. The pagan lacked the spirit's definition of the self, therefore he expressed such a judgment of self-slaughter -- and this the same pagan did who condemned with moral severity theft, unchastity, etc. He lacked the point of view for regarding self-slaughter, he lacked the Godrelationship and the self. From a purely pagan point of view selfslaughter is a thing indifferent, a thing every man may do if he likes, because it concerns nobody else. If from a pagan point of view one were to warn against self-slaughter, it must be by a long detour, by showing that it was breach of duty toward one's fellow-men. The point in self-slaughter, that it is a crime against God, entirely escapes the pagan. One cannot say, therefore, that the self-slaughter was despair, which would be a thoughtless hysteron proteron; one must say that the fact that the pagan judged self-slaughter as he did was despair.

Nevertheless there is and remains a distinction, and a qualitative one, between paganism in the narrowest sense, and paganism within Christendom. The distinction (as Vigilius Haufniensis has pointed out in relation to dread) is this, that paganism, though to be sure it lacks spirit, is definitely oriented in the direction of spirit, whereas paganism within Christendom lacks spirit with a direction away from it, or by apostasy, and hence in the strictest sense is spiritlessness.

(b). The Despair which is Conscious of being Despair, as also it is Conscious of being a Self wherein there is after all something Eternal, and then is either in despair at not willing to be itself, or in despair at willing to be itself.

A distinction of course must be made as to whether he who is conscious of his despair has the true conception of what despair is. Thus a man may be right, according to the conception he has, in asserting that he is in despair, it may be true that he is in despair, and yet this is not to say that he has the true conception of despair, it may be that one who contemplated this man's life in the light of the true conception would say, "You are far more in despair than you are aware, the despair lies far deeper." So with the pagan (to recall the foregoing instance), when in comparison with others he considered himself in despair, he doubtless was right in thinking that he was in despair, but he was wrong in thinking that the others were not; that is to say, he had not the true conception of despair.

So then, for conscious despair there is requisite on the one hand the true conception of what despair is. On the other hand, clearness is requisite about oneself -- in so far, that is to say, as clearness and despair are compatible. How far complete clarity about oneself, as to whether one is in despair, may be united with being in despair, where this knowledge and self-knowledge might not avail precisely to tear a man out of his despair, to make him so terrified about himself that he would cease to be in despair -- these questions we shall not decide here, we shall not even attempt to do so, since in the sequel we shall find a place for this whole investigation. But without pursuing the thought to this extremest point, we here merely call attention to the fact that, although the degree of consciousness as to what despair is may be very various, so also may be the degree of consciousness touching one's own condition, the consciousness that it is despair. Real life is far too multifarious to be portrayed by merely exhibiting such abstract contrasts as that between a despair which is completely unconscious, and one which is completely conscious of being such. Most frequently, no doubt, the condition of the despairing man, though characterized by multiform nuances, is that of a half obscurity about his own condition. He himself knows well enough in a way up to a certain point that he is in despair, he notices it in himself, as one notices in oneself that one is going about with an illness as yet unpronounced, but he will not quite admit what illness it is. At one moment it has almost become clear to him that he is in despair; but then at another moment it appears to him after all as though his indisposition might have another ground, as though it were the consequence of something external, something outside himself, and that if this were to be changed, he would not be in despair. Or perhaps by diversions, or in other ways, e.g., by work and busy occupations as means of distraction, he seeks by his own effort to preserve an obscurity about his condition, yet again in such a way that it does not become quite clear to him that he does it for this reason, that he does what he does in order to bring about obscurity. Or perhaps he even is conscious that he labors thus in order to sink the soul into obscurity, does this with a certain acuteness and shrew calculation, with psychological insight, but is not in a deeper sense clearly conscious of what he does, of how despairingly he labors etc. For in fact there is in all obscurity a dialectical interplay of knowledge and will, and in interpreting a man one may err, either by emphasizing knowledge merely, or merely the will.

But, as was pointed out above, the degree of consciousness potentiates despair. In the same degree that a man has a truer conception of despair while still remaining in it, and in the same degree that he is more conscious of being in despair, in that same degree is his despair more intense. He who with the consciousness that suicide is despair, and to that extent with the true conception of what despair is, then Commits suicide -- that man has a more intense despair than the man who commits suicide without having the true conception that suicide is despair; but, conversely, the less true his conception of suicide is, the less intense his despair. On the other hand, the clearer consciousness of himself (self-consciousness) a man has in committing suicide, the more intense is his despair, in comparison with that of the man whose soul, compared with his, is in a confused and obscure condition.

In what follows I shall go on to examine the two forms of conscious despair, in such a way as to display at the same time a heightening of the consciousness of what despair is, and of the consciousness of the fact that one's own condition is despair -- or, what is the same thing and the decisive thing, a heightening of the consciousness of the self. But the opposite of being in despair is believing; hence we may perceive the justification for what was stated above (I.A) as the formula which describes a condition in which no despair at all exists, for this same formula is also the formula for believing: by relating itself to its own self, and by willing to be itself, the self is grounded transparently in the Power which constituted it.

(1). In Despair at not Willing to be Oneself, the Despair of Weakness.

When this form of despair is called the despair of weakness, there is already contained in this a reflection upon the second form (2), the despair of willing despairingly to be oneself -- defiance. So the contrast here is only relative. No despair is entirely without defiance: in fact defiance is implied in the very expression, "Not to will to be." On the other hand, even the extremest defiance of despair is after all never without some weakness. The difference is therefore only relative. The one form is, so to speak, the despair of womanliness, the other of manliness.*

(*If psychologically one will take a look around in real life, one will from time to time have opportunity to convince oneself that this distinction, which is logically correct and so shall and must be pertinent, is in fact pertinent, and that this classification embraces the whole reality of despair. For so far as the child is concerned, one does not talk about despair but only about ill-temper, because one has only a right to assume that the eternal is present in the child , and has never a right to demand it of the child, as one has a right to demand it of the grown man, to whom it applies that he shall have it. However, I do not by any means wish to deny that on the part of women there may occur forms of manly despair, and conversely forms of womanly despair on the part of men. But these are exceptions. And this is a matter of course, the ideal also is rare; and only in a purely ideal sense is this distinction between manly and womanly despair entirely true. Woman has neither the selfishly developed conception of the self nor the intellectuality of man, for all that she is his superior in tenderness and fineness of feeling. On the other hand, woman s nature is devotion (Hengivenhed), submission (Hengivelse), and it is unwomanly if it is not so. Strangely enough, no one can be so pert (a word which language has expressly coined for woman), so almost cruelly particular as a woman -- and yet her nature is devotion, and yet (here is the marvel) all this is really the expression for the fact that her nature is devotion. For just because in her nature she carries the whole womanly devotion, nature has lovingly equipped her with an instinct, in comparison with which in point of delicacy the most eminently developed male reflection is as nothing. This devotion of woman, this (to speak as a Greek) divine dowry and riches, is too great a good to be thrown away blindly; and yet no clear-sighted manly reflection is capable of seeing sharply enough to be able to dispose of it rightly. Hence nature has taken care of her: instinctively she sees blindly with greater clarity than the most sharpsighted reflection, instinctively she sees where it is she is to admire, what it is she ought to devote herself to. Devotion is the only thing woman has, therefore nature undertook to be her guardian. Hence it is too that womanliness first comes into existence through a metamorphosis; it comes into existence when the infinite pertness is transfigured in womanly devotion. But the fact that devotion is woman's nature comes again to evidence in despair. By devotion Ithe word literally means giving away] she has lost herself, and only thus is she happy, only thus is she herself; a woman who is happy without devotion, that is, without giving herself away (to whatever it may be she gives herself) is unwomanly. A man also devotes himself (gives himself away), and it is a poor sort of a man who does not do it; but his self is not devotion (this is the expression for womanly substantial devotion), nor does he acquire himself by devotion, as in another sense a woman does, he has himself; he gives himself away, hut his self still remains behind as a sober consciousness of devotion, whereas woman, with genuine womanliness, plunges her self into that to which she devotes herself . -- In such a way man does not devote himself; but the second form of despair expressed also the manly nature: in despair at willing to be oneself.

So far with respect to the relation between the manly and the womanly despair. It mnst be remembered, however, that we are not speaking here of devotion to God or of the Cod-relationship, which is not to be dealt with till we come to Part Second. In the relationship to God, where such a distinction as man/woman vanishes, it is true of man as of woman that devotion is the self, and that by devotion the self is acquired. This is true equally for man and woman, although most frequently in real life woman is related to God only through man.)

(i). Despair Over the Earthly or Over Something Earthly.

This is pure immediacy, or else an immediacy which contains a quantitative reflection. -- Here there is no infinite consciousness of the self, of what despair is, or of the fact that the condition is one of despair; the despair is passive, succumbing to the pressure of the outward circumstance, it by no means comes from within as action. It is, if I may say so, by an innocent misuse of language, a play upon words, as when children play at being soldiers, that in the language of immediacy such words as the self and despair occur.

The immediate man (in so far as immediacy is to be found without any reflection) is merely soulishly determined, his self or he himself is a something included along with "the other" in the compass of the temporal and the worldly, and it has only an illusory appearance of possessing in it something eternal. Thus the self coheres immediately with "the other," wishing, desiring, enjoying, etc., but passively; even in desiring, the self is in the dative case, like the child when it says "me" for I. Its dialectic is: the agreeable and the disagreeable; its concepts are: good fortune, misfortune, fate.

Now then there happens, befalls (falls upon) this immediate self something which brings it to despair; in no other way can this come about, since the self has no reflection in itself, that which brings it to despair must come from without, and the despair is merely passive. That wherein immediacy has its being, or (supposing that after all it has a little bit of reflection in itself) that part thereof to which it especially clings, a man is deprived of by "a stroke of fate," in short, he becomes, as he calls it, unfortunate, that is, the immediacy in him receives such a shock that it cannot recover itself -- he despairs. Or (to mention a case which is more rarely to be seen in real life, but which dialectically is entirely correct) this despair of immediacy occurs through what the immediate man calls an all-too-great good fortune; for it is a fact that immediacy as such is prodigiously fragile, and every quid nimis [excess] which demands of it reflection brings it to despair.

So then he despairs, that is to say, by a strangely preposterous attitude and a complete mystification with regard to himself, he calls this despair. But to despair is to lose the eternal -- and of this he does not speak, does not dream. The loss of the earthly as such is not the cause of despair, and yet it is of this he speaks, and he calls it despairing. What he says is in a certain sense true, only it is not true in the sense in which he understands it; he stands with his face inverted, and what he says must be understood inversely; he stands and points at that which is not a cause of despair, and he declares that he is in despair, and nevertheless it is quite true that despair is going on behind him without his knowing it. It is as if one were to stand with one's back toward the City Hall and the Court House, and pointing straight before him were to say, "There is the City Hall and the Court House." The man is right, there it is . . . if he turns around. It is not true, he is not in despair, and yet he is right when he says it. But he calls himself "in despair," he regards himself as dead, as a shadow of himself. But dead he is not; there is, if you will, life in the characterization. In case everything suddenly changes, everything in the outward circumstances, and the wish is fulfilled, then life enters into him again, immediacy rises again, and he begins to live as fit as a fiddle. But this is the only way immediacy knows how to fight, the one thing it knows how to do: to despair and swoon -- and yet it knows what despair is less than anything else. It despairs and swoons, and thereupon it lies quite still as if it were dead, like the childish play of "lying dead"; immediacy is like certain lower animals which have no other weapon or means of defense but to lie quite still and pretend they are dead.

Meanwhile time passes. If outward help comes, then life returns to the despairer, he begins where he left off; he had no self, and a self he did not become, but he continues to live on with only the quality of immediacy. If outward help does not come, then in real life something else commonly occurs. Life comes back into him after all, but "he never will be himself again," so he says. He now acquires some little understanding of life, he learns to imitate the other men, noting how they manage to live, and so he too lives after a sort. In Christendom he too is a Christian, goes to church every Sunday, hears and understands the parson, yea, they understand one another; he dies; the parson introduces him into eternity for the price of $10 -- but a self he was not, and a self he did not become.

This form of despair is: despair at not willing to be oneself; or still lower, despair at not willing to be a self; or lowest of all, despair at willing to be another than himself, wishing for a new self. Properly speaking, immediacy has no self, it does not recognize itself, so neither can it recognize itself again, it terminates therefore preferably in the romantic. When immediacy despairs it possesses not even enough self to wish or to dream that it had become what it did not become. The immediate man helps himself in a different way: he wishes to be another. Of this one may easily convince oneself by observing immediate men. At the moment of despair no wish is so natural to them as the wish that they had become or might become another. In any case one can never forbear to smile at such a despairer, who, humanly speaking, although he is in despair, is so very innocent. Commonly such a despairer is infinitely comic. Think of a self (and next to God there is nothing so eternal as a self), and then that this self gets the notion of asking whether it might not let itself become or be made into another. . . than itself. And yet such a despairer, whose only wish is this most crazy of all transformations, loves to think that this change might be accomplished as easily as changing a coat. For the immediate man does not recognize his self, he recognizes himself only by his dress, he recognizes (and here again appears the infinitely comic trait) he recognizes that he has a self only by externals. There is no more ludicrous confusion, for a self is just infinitely different from externals. When then the whole of existence has been altered for the immediate man and he has fallen into despair, he goes a step further, he thinks thus, this has become his wish: "What if I were to become another, were to get myself a new self?" Yes, but if he did become another, I wonder if he would recognize himself again! It is related of a peasant who came cleanly shaven to the Capital, and had made so much money that he could buy himself a pair of shoes and stockings and still had enough left over to get drunk on -- it is related that as he was trying in his drunken state to find his way home he lay down in the middle of the highway and fell asleep. Then along came a wagon, and the driver shouted to him to move or he would run over his legs. Then the drunken peasant awoke, looked at his legs, and since by reason of the shoes and stockings he didn't recognize them, he said to the driver, "Drive on, they are not my legs." So in the case of the immediate man when he is in despair it is impossible to represent him truly without a touch of the comic; it is, if I may say so, a clever trick to talk in this jargon about a self and about despair.

When immediacy is assumed to have self-reflection, despair is somewhat modified; there is somewhat more consciousness of the self, and therewith in turn of what despair is, and of the fact that one's condition is despair; there is some sense in it when such a man talks of being in despair: but the despair is essentially that of weakness, a passive experience; its form is, in despair at not wanting to be oneself.

The progress in this case, compared with pure immediacy, is at once evident in the fact that the despair does not always come about by reason of a blow, by something that happens, but may be occasioned by the mere reflection within oneself, so that in this case despair is not a purely passive defeat by outward circumstances, but to a certain degree is self-activity, action. Here there is in fact a certain degree of self-reflection, and so a certain degree of observation of oneself. With this certain degree of self-reflection begins the act of discrimination whereby the self becomes aware of itself as something essentially different from the environment, from externalities and their effect upon it. But this is only to a certain degree. Now when the self with a certain degree of self-reflection wills to accept itself, it stumbles perhaps upon one difficulty or another in the composition of the self.

For as no human body is perfection, so neither is any self. This difficulty, be it what it may, frightens the man away shudderingly. Or something happens to him which causes within him a breach with immediacy deeper than he has made by reflection. Or his imagination discovers a possibility which, if it were to come to pass, would likewise become a breach with immediacy.

So he despairs. His despair is that of weakness, a passive suffering of the self, in contrast to the despair of self-assertion; but, by the aid of relative self-reflection which he has, he makes an effort (which again distinguishes him from the purely immediate man) to defend his self. He understands that the thing of letting the self go is a pretty serious business after all, he is not so apoplectically muddled by the blow as the immediate man is, he understands by the aid of reflection that there is much he may lose without losing the self; he makes admissions, is capable of doing so -- and why? Because to a certain degree he has dissociated his self from external circumstances, because he has an obscure conception that there may even be something eternal in the self. But in vain he struggles thus; the difficulty he stumbled against demands a breach with immediacy as a whole, and for that he has not sufficient self-reflection or ethical reflection; he has no consciousness of a self which is gained by the infinite abstraction from everything outward, this naked, abstract self (in contrast to the clothed self of immediacy) which is the first form of the infinite self and the forward impulse in the whole process whereby a self infinitely accepts its actual self with all its difficulties and advantages.

So then he despairs, and his despair is: not willing to be himself. On the other hand, the ludicrous notion of wanting to be another never occurs to him; he maintains the relationship to his self -- to that extent reflection has identified him with the self. He then is in just such a situation with regard to the self as a man may be with regard to his dwelling-place. The comic feature is that a self certainly does not stand in such a casual relation to itself as does a man to his dwellingplace. A man finds his dwelling-place distasteful, either because the chimney smokes, or for any other reason whatsoever; so he leaves it, but he does not move out, he does not engage a new dwelling, he continues to regard the old one as his habitation; he reckons that the offense will pass away. So it is with the despairer. As long as the difficulty lasts he does not dare to come to himself (as the common phrase expresses it with singular pregnancy), he does not want to be himself -- but that surely will pass by, perhaps things will change, the dark possibility will surely be forgotten. So meanwhile he comes to himself only once in a while, as it were on a visit, to see whether the change has not occurred, and so soon as it has occurred he moves home again, "is again himself," so he says. However, this only means that he begins again where he left off; he was to a certain degree a self of a sort, and he became nothing more.

But if no change occurs, he helps himself in another way. He swings away entirely from the inward direction which is the path he ought to have followed in order to become truly a self. The whole problem of the self in a deeper sense becomes a sort of blind door in the background of his soul behind which there is nothing. He accepts what in his language he calls his self, that is to say, whatever abilities, talents, etc. may have been given him; all this he accepts, yet with the outward direction toward what is called life, the real, the active life; he treats with great precaution the bit of self-reflection which he has in himself, he is afraid that this thing in the background might again emerge. So little by little he succeeds in forgetting it; in the course of years he finds it almost ludicrous, especially when he is in good company with other capable and active men who have a sense and capacity for real life. Charmant! He has now, as they say in romances, been happily married for a number of years, is an active and enterprising man, a father and a citizen, perhaps even a great man; at home in his own house the servants speak of him as "himself"; in the city he is among the honoratiores; his bearing suggests "respect of persons," or that he is to be respected as a person, to all appearance he is to be regarded as a person. In Christendom he is a Christian (quite in the same sense in which in paganism he would have been a pagan, and in England an Englishman), one of the cultured Christians. The question of immortality has often been in his mind, more than once he has asked the parson whether there really was such an immortality, whether one would really recognize oneself again -- which indeed must have for him a very singular interest, since he has no self.

It is impossible to represent truly this sort of despair without a certain admixture of satire. The comical thing is that he will talk about having been in despair; the dreadful thing is that after having, as he thinks, overcome despair, he is then precisely in despair. It is infinitely comic that at the bottom of the practical wisdom which is so much extolled in the world, at the bottom of all the devilish lot of good counsel and wise saws and "wait and see" and "put up with one's fate" and "write in the book of forgetfulness" -- that at the bottom of all this, ideally understood, lies complete stupidity as to where the danger really is and what the danger really is. But again this ethical stupidity is the dreadful thing.

Despair over the earthly or over something earthly is the commonest sort of despair, especially in the second form of immediacy with a quantitative reflection. The more thoroughly reflected the despair is, the more rarely it occurs in the world. But this proves that most men have not become very deep even in despair; it by no means proves, however, that they are not in despair. There are very few men who live even only passably in the category of spirit; yea, there are not many even who merely make an attempt at this life, and most of those who do so, shy away. They have not learned to fear, they have not learned what "must" means, regardless, infinitely regardless of what it may be that comes to pass. Therefore they cannot endure what even to them seems a contradiction, and which as reflected from the world around them appears much more glaring, that to be concerned for one's own soul and to want to be spirit is a waste of time, yes, an inexcusable waste of time, which ought if possible to be punishable by law, at all events is punished by contempt and ridicule as a sort of treason against men, as a froward madness which crazily fills up time with nothing. Then there is a period in their lives (alas, their best period) when they begin after all to take the inward direction. They get about as far as the first difficulties, there they veer away; it seems to them as though this road were leading to a disconsolate desert -- und rings umher liegt schöne grüne Weide [and all about lie beautiful green pastures]. So they are off, and soon they forget that best period of theirs; and, alas, they forget it as though it were a bit of childishness. At the same time they are Christians, tranquilized by the parson with regard to their salvation. This despair, as I have said, is the commonest, it is so common that only thereby can one explain the rather common opinion in common intercourse that despair is something belonging to youth, which appears only in youthful years, but is not to be found in the settled man who has come to the age of maturity and the years of wisdom. This is a desperate error, or rather a desperate mistake, which overlooks (yes, and what is worse, it overlooks the fact that what it overlooks is pretty nearly the best thing that can be said of a man, since far worse often occurs) -- it overlooks the fact that the majority of men do never really manage in their whole life to be more than they were in childhood and youth, namely, immediacy with the addition of a little dose of self-reflection. No, despair verily is not something which appears only in the young, something out of which one grows as a matter of course -- "as one grows out of illusion." But neither is illusion something one grows out of, though people are foolish enough to think so. On the contrary, one encounters grown men and women and aged persons who have as much childish illusion as any youth. People overlook the fact that illusion has essentially two forms: that of hope, and that of recollection. But just because the older person is under illusion, he has also an entirely onesided conception of what illusion is, thinking that it is only the illusion of hope. And this is natural. The older man is not plagued by the illusion of hope, but he is on the other hand by the whimsical idea of looking down at the illusion of youth from a supposedly superior standpoint which is free from illusion. The youth is under illusion, he hopes for the extraordinary from life and from himself. By way of compensation, one often finds in an older man illusion with respect to the recollections of his youth. An elderly woman who has now supposedly given up all illusions is often found to be as fantastic in her illusion as any young girl, with respect to how she remembers herself as a girl, how happy she once was, how beautiful, etc. This fuimus [we have been] which is so often heard from old people is fully as great an illusion as the futuristic illusion of the youth. They both of them are lying or poetizing.

But far more desperate than this is the mistake that despair belongs only to youth. In the main it is a great folly, and precisely it is a lack of sense as to what spirit is, and moreover it is failure to appreciate that man is spirit, not merely an animal, when one supposes that it might be such an easy matter to acquire faith and wisdom which come with the years as a matter of course, like teeth and a beard and such like. No, whatever it may be that a man as a matter of course comes to, and whatever it may be that comes to a man as a matter of course -- one thing it is not, namely, faith and wisdom. But the thing is this: with the years man does not, spiritually understood, come to anything; on the other hand, it is very easy with the years to go from something. And with the years one perhaps goes from the bit of passion, feeling, imagination, the bit of inwardness, which one had, and goes as a matter of course (for such things go as a matter of course) under triviality's definition of understanding of life. This . . . improved condition, which true enough has come about with the years, he now in despair regards as a good, he readily assures himself (and in a certain satirical sense there is nothing more sure) that it now never could occur to him to despair -- no, he has assured himself against this, yet he **is** in despair, spiritually in despair. Why I wonder did Socrates love youths -- unless it was because he knew men!

And if it does not so happen that a man with the years sinks into the most trivial kind of despair, from this it does not by any means follow that despair might belong only to youth. If a man really develops with the years, if he ripens into essential consciousness of the self, he may perhaps despair in a higher form. And if he does not essentially develop with the years, nor yet sink into sheer triviality, that is to say, if he remains pretty much a young man, a youth, although he is mature, a father and gray-haired, retaining therefore something of the good traits of youth, then indeed he will be exposed also to the possibility of despairing as a youth over the earthly or over something earthly.

So a difference there may well be between the despair of an older man and a youth, but no essential difference, only a fortuitous one. The youth despairs over the future, as a present tense in futuro; there is something in the future he is not willing to accept, with this he will not be himself. The older man despairs over the past, as a present in praeterito, which refuses to become more and more past -- for so desperate he is not that he entirely succeeds in forgetting it. This past is perhaps something even which repentance should have taken in hand. But if repentance were to emerge, one would first have to despair completely, to despair out and out, and then the spirit-life might break through from the very bottom. But desperate as he is, he dare not let the thing come to such a pass. So there he remains standing, time goes on -- unless he succeeds, still more desperately, by the help of forgetfulness, in healing it, so that instead of becoming a repenter, he becomes his own healer [or accomplice, as the word would be more commonly understood]. But such despair, whether it be of the youth or of the man, is essentially the same, it does not reach any metamorphosis in which the consciousness of the eternal in the self breaks through, so that the battle might begin which either potentiates despair to a higher power or leads to faith.

But is there no essential difference between the two expressions hitherto used as identical: to despair over the earthly (the determinant of totality), and to despair over something earthly (the particular)?

Indeed there is. When with infinite passion the self by means of imagination despairs over something earthly, this infinite passion transforms this particular, this something, into the earthly in toto, that is to say, the determinant of totality inheres in and belongs to the despairer. The earthly and temporal as such are precisely what falls apart into the particular. It is impossible actually to lose or be deprived of all that is earthly, for the determinant of totality is a thoughtdeterminant. So the self first increases infinitely the actual loss, and then it despairs over the earthly in toto. But so soon as this distinction (between despairing over the earthly and over something earthly) is essentially armed there is also an essential advance made in the consciousness of the self. This formula, "to be in despair over the earthly" is a dialectic first expression for the next form of despair.

(ii). Despair about the eternal or over oneself.

Despair over the earthly or over something earthly is really despair also about the eternal and over oneself, in so far as it is despair, for this is the formula for all despair.("Therefore it is linguistically correct to say, "in despair over the earthly" (the occasion), and "about the eternal," but "over oneself," because this is again another expression for the occasion of despair, which in its concept is always about the eternal, whereas that over which one despairs may be of the most various sorts. One despairs over that which fixes one in despair, over one's misfortune, for example, over the earthly, over the loss of one's fortune, but about that which, rightly understood, releases one from despair, therefore about the eternal, about one's salvation, about one's own rower, etc. In relation to the self one employs both words: to despair over and about oneself, because the self is doubly dialectic. And herein consists the obscurity, especially in all lower forms of despair, and in almost all despairers, that with such passionate clearness a man sees and knows over what he is in despair, but about what it is escapes his notice. The condition requisite for healing it always this about-face, and from a purely philosophical point of view it might be a subtle question whether it is possible for one to be in despair with full consciousness of what it is about which one despairs.) But the despairer, as he was depicted in the foregoing, did not observe what was happening behind him, so to speak; he thinks he is in despair over something earthly and constantly talks about what he is in despair over, and yet he is in despair about the eternal; for the fact that he ascribes such great value to the earthly, or, to carry the thought further, that he ascribes to something earthly such great value, or that he first transforms something earthly into everything earthly, and then ascribes to the earthly such great value, is precisely to despair about the eternal.

This despair is now well in advance. If the former was the despair of weakness, this is despair over his weakness, although it still remains as to its nature under the category "despair of weakness," as distinguished from defiance in the next section. So there is only a relative difference. This difference consists in the fact that the foregoing form has the consciousness of weakness as its final consciousness, whereas in this case consciousness does not come to a stop here but potentiates itself to a new consciousness, a consciousness of its weakness. The despairer understands that it is weakness to take the earthly so much to heart, that it is weakness to despair. But then, instead of veering sharply away from despair to faith, humbling himself before God for his weakness, he is more deeply absorbed in despair and despairs over his weakness. Therewith the whole point of view is inverted, he becomes now more clearly conscious of his despair, recognizing that he is in despair about the eternal, he despairs over himself that he could be weak enough to ascribe to the earthly such great importance, which now becomes his despairing expression for the fact that he has lost the eternal and himself.

Here is the scale of ascent. First, in consciousness of himself: for to despair about the eternal is impossible without having a conception about the sell, that there is something eternal in it, or that it has had something eternal in it. And if a man is to despair over himself, he must indeed be conscious also of having a self; that, however, is the thing over which he despairs -- not over the earthly or over something earthly, but over himself. Moreover there is in this case a greater consciousness of what despair is; for despair is precisely to have lost the eternal and oneself. As a matter of course there is greater consciousness of the fact that one's condition is that of despair. Furthermore, despair in this case is not merely passive suffering but action. For when the earthly is taken away from the self and a man despairs, it is as if despair came from without, though it comes nevertheless always from the self, indirect-directly from the self, as counter-pressure (reaction), differing in this respect from defiance, which comes directly from the self. Finally, there is here again, though in another sense, a further advance. For just because this despair is more intense, salvation is in a certain sense nearer. Such a despair will hardly forget, it is too deep; but despair is held open every instant, and there is thus possibility of salvation.

For all that, this despair is to be referred to the formula: in despair at not willing to be oneself. Just as a father disinherits a son, so the self is not willing to recognize itself after it has been so weak. In its despair it cannot forget this weakness, it hates itself in a way, it will not humble itself in faith under its weakness in order to gain itself again; no, in its despair it will not hear of itself, so to speak, will not know anything about itself. But there can be no question of being helped by forgetfulness, no question of slipping by the aid of forgetfulness under the determinant of selflessness, and so being a man and a Christian like other men and Christians; no, for this the self is too much a self. As it often was the case with the father who disinherited his son that the outward fact was of little avail to him, he did not by this get free of his son, at least his thought did not; as is often the case with the lover's curse upon the hated one (i.e. the loved one) that it does not help much, it almost imprisons him the more -- so it is in the case of the despairing self with relation to itself.

This despair is one quality deeper than the foregoing and is a sort which rarely is met with in the world. That blind door behind which there was nothing is in this case a real door, a door carefully locked to be sure, and behind it sits as it were the self and watches itself, employed in filling up time with not willing to be itself, and yet is self-enough to love itself. This is what is called introversion. And from now on we shall be dealing with introversion, which is the direct opposite to immediacy and has a great contempt for it, in the sphere of thought more especially.

But does there then in the realm of reality exist no such self? Has he fled outside of reality to the desert, to the cloister, to the mad-house? Is he not a real man, clothed like others, or like others clad in the customary outer-garments? Yes, certainly there is! Why not? But with respect to this thing of the self he initiates no one, not a soul, he feels no urge to do this, or he has learnt to suppress it. Hear how he talks about it. "After all it's only the purely immediate men -- who so far as spirit is concerned are about at the same point as the child in the first period of earliest infancy when with a thoroughly endearing nonchalance it lets everything pass out -- it's the purely immediate men who can't retain anything. It is this sort of immediacy which often with great pretentiousness proclaims itself 'truth,' that one is 'a true man and just like people generally are' -- which is just as true as it is untrue that a grown man as soon as he feels a corporal need at once yields to it. Every self which is even a little bit reflective has surely a notion of what it is to repress the self." And our despairer is introverted enough to be able to keep every intruder (that is, every man) at a distance from the topic of the self, whereas outwardly he is completely "a real man" He is a university man, husband and father, an uncommonly competent civil functionary even, a respectable father, very gentle to his wife and carefulness itself with respect to his children. And a Christian? Well, yes, he is that too after a sort however, he preferably avoids talking on the subject, although he willingly observes and with a melancholy joy that his wife for her edification engages in devotions. He very seldom goes to church, because it seems to him that most parsons really don't know what they are talking about. He makes an exception in the case of one particular priest of whom he concedes that he knows what he is talking about, but he doesn't want to hear him for another reason, because he has a fear that this might lead him too far. On the other hand, he often feels a need of solitude, which for him is a vital necessity -- sometimes like breathing, at other times like sleeping. The fact that he feels this vital necessity more than other men is also a sign that he has a deeper nature. Generally, the need of solitude is a sign that there is spirit in a man after all, and it is a measure for what spirit there is. The purely twaddling inhuman and too-human men are to such a degree without feeling for the need of solitude that like a certain species of social birds (the so-called love birds) they promptly die if for an instant they have to be alone. As the little child must be put to sleep by a lullaby, so these men need the tranquilizing hum of society before they are able to eat, drink, sleep, pray, fall in love, etc. But in ancient times as well as in the Middle Ages people were aware of the need of solitude and had respect for what it signifies. In the constant sociability of our age people shudder at solitude to such a degree that they know no other use to put it to but (oh, admirable epigram!) as a punishment for criminals. But after all it is a fact that in our age it is a crime to have spirit, so it is natural that such people, the lovers of solitude, are included in the same class with criminals.

The introverted despairer thus lives on horis succesivis [successive hours], through hours which, though they are not lived for eternity, have nevertheless something to do with the eternal, being employed about the relationship of one's self to itself -- but he really gets no further than this. So when this is done, when the need for solitude is satisfied, he goes outside as it were -- even when he goes in to converse with wife and children. That which as a husband makes him so gentle and as a father so careful is, apart from his good-nature and his sense of duty, the admission he has made to himself in his most inward reserve concerning his weakness.

If it were possible for anyone to be privy to his introversion and were to say to him, "This is in fact pride, thou art proud of thyself," he would hardly be likely to admit it to another. When he was alone with himself he would likely admit that there was something in it; but the passionateness with which his self-had pictured his weakness would quickly make him believe again that it could not possibly be pride, for it was in fact precisely over his weakness he was in despair -- just as if it were not pride which attached such prodigious weight to weakness, just as if it were not because he wanted to be proud of himself that he could not endure this consciousness of weakness -- If one were to say to him, "This is a strange complication, a strange sort of knot; for the whole misfortune consists in the way thought is twined; otherwise the direction is quite normal, it is just this path you must travel through the despair of the self to faith. It is true enough about the weakness, but it is not over this you must despair the self must be broken in order to become a self, so cease to despair over it." If one were to talk to him thus, he would perhaps understand it in a dispassionate moment, but soon passion would again see falsely, and so again he takes the wrong turn into despair.

As I have said, such despair is rather rare. If it does not stay at that point, merely marking time, and if on the other hand there does not occur a radical change in the despairer so that he gets on the right path to faith, then such despair will either potentiate itself to a higher form and continue to be introversion, or it breaks through to the outside and demolishes the outward disguise under which the despairing man has been living in his incognito. In the latter case such a despairer will then plunge into life, perhaps into the distractions of great undertakings, he will become a restless spirit which leaves only too clear a trace of its actual presence, a restless spirit which wants to forget, and inasmuch as the noise within is so loud stronger means are needed, though of a different sort, than those which Richard III employs in order not to hear his mother's curses. Or he will seek forgetfulness in sensuality, perhaps in debauchery, in desperation he wants to return to immediacy, but constantly with consciousness of the self, which he does not want to have. In the first case, when despair is potentiated, it becomes defiance, and it now becomes manifest how much truth there was in this notion of weakness, it becomes manifest how dialectically correct it is to say that the first expression of defiance is precisely despair over one's weakness.

However, let us in conclusion take another little look at the introvert who in his introversion marks time on the spot. If this introversion is absolutely maintained, omnibus numeris absoluta [perfect in every respect], then suicide will be the danger nearest to him. The common run of men have of course no presentiment of what such an introvert is capable of bearing; if they were to come to know it, they would be astonished. If on the other hand he talks to someone, if to one single man he opens his heart, he is in all probability strained to so high a tension, or so much let down, that suicide does not result from introversion. Such an introvert with one person privy to his thought is a whole tone milder than the absolute case. He probably will shun suicide. It may happen, however, that he falls into despair just for the fact that he has opened his heart to another; it may be that he thinks it would have been infinitely preferable to maintain silence rather than have anyone privy to his secret. There are examples of introverts who are brought to despair precisely because they have acquired a confidant. So after all suicide may be the consequence. Poetically the catastrophe (assuming poetice that the protagonist was e.g. a king or emperor) might be fashioned in such a way that the hero had the confidant put to death. One could imagine such a demoniacal tyrant who felt the need of talking to a fellow-man about his torment, and in this way consumed successively a whole lot of men; for to be his confidant was certain death. -- It would be the task for a poet to represent this agonizing self-contradiction in a demoniac man who is not able to get along without a confidant, and not able to have a confidant, and then resolving it in such a way as this.

(2) The despair of willing despairingly to be oneself -- defiance.

As it was shown that one might call the despair dealt with in section 1 the despair of womanliness, so one might call the despair now to be considered the despair of manliness. In connection with the kind just described it may be called: despair viewed under the determinant of spirit. But this manliness belongs more precisely under the determinant of spirit, and womanliness is a lower synthesis.

The despair described in section 1 (ii) was despair over one's weakness, the despairer does not want to be himself. But if one goes one single dialectical step further, if despair thus becomes conscious of the reason why it does not want to be itself, then the case is altered, then defiance is present, for then it is precisely because of this a man is despairingly determined to be himself.

First comes despair over the earthly or something earthly, then despair over oneself about the eternal. Then comes defiance, which really is despair by the aid of the eternal, the despairing abuse of the eternal in the self to the point of being despairingly determined to be oneself. But just because it is despair by the aid of the eternal it lies in a sense very close to the true, and just because it lies very close to the true it is infinitely remote. The despair which is the passageway to faith is also by the aid of the eternal: by the aid of the eternal the self has courage to lose itself in order to gain itself. Here on the contrary, it is not willing to begin by losing itself but wills to be itself.

In this form of despair there is now a mounting consciousness of the self, and hence greater consciousness of what despair is and of the fact that one's condition is that of despair. Here despair is conscious of itself as a deed, it does not come from without as a suffering under the pressure of circumstances, it comes directly from the self. And so after all defiance is a new qualification added to despair over one weakness.

In order to will in despair to be oneself there must be consciousness of the infinite self. This infinite self, however, is really only the abstractest form, the abstractest possibility of the self, and it is this self the man despairingly wills to be, detaching the self from every relation to the Power which posited it, or detaching it from the conception that there is such a Power in existence. By the aid of this infinite form the self despairingly wills to dispose of itself or to create itself, to make itself the self it wills to be, distinguishing in the concrete self what it will and what it will not accept. The man's concrete self, or his concretion, has in fact necessity and limitations, it is this perfectly definite thing, with these faculties, dispositions, etc. But by the aid of the infinite form, the negative self, he wills first to undertake to refashion the whole thing, in order to get out of it in this way a self such as he wants to have, produced by the aid of the infinite form of the negative self -- and it is thus he wills to be himself. That is to say, he is not willing to begin with the beginning but "in the beginning." He is not willing to attire himself in himself, nor to see his task in the self given him; by the aid of being the infinite form he wills to construct it himself.

If one would have a common name for this despair, one might call it Stoicism -- yet without thinking only of this philosophic sect. And to illuminate this sort of despair more sharply one would do well to distinguish between the active and the passive self, showing how the self is related to itself when it is active, and how it is related to itself in suffering when it is passive, and showing that the formula constantly is: in despair to will to be oneself.

If the despairing self is active, it really is related to itself only as experimenting with whatsoever it be that it undertakes, however great it may be, however astonishing, however persistently carried out. It acknowledges no power over it, hence in the last resort it lacks seriousness and is able only to conjure up a show of seriousness when the self bestows upon its experiments its utmost attention. Like the fire which Prometheus stole from the gods, so does this mean to steal from God the thought which is seriousness, that God is regarding one, instead of which the despairing self is content with regarding itself, and by that it is supposed to bestow upon its undertakings infinite interest and importance, whereas it is precisely this which makes them mere experiments. For though this self were to go so far in despair that it becomes an experimental god, no derived self can by regarding itself give itself more than it is: it nevertheless remains from first to last the self, by self-duplication it becomes neither more nor less than the self. Hence the self in its despairing effort to will to be itself labors itself into the direct opposite, it becomes really no self. In the whole dialectic within which it acts there is nothing firm, what the self is does not for an instant stand firm, that is, eternally firm. The negative form of the self exercises quite as much the power of loosing as of binding, every instant it can quite arbitrarily begin all over again, and however far a thought may be pursued, the whole action is within a hypothesis. It is so far from being true that the self succeeds more and more in becoming itself, that in fact it merely becomes more and more manifest that it is a hypothetical self. The self is its own lord and master, so it is said, absolutely its own lord, and precisely this is despair, but it also is what it regards as its pleasure and enjoyment. However, by closer inspection one easily ascertains that this ruler is a king without a country, he rules really over nothing; his condition, his dominion, is subjected to the dialectic that every instant revolution is legitimate. For in the last resort this depends arbitrarily upon the self.

So the despairing self is constantly building nothing but castles in the air, it fights only in the air. All these experimented virtues make a brilliant showing; for an instant they are enchanting like an oriental poem: such self-control, such firmness, such ataraxia, etc., border almost on the fabulous. Yes, they do to be sure; and also at the bottom of it all there is nothing. The self wants to enjoy the entire satisfaction of making itself into itself, of developing itself, of being itself; it wants to have the honor of this poetical, this masterly plan according to which it has understood itself. And yet in the last resort it is a riddle how it understands itself; just at the instant when it seems to be nearest to having the fabric finished it can arbitrarily resolve the whole thing into nothing.

If the despairing self is a passive sufferer, we have still the same formula: in despair at willing to be oneself. Perhaps such an experimenting self which in despair wills to be itself, at the moment when it is making a preliminary exploration of its concrete self, stumbles upon one or another hardship of the sort that the Christian would call a cross, a fundamental defect, it matters not what. The negative self, the infinite form of the self, will perhaps cast this clean away, pretend that it does not exist, want to know nothing about it. But this does not succeed, its virtuosity in experimenting does not extend so far, nor does its virtuosity in abstraction; like Prometheus the infinite, negative self feels that it is nailed to this servitude. So then it is a passively suffering self. How then does the despair which despairingly wills to be itself display itself in this case?

Note that in the foregoing the form of despair was represented which is in despair over the earthly or over something earthly, so understood that at bottom this is and also shows itself to be despair about the eternal, i.e. despair which wills not to let itself be comforted by the eternal, which rates the earthly so high that the eternal can be of no comfort. But this too is a form of despair: not to be willing to hope that an earthly distress, a temporal cross, might be removed. This is what the despair which wills desperately to be itself is not willing to hope. It has convinced itself that this thorn in the flesh gnaws so profoundly that he cannot abstract it -- no matter whether this is actually so or his passion makes it true for him,(From this standpoint, it is well to note here, one will see also that much which is embellished by the name of resignation is a kind of despair, that of willing despairingly to be one's abstract self, of willing despairingly to be satisfied with the eternal and thereby be able to defy or ignore suffering in the earthly and temporal sphere. The dialectic of resignation is commonly this: to will to be one's eternal self, and then with respect to something positive wherein the self suffers, not to will to be oneself, contenting oneself with the thought that after all this will disappear in eternity, thinking itself therefore justified in not accepting it in time, so that, although suffering under it, the self will not make to it the concession that it properly belongs to the self, that is, it will not humble itself under it in faith. Resignation regarded as despair is essentially different from the form, "in despair at not willing to be oneself," for it wills desperately to be itself -- with exception, however, of one particular, with respect to which it wills despairingly not to be itself.) and so he is willing to accept it as it were eternally. So he is offended by it, or rather from it he takes occasion to be offended at the whole of existence, in spite of it he would be himself, not despitefully be himself without it (for that is to abstract from it, and that he cannot do, or that would be a movement in the direction of resignation); no, in spite of or in defiance of the whole of existence he wills to be himself with it, to take it along, almost defying his torment. For to hope in the possibility of help, not to speak of help by virtue of the absurd, that for God all things are possible -- no, that he will not do. And as for seeking help from any other -- no, that he will not do for all the world; rather than seek help he would prefer to be himself -- with all the tortures of hell, if so it must be.

And of a truth it is not quite so true after all when people say that "it is a matter of course that a sufferer would be so glad to be helped, if only somebody would help him" -- this is far from being the case, even though the opposite case is not always so desperate as this. The situation is this. A sufferer has one or more ways in which he would be glad to be helped. If he is helped thus, he is willing to be helped. But when in a deeper sense it becomes seriousness with this thing of needing help, especially from a higher or from the highest source -- this humiliation of having to accept help unconditionally and in any way, the humiliation of becoming nothing in the hand of the Helper for whom all things are possible, or merely the necessity of deferring to another man, of having to give up being oneself so long as one is seeking help -- ah, there are doubtless many sufferings, even protracted and agonizing sufferings, at which the self does not wince to this extent, and which therefore at bottom it prefers to retain and to be itself.

But the more consciousness there is in such a sufferer who in despair is determined to be himself, all the more does despair too potentiate itself and become demoniac. The genesis of this is commonly as follows. A self which in despair is determined to be itself winces at one pain or another which simply cannot be taken away or separated from its concrete self. Precisely upon this torment the man directs his whole passion, which at last becomes a demoniac rage. Even if at this point God in heaven and all his angels were to offer to help him out of it -- no, now he doesn't want it, now it is too late, he once would have given everything to be rid of this torment but was made to wait, now that's all past, now he would rather rage against everything, he, the one man in the whole of existence who is the most unjustly treated, to whom it is especially important to have his torment at hand, important that no one should take it from him -- for thus he can convince himself that he is in the right. This at last becomes so firmly fixed in his head that for a very peculiar reason he is afraid of eternity -- for the reason, namely, that it might rid him of his (demoniacally understood) infinite advantage over other men, his (demoniacally understood) justification for being what he is. It is himself he wills to be; he began with the infinite abstraction of the self, and now at last he has become so concrete that it would be an impossibility to be eternal in that sense, and yet he wills in despair to be himself. Ah, demoniac madness! He rages most of all at the thought that eternity might get it into its head to take his misery from him!

This sort of despair is seldom seen in the world, such figures generally are met with only in the works of poets, that is to say, of real poets, who always lend their characters this "demoniac" ideality (taking this word in the purely Greek sense). Nevertheless such a despairer is to be met with also in real life. What then is the corresponding outward mark? Well, there is no "corresponding" mark, for in fact a corresponding outward expression corresponding to close reserve is a contradiction in terms; for if it is corresponding, it is then of course revealing. But outwardness is the entirely indifferent factor in this case where introversion, or what one might call inwardness with a jammed lock, is so much the predominant factor. The lowest forms of despair, where there really was no inwardness, or at all events none worth talking about, the lowest forms of despair one might represent by describing or by saying something about the outward traits of the despairer. But the more despair becomes spiritual, and the more inwardness becomes a peculiar world for itself in introversion, all the more is the self alert with demoniac shrewdness to keep despair shut up in close reserve, and all the more intent therefore to set the outward appearance at the level of indifference, to make it as unrevealing and indifferent as possible. As according to the report of superstition the troll disappears through a crack which no one can perceive, so it is for the despairer all the more important to dwell in an exterior semblance behind which it ordinarily would never occur to anyone to look for it. This hiddenness is precisely something spiritual and is one of the safety-devices for assuring oneself of having as it were behind reality an enclosure, a world for itself locking all else out, a world where the despairing self is employed as tirelessly as Tantalus in willing to be itself.

We began in section 1 (ii) with the lowest form of despair, which in despair does not will to be itself. The demoniac despair is the most potentiated form of the despair which despairingly wills to be itself. This despair does not will to be itself with Stoic doting upon itself, nor with self-deification, willing in this way, doubtless mendaciously, yet in a certain sense in terms of its perfection; no, with hatred for existence it wills to be itself, to be itself in terms of its misery; it does not even in defiance or defiantly will to be itself, but to be itself in spite; it does not even will in defiance to tear itself free from the Power which posited it, it wills to obtrude upon this Power in spite, to hold on to it out of malice. And that is natural, a malignant objection must above all take care to hold on to that against which it is an objection. Revolting against the whole of existence, it thinks it has hold of a proof against it, against its goodness. This proof the despairer thinks he himself is, and that is what he wills to be, therefore he wills to be himself, himself with his torment, in order with this torment to protest against the whole of existence. Whereas the weak despairer will not hear about what comfort eternity has for him, so neither will such a despairer hear about it, but for a different reason, namely, because this comfort would be the destruction of him as an objection against the whole of existence. It is (to describe it figuratively) as if an author were to make a slip of the pen, and that this clerical error became conscious of being such -- perhaps it was no error but in a far higher sense was an essential constituent in the whole exposition -- it is then as if this clerical error would revolt against the author, out of hatred for him were to forbid him to correct it, and were to say, "No, I will not be erased, I will stand as a witness against thee, that thou art a very poor writer."

Part 2: Despair is Sin

Chapter 1: Despair is Sin

Sin is this: before God, or with the conception of God, to be in despair at not willing to be oneself, or in despair at willing to be oneself.

Thus sin is potentiated weakness or potentiated defiance: sin is the potentiation of despair. The point upon which the emphasis rests is before God, or the fact that the conception of God is involved; the factor which dialectically, ethically, religiously, makes "qualified" despair (to use a juridical term) synonymous with sin is the conception of God.

Although in this Second Part, and especially in this section, there is no place or occasion for psychological description, there here may be introduced, as the most dialectical borderline between despair and sin, what one might call a poet-existence in the direction of the religious, an existence which has something in common with the despair of resignation, only that the conception of God is involved. Such an existence (as is to be seen from the conjunction and position of the categories) will be the most eminent poet-existence. From a Christian standpoint such an existence (in spite of all aesthetic) is sin, it is the sin of poetizing instead of being, of standing in relation to the Good and the True through imagination instead of being that, or rather existentially striving to be it. The poet-existence here in question is distinguished from despair by the fact that it includes the conception of God or is before God; but it is prodigiously dialectical, and is in an impenetrable dialectical confusion as to how far it is conscious of being sin. Such a poet may have a very deep religious need, and the conception of God is included in his despair. He loves God above everything, God is for him the only comfort in his secret torment, and yet he loves the torment, he will not let it go. He would so gladly be himself before God, but not with respect to this fixed point where the self suffers, there despairingly he will not be himself; he hopes that eternity will remove it, and here in the temporal, however much he suffers under it, he cannot will to accept it, cannot humble himself under it in faith. And yet he continues to hold to God, and this is his only happiness, for him it would be the greatest horror to have to do without God, "it would be enough to drive one to despair"; and yet he permits himself commonly, but perhaps unconsciously, to poetize. God, making him a little bit other than He is, a little bit more like a loving father who all too much indulges the child's "only wish." He who became unhappy in love, and therefore became a poet, blissfully extolls the happiness of love -- so he became a poet of religiousness, he understands obscurely that it is required of him to let this torment go, that is, to humble himself under it in faith and to accept it as belonging to the self -- for he would hold it aloof from him, and thereby precisely he holds it fast, although doubtless he thinks (and this, like every other word of despair, is correct in the opposite sense and therefore must be understood inversely) that this must mean separating himself from it as far as possible, letting it go as far as it is possible for a man to do so. But to accept it in faith, that he cannot do, or rather in the last resort he will not, or here is where the self ends in obscurity. But like that poet's description of love, so this poet's description of the religious possesses an enchantment, a lyrical flight, such as no married man's description has, nor that of his Reverence. What he says is not untrue, by no means, his representation reflects his happier, his better ego. With respect to the religious he is an unhappy lover, that is, he is not in a strict sense a believer, he has only the first prerequisite of faith, and with that an ardent longing for the religious. His collision is essentially this: is he the elect, is the thorn in the flesh the expression for the fact that he is to be employed as the extraordinary, is it before God quite as it should be with respect to the extraordinary figure he has become? or is the thorn in the flesh the experience he must humble himself under in order to attain the universal human? But enough of this. I can say with the emphasis of truth, "To whom am I talking?" Who will bother about such psychological investigations carried to the nth power? The Nüremburg Picture Books painted by priests are easily understood; one and all, they resemble, deceptively, people as they generally are, and, spiritually understood, nothing.

1. Gradations in the Consciousness of the Self (The Qualification "before God")

In the foregoing there is steadily pointed out a gradation in the consciousness of the self: first came unconsciousness of being-an eternal self (III.B a), then a knowledge of having a self in which there is after all something eternal (III.B b), and under this (1 i and ii, 2) there were again pointed out gradations. This whole situation must now be turned about and viewed in a new way. The point is this. The gradations in the consciousness of the self with which we have hitherto been employed are within the definition of the human self, or the self whose measure is man. But this self acquires a new quality or qualification in the fact that it is the self directly in the sight of God. This self is no longer the merely human self but is what I would call, hoping not to be misunderstood, the theological self, the self directly in the sight of God. And what an infinite reality this self acquires by being before God! A herdsman who (if this were possible) is a self only in the sight of cows is a very-low self, and so also is a ruler who is a self in the sight of slaves -- for in both cases the scale or measure is lacking. The child who hitherto has had only the parents to measure himself by, becomes a self when he is a man by getting the state as a measure. But what an infinite accent falls upon the self by getting God as a measure! The measure for the self always is that in the face of which it is a self; but this does not define what "measure" is. As one can add up only magnitudes of the same order, so each thing is qualitatively that by which it is measured; and that which is qualitatively its measure (Maalestok) is ethically its goal (Maal); and the measure and goal are qualitatively that which something is -- with exception of the relation which obtains in the world of freedom, where a man by not being qualitatively that which is his goal and his measure must himself have deserved this disqualification, so that the goal and the measure remains the same . . . condemningly, making manifest what it is he is not: that, namely which is his goal and his measure.

It was a very just thought to which the older dogmatic frequently recurred, whereas a later dogmatic so often censored it for lack of understanding and a proper sense of its meaning -- it was a very just thought, although sometimes a wrong application was made of it: the thought that what makes sin so frightful is that it is before God. From this the theologians proved the eternity of hell-punishment. Subsequently they became shrewder and said, "Sin is sin; sin is not greater because it is against God or before God." Strange! For even the jurists talk about "qualified" crimes and extenuating circumstances, even the jurists make distinction with regard to a crime, inquiring, for example, whether it is committed against a public functionary or a private person, they prescribe a different punishment for the murder of a father and an ordinary murder.

No, the earlier dogmatic was right in asserting that the fact that the sin was before God infinitely potentiated it. Their fault lay in regarding God as something external, and in assuming that it was only now and then men sinned against God. But God is not something external in the sense that a policeman is. What we need to emphasize is that the self has the conception of God, and that then it does not will as He wills, and so is disobedient. Nor is it only now and then one sins before God; for every sin is before God, or rather it is this which properly makes human guilt to be sin.

Despair is potentiated in proportion to consciousness of self; but the self is potentiated in the ratio of the measure proposed for the self, and infinitely potentiated when God is the measure. The more conception of God, the more self; the more self, the more conception of God. Only when the self as this definite individual is conscious of existing before God, only then is it the infinite self; and then this self-sins before God. The selfishness of paganism, therefore, in spite of all that can be said about it, is not nearly so "qualified" as that of Christendom, in so far as here also there is selfishness; for the pagan did not possess his self directly in the face of God. The pagan and the natural man have as their measure the merely human self. One may be right therefore from a higher standpoint in regarding paganism as lying in sin, but properly the sin of paganism was the despairing unawareness of God, unawareness of existing before God; this means to be "without God in the world." On the other hand, it is for this reason true that the pagan did not sin in the strictest sense, for he did not sin before God. Moreover, it is also in a sense quite certain that many a time a pagan is enabled in a way to slip through the world irreproachably precisely because his light-minded Pelagian interpretation saved him; but then his sin is a different one, namely, this light-minded interpretation. On the other hand and in a different aspect it is quite certain that just by being brought up strictly in Christianity a man has in a certain sense been plunged into sin, because the whole Christian view was too serious for him, especially in an earlier period of his life; but then in another sense this is again of some help to him, this deeper apprehension of what sin is.

Sin is: before God in despair not to will to be oneself, or before God in despair to will to be oneself. But is not this definition, even though in other aspects it may be conceded to have advantages (and among them this which is the weightiest of all, that it is the only Scriptural definition, for the Scripture always defines sin as disobedience), is it not after all too spiritual? To this one must first of all make answer that a definition of sin can never be too spiritual (unless it becomes so spiritual that it does away with sin); for sin is precisely a determinant of spirit. And in the next place, why should it then be too spiritual? Because it does not talk about murder, theft, unchastity, etc.? But does it not talk of them? Is it not also self-assertion against God when one is disobedient and defies His commandment? But on the other hand, when in talking about sin one talks only of such sins, it is so easily forgotten that in a way it may be all right, humanly speaking, with respect to all such things up to a certain point, and yet the whole life may be sin, the well-known kind of sin: glittering vices, willfulness, which either spiritlessly or impudently continues to be or wills to be unaware in what an infinitely deeper sense a human self is morally under obligation to God with respect to every most secret wish and thought, with respect to quickness in comprehending and readiness to follow every hint of God as to what His will is for this self. The sins of the flesh are the self-assertion of the lower self; but how often one devil is cast out by the devil's help, and the last state becomes worse than the first. For so it is with men in this world: first a man sins from frailty and weakness; and then -- yes, then perhaps he learns to flee to God and to be helped by faith which saves from all sin; but of this we are not talking here -- then he despairs over his weakness and becomes, either a Pharisee who in despair manages to attain a certain legal righteousness, or he despairs and plunges again into sin.

The definition therefore certainly embraces every conceivable and actual form of sin; it certainly throws into relief the decisive fact that sin is despair (for sin is not the wildness of flesh and blood, but it is the spirit's consent thereto), and it is . . . before God. As a definition it is algebraic. In this little work it would be out of place, and an effort moreover which perhaps would not succeed, were I to begin by describing the particular sins. The principal thing here is that the definition like a net must embrace all forms. And that it does, as can be seen when one tests it by setting up the opposite, namely, the definition of faith, by which I steer my course in the whole of this work, as by a sure mariners' mark. Faith is: that the self in being itself and in willing to be itself is grounded transparently in God.

But too often it has been overlooked that the opposite of sin is not virtue, not by any manner of means. This is in part a pagan view which is content with a merely human measure and properly does not know what sin is, that all sin is before God. No, the opposite of sin is faith, as is affirmed in Rom. 14:23, "whatsoever is not of faith is sin." And for the whole of Christianity it is one of the most decisive definitions that the opposite of sin is not virtue but faith.

Appendix: That the Definition of Sin Contains the Possibility of the

Offense -- A General Observation about Offense

The opposition sin/faith is the Christian one, which in a Christian way transforms the definition of all ethical concepts, giving them one distillation the more. At the bottom of this opposition lies the decisive Christian concept, "before God," a determinant which in turn stands in relation to the decisive criterion of Christianity: the absurd, the paradox, the possibility of offense. And that this should be indicated in every definition of Christianity is of the utmost importance, for the offense is Christianity's defense against all speculation. In this instance where is the possibility of the offense? It lies in the fact that a man, as a particular individual, should have such a reality as is implied by existing directly in the sight of God; and then again, and as a consequence of this, that a man s sin should concern God. This notion of the particular man . . . before God speculative philosophy never gets into its head, it can only universalize the particular man fantastically. It was just for this reason also that an incredulous Christianity made out that sin is sin, no matter whether it is directly in the sight of God or not. That is to say, they wanted to do away with the determinant "before God," and to this end they discovered a higher wisdom -- which, however, strangely enough, was neither more nor less than what the higher wisdom no doubt generally is . . . the old paganism.

There is so much said now about people being offended at Christianity because it is so dark and gloomy, offended at it because it is so severe, etc. It is now high time to explain that the real reason why man is offended at Christianity is because it is too high, because its goal is not man's goal, because it would make of a man something so extraordinary that he is unable to get it into his head. A perfectly simple psychological investigation of what offense is will explain this, and at the same time it will show how infinitely silly their behavior has been who defended Christianity by taking away the offense, how stupidly or impudently they have ignored Christ's own instruction, who often and with such deep concern warns against the offense, that is, intimates that the possibility of the offense is present, and must be ever-present, for if it is not present, if it is not an eternally essential constituent of Christianity. it is nonsense, humanly speaking, for Christ, instead of taking it away, to be distressed about it and to give warning against it.

If I were to imagine to myself a day-laborer and the mightiest emperor that ever lived, and were to imagine that this mighty Emperor took a notion to send for the poor man, who never had dreamed, "neither had it entered into his heart to believe," that the Emperor knew of his existence, and who therefore would think himself indescribably fortunate if merely he was permitted once to see the

Emperor, and would recount it to his children and children's children as the most important event of his life -- but suppose the Emperor sent for him and informed him that he wished to have him for his son-in-law . . . what then? Then the laborer, humanly, would become somewhat or very much puzzled, shame-faced, and embarrassed, and it would seem to him, quite humanly (and this is the human element in it), something exceedingly strange, something quite mad, the last thing in the world about which he would say a word to anybody else, since he himself in his own mind was not far from explaining it by supposing (as his neighbors would be busily doing as soon as possible) that the Emperor wanted to make a fool of him, so that the poor man would be the laughing-stock of the whole town, his picture in the papers, the story of his espousal to the Emperor's daughter the theme of balladmongers. This thing, however, of becoming the Emperor's son-in-law might readily be subjected to the tests of reality, so that the laborer would he able to ascertain how far the Emperor was serious in this matter, or whether he merely wanted to make fun of the poor fellow, render him unhappy for the rest of his life, and help him to find his way to the mad-house; for the quid nimis is in evidence, which with such infinite ease can turn into its opposite. A small expression of favor the laborer would be able to get through his head; it would be understood in the market-town by "the highly respected cultured public," by all ballad-mongers, in short, by the 5 times 100,000 persons who dwelt in that market-town, which with respect to its population was even a very big city, but with respect to possessing understanding of and sense for the extraordinary was a very small market-town -- but this thing of becoming the Emperor's son-in-law was far too much. And suppose now that this was not an external reality but an inward thing, so that factual proofs could not help the laborer to certitude, but faith itself was the facticity, and so it was all left to faith whether he possessed humble courage enough to dare to believe it (for impudent courage cannot help one to believe)-- how many laboring men were there likely to be who possessed this courage? But he who had not this courage would be offended; the extraordinary would seem to him almost like mockery of him. He would then perhaps honestly and plainly admit, "Such a thing is too high for me, I cannot get it into my head; it seems to me, if I may blurt it straight out, foolishness."

And now for Christianity! Christianity teaches that this particular individual, and so every individual, whatever in other respects this individual may be, man, woman, serving-maid, minister of state, merchant, barber, student, etc. -- this individual exists before God -- this individual who perhaps would be vain for having once in his life talked with the King, this man who is not a little proud of living on intimate terms with that person or the other, this man exists before God, can talk with God any moment he will, sure to be heard by Him; in short, this man is invited to live on the most intimate terms with God! Furthermore, for this man's sake God came to the world, let himself be born, suffers and dies; and this suffering God almost begs and entreats this man to accept the help which is offered him! Verily, if there is anything that would make a man lose his understanding, it is surely this! Whosoever has not the humble courage to dare to believe it, must be offended at it. But why is he offended? Because it is too high for him, because he cannot get it into his head, because in the face of it he cannot acquire frank-heartedness, and therefore must have it done away with, brought to naught and nonsense, for it is as though it would stifle him.

For what is offense? Offense is unhappy admiration. It is therefore akin to envy, but it is an envy which is turned against oneself, or, more exactly, envy which is worst of all against oneself. The narrowmindedness of the natural man cannot welcome for itself the extraordinary which God has intended for him; so he is offended.

The degree of the offense depends upon what passion a man has for admiration. The more prosaic men, devoid of imagination and passion, and who therefore are not apt to admire, they too may be offended, but they confine themselves to saying, "Such a thing I can't get through my head, I let it alone." These are the skeptics. But the more passion and imagination a man has, the nearer consequently he is in a certain sense (that is, in possibility) to being able to become a believer -- nota bene! by adoringly humbling himself under the extraordinary - all the more passionate is the offense, which at last cannot be contented with less than getting this thing rooted out, annihilated and trodden in the dust.

If one would learn to understand offense, let him study human envy, a subject which I offer as an extra course, pluming myself upon having studied it profoundly. Envy is concealed admiration. An admirer who feels that he cannot be happy by surrendering himself elects to become envious of that which he admires. So he speaks another language, and in that language of his the thing which he really admires is called a stupid, insipid and queer sort of thing. Admiration is happy selfsurrender; envy is unhappy self-assertion.

So also it is with offense: that which in the relation between man and man is known as admiration/envy, in the relation between man and God is adoration/offense. The summa summarum of all human wisdom is this "golden," or perhaps more properly the gilded, ne quid nimis [nothing to excess], too much or too little spoils the broth. This is given and taken between man and man as wisdom and is honored by admiration, its quotation never fluctuates, the whole of humanity guarantees its value. So if once in a while there lives a genius who goes a little bit beyond it, he is declared mad . . . by the wise. But Christianity takes a prodigious giant-stride beyond this ne quid nimis, a stride into the absurd -- there Christianity begins . . . and the offense.

One sees now how extraordinarily (that there might be something extraordinary left) -- how extraordinarily stupid it is to defend Christianity, how little knowledge of men this betrays, and how truly, even though it be unconsciously, it is working in collusion with the enemy, by making of Christianity a miserable something or another which in the end has to be rescued by a defense. Therefore, it is certain and true that he who first invented the notion of defending Christianity in Christendom is de facto Judas No. 2; he also betrays with a kiss, only his treachery is that of stupidity. To defend anything is always to discredit it. Let a man have a storehouse full of gold, let him be willing to dispense every ducat to the poor -- but let him besides that be stupid enough to begin this benevolent undertaking with a defense in which he advances three reasons to prove that it is justifiable -- and people will be almost inclined to doubt whether he is doing any good. But now for Christianity! Yea, he who defends it has never believed in it. If he believes, then the enthusiasm of faith is . . . not defense, no, it is attack and victory. The believer is a victor.

Thus it stands with Christianity and the offense. The possibility of the offense is quite rightly included in the Christian definition of sin -- in this phrase, "before God." A. pagan, the natural man, is very willing to admit that sin exists, but this "before God," which really is what makes sin to be sin, is for him too much, it seems to him (though in a different sense from that pointed out here) to make too much of what it is to be a man; a little less, and then he is willing to agree to it -- "but too much is too much."

2. The Socratic Definition of Sin

Sin is ignorance. This is the well-known Socratic definition of sin, which, like everything Socratic, is an opinion always worthy of attention. However, with respect to this Socratic position, as with respect to many other Socratic positions, how many men have felt a need of going further? What an innumerable number have felt the need of going further than the Socratic ignorance -- presumably because they felt that it was impossible for them to stay there; for in every generation how many men are there that are capable, even for only a month, of enduring and existentially expressing ignorance about everything?

Therefore, I do not by any means intend to dispose of the Socratic definition on the ground that one cannot stop with it but, having the Christian definition in mente [in mind], I would make use of it to bring the other out sharply (just because the Socratic definition is so genuinely Greek), so that here as always the hollowness of every other definition which is not in the strictest sense Christian (that is, of every partial definition) may become manifest.

The difficulty with the Socratic definition is that it leaves undetermined how ignorance itself is to be more precisely understood, the question of its origin, etc. That is to say, even if sin be ignorance (or what Christianity would perhaps prefer to call stupidity), which in one sense cannot be denied, we have to ask, is this an original ignorance, is it always the case that one has not known and hitherto could not know anything about the truth, or is it a superinduced, a subsequent ignorance? If it is what the last question implies, then sin must properly have its ground in something else, it must have its ground in the activity with which a man has labored to obscure his intelligence. But also when this is assumed, the stiff-necked and tough-lived difficulty returns, prompting the question whether at the instant a man began to obscure his intelligence he was distinctly conscious of what he was doing. If he was not distinctly conscious of this, then his intelligence was already somewhat obscured before he began, and the question merely returns again. If it is assumed on the contrary that when he began to obscure his intelligence he was distinctly conscious of it, then sin (even though it be unconsciousness, seeing that this was an induced state) would not lie in the intelligence but in the will, and the question which must be raised is about the relation of the intelligence and the will to one another. With such questions as these (and one might continue to augment them for many a day) the Socratic definition does not deal. Socrates was certainly an ethical teacher (the Classical age claims him absolutely as the discoverer of ethics), he was the first one, as he is and remains the first in his class; but he begins with ignorance. Intellectually, it is toward ignorance he tends, toward the position of knowing nothing.

Ethically, he understands by ignorance quite a different thing, and so he begins with that.

But on the other hand, as a matter of course, Socrates is not an essentially religious ethicist, still less a dogmatic one, as the Christian ethicist is. Hence, he does not really enter into the whole investigation with which Christianity begins, into the prius [before] in which sin presupposes itself, and which is Christianly explained by the doctrine of original sin -- a dogma to the border of which only we come in this investigation.

Socrates therefore never really gets to the determinant we know as sin, which is surely a defect in a definition of sin. Why is this? For if sin is indeed ignorance, then sin properly does not exist, since sin is definitely consciousness. I-f sin consists in being ignorant of what is right, so that one consequently does what is wrong, sin does not exist. If this is sin, then it must be assumed, as Socrates also assumed, that the case does not occur of a man knowing what is right and doing what is wrong, or knowing that a thing is wrong and doing the wrong. So then, if the Socratic definition is correct, sin does not exist. But, lo, precisely this is, Christianity understood, just as it should be, in a deeper sense it is quite correct, in the interest of Christianity it is quadrat demonstrandum. Precisely the concept by which Christianity distinguishes itself qualitatively and most decisively from paganism is the concept of sin, the doctrine of sin; and therefore Christianity also assumes quite consistently that neither paganism nor the natural man knows what sin is; yea, it assumes that there must be a revelation from God to make manifest what sin is. For it is not true, as a superficial view assumes, that the doctrine of the atonement is the qualitative difference between paganism and Christianity. No, the beginning must be made far deeper, with sin, with the doctrine of sin, as Christianity also does. What a dangerous objection therefore against Christianity if paganism had a definition of sin which Christianity must admit is correct!

What determinant is it then that Socrates lacks in determining what sin is? It is will, defiant will. The Greek intellectualism was too happy, too naive, too aesthetic, too ironical, too witty . . . too sinful to be able to get it into its head that a person knowingly could fail to do the good, or knowingly. with knowledge of what was right, do what was wrong.

The Greek spirit proposes an intellectual categorical imperative.

The truth in this definition must by no means be overlooked, and it needs to be enforced in times such as these which have gone astray in so much flatulent and unfruitful knowledge, so that doubtless now, just as in Socrates' age, only much more, it is advisable that people should be starved a little bit Socratically. It is enough to provoke both laughter and tears -- not only all these protestations about having understood and comprehended the highest thought, but also the virtuosity with which many know how to present it in abstracto, and in a certain sense quite correctly -- it is enough to provoke both laughter and tears when one sees then that all this knowing and understanding exercises no influence upon the lives of these men, that their lives do not in the remotest way express what they have understood, but rather the contrary. One involuntarily exclaims at the sight of a disproportion at once so sorrowful and so ludicrous. But how in the world is it possible that they have understood it? And is it true that they have understood? Here the ancient ironist and ethicist makes answer: "My dear man, never believe it, for if they truly had understood, their lives also would have expressed it, they would have done what they understood."

To understand/and to understand are therefore two things? Certainly they are; and he who has understood this (but not, be it noted, in the sense of the first sort of understanding) is initiated into all the secret mysteries of irony. It is with this contradiction irony is properly employed. To perceive the comic in the fact that a person is actually ignorant of something means a very low sort of comic, beneath the dignity of irony. There is properly no profound comic in the fact that people once lived who assumed that the earth stands still -- when nobody knew any better. The same thing will presumably befall our age in contrast with an age which knows more of physical law. The contradiction is one between two different ages, there is lacking a deeper point of coincidence; such a contradiction is not essential, and hence neither is it essentially comic. No, but that a man stands up and says the right thing . . . and so has understood it, and then when he has to act does the wrong thing . . . and so shows that he has not understood it -- yes, that is comic. It is infinitely comic that a man, moved unto tears, so much moved that not only tears but sweat trickle from him, can sit and read, or hear, representations of self-denial, of the nobility of sacrificing one's life for the truth -- and then the next instant -- one, two, three, slap-dash, almost with the tears still in his eyes -- is in full swing, in the sweat of his brow, with all his might and main, helping falsehood to conquer. It is infinitely comic that an orator, with truth in his voice and in the expression of his features, profoundly touched and profoundly touching, can present the truth in a heart-rending way, can tread all evil and all the powers of hell under his feet, with an aplomb in his attitude, an assurance in his glance, a resoluteness in his step, which is altogether admirable -- it is infinitely comic that almost at the same moment, almost "with his dressinggown still on," he can run cowardly and timidly out of the way of the least inconvenience. It is infinitely comic that a man can understand the whole truth about how wretched and petty this world is, etc. -- that he can understand this, and then cannot recognize again what he understood; for almost in the same moment he himself goes off and takes part in the same pettiness and wretchedness, takes glory in it and receives glory from it, that is, accepts it. O when one beholds a man who protests that he has entirely understood how Christ went about in the form of a lowly servant, poor, despised, and, as the Scripture says, spat upon -- when I see the same man so careful to betake himself thither where in a worldly sense it is good to be, and accommodate himself there in the utmost security, when I see him apprehensive of every puff of wind from right or left, as though his life depended upon it, and so blissful, so utterly blissful, so awfully glad -- yes, to make the thing complete, so awfully glad that he is able to thank God for it -- glad that he is held in honor by all men -- then I have often said to myself and by myself, "Socrates, Socrates, Socrates, can it be possible that this man has understood what he says he has understood?" So I have said, and at the same time I have wished that Socrates might be right. For it seemed to me after all as though Christianity were too severe, nor can I bring it into accord with my experience to treat such a man as a hypocrite. No, Socrates, thee I can understand; thou dost treat him as a wag, as a sort of merry Andrew, thou dost treat him as a butt for laughter, thou hast no objection, it has even thine approval, that I prepare and serve him up as a comic dish -- provided I do it well.

Socrates, Socrates, Socrates! Yes, one may well call thy name thrice, it would not be too much to call it ten times, if that would do any good. People think that the world needs a republic, and they think that it needs a new social order, and a new religion -- but it never occurs to anybody that what the world now needs, confused as it is by much knowing, is a Socrates. But that is perfectly natural, for if anybody had this notion, not to say if many were to have it, there would be less need of a Socrates. What a delusion most needs is the very thing it least thinks of -- naturally, for otherwise it would not be a delusion.

So then, such an ironic-ethical correction might very well be what our age needs, and perhaps the only thing it really needs; for it is evident that this is the thing it least thinks of. It is highly important that, instead of going further than Socrates, we simply return to the Socratic dictum that to understand/and to understand are two things -- not returning to it as a result [once for all acquired], for in the end that only helps men into the deepest wretchedness, since it simply abolishes the distinction between understanding/and understanding, but returning to it as the ethical interpretation of every-day life.

The Socratic definition helps itself out as follows. When a person doesn't do the right thing; why then, neither has he understood it; his understanding is a vain conceit, his assertion that he has understood it is a false indication of the way, his repeated assertion that the devil take him if he has not understood it is a prodigious remoteness along the greatest possible detour. But then indeed the definition is correct. If a man does the right thing, then surely he doesn't sin; and if he doesn't do the right thing, then neither has he understood it; if in truth he had understood it, this would at once have moved him to do it, would at once make him an echo of his understanding -- ergo sin is ignorance.

But where does the difficulty lie? It is to be ascribed to a fact of which the Socratic view itself was aware (though only to a certain degree) and sought to remedy, that it lacks a dialectical determinant for the transition from having understood something to the doing of it. In this transition Christianity makes its start; by proceeding along this path it proves that sin lies in the will, thus attaining the concept of defiance; and then, in order to make the end thoroughly fast, it adjoins to this the dogma of original sin -- for, alas, the secret of Speculation's success in comprehending is just this, of sewing without making the end fast and without knotting the thread, and therefore it can marvelously keep on sewing, i.e. keep on pulling the end through. Christianity, on the contrary, fastens the end by means of the paradox.

In pure ideality, where there is no question of the real individual man, the transition is accomplished by necessity (in the System indeed everything comes about by necessity), in other words, there is no difficulty at all connected with the transition from understanding to doing. This is purely in the Greek spirit -- yet not Socratic, for Socrates was too much of an ethicist for that. And quite the same thing is really the secret of the whole of recent philosophy: cogito ergo sum, to think is to be. The Christian motto, on the contrary, is: As thou believest, so it comes to pass; or As thou believest, so art thou; to believe is to be. So one can see that modern philosophy is neither more nor less than paganism. But this is not the worst, to be akin to Socrates is not the meanest position. But the entirely unsocratic trait of modern philosophy is that it wants to make itself and us believe that it is Christianity.

In the world of reality, on the other hand, where it is a question of the individual man, there is this little tiny transition from having understood to doing; it is not always cito citissime [as quickly as possible], not geschwind wie der Wind [fast as the wind], if I may speak German for lack of philosophic terms. On the contrary, here begins a very prolix story.

In the life of spirit, on the other hand, there is no stopping [Stilstand] (nor in reality is there any condition [Tilstand], everything is actuality): in case then a man the very same second he has known what is right does not do it -- well then, first of all, the knowledge stops boiling. And next comes the question how the will likes this thing that is known. If it does not like it, it does not follow that the will goes ahead and does the opposite of that which the intelligence understood, such strong contrasts occur doubtless rather seldom; but the will lets some time pass, there is an interim, that means, "We'll see about that tomorrow." All this while the intelligence becomes more and more obscured, and the lower nature triumphs more and more. For, alas, the good must be done at once -- at once, the moment it is known (and hence the transition goes so easily in the pure ideality where everything is "at once"), but the strength of the lower nature consists in dragging a thing out. The will has no particular objection to it -- so it says with its fingers crossed. And then when the intelligence has become duly darkened, the intelligence and the will can understand one another better; at last they agree entirely, for now the intelligence has gone over to the side of the will and acknowledges that the thing is quite right as it would have it. And so there live perhaps a great multitude of men who labor off and on to obscure their ethical and religious understanding which would lead them out into decisions and consequences which the lower nature does not love, extending meanwhile their aesthetic and metaphysical understanding, which ethically is a distraction.

However, with all this we have not yet got any further than the Socratic position; for, as Socrates would say, if this comes about, then it only shows that such a man had not understood what is right. That is to say, the Greek spirit had not the courage to assert that a man knowingly does what is wrong, with knowledge of the right does what is wrong; so Socrates comes to its aid and says, When a man does wrong, he has not understood what is right.

Quite correct, and further than that no man can go: no man by himself and of himself can explain what sin is, precisely because he is in sin. All his talk about sin is at bottom palliation for sin, an excuse, a sinful mitigation. Hence Christianity begins also in another way, by declaring that there must be a revelation from God in order to instruct man as to what sin is, that sin does not consist in the fact that man has not understood what is right, but in the fact that he will not understand it, and in the fact that he will not do it.

With respect to the distinction between not being able to understand/and not being willing to understand, even Socrates furnishes no real enlightenment, whereas he is Grand Master above all ironists in operating by means of the distinction between understanding/and understanding. Socrates explains that he who does not do the right thing has not understood it; but Christianity goes a little further back and says, it is because he will not understand it, and this in turn is because he does not will the right. And in the next place, describing what properly is defiance, it teaches that a man does wrong although he understands what is right, or forbears to do right although he understands what is right; in short, the Christian doctrine of sin is pure impertinence against man, accusation upon accusation; it is the charge which the Deity as prosecutor takes the liberty of lodging against man.

But can anyone comprehend this Christian doctrine? By no means -- this too is Christian, and so is an offense. It must be believed. Comprehension is conterminous with man's relation to the human, but faith is man's relation to the divine. How then does Christianity explain this incomprehensible? Quite consistently, in an equally incomprehensible way, by means of the fact that it is revealed.

So then, Christianly understood, sin lies in the will, not in the intellect; and this corruption of the will goes well beyond the consciousness of the individual. This is the perfectly consistent declaration, for otherwise the question how sin began must arise with respect to each individual.

Here again we have the criterion of the offense. The possibility of the offense consists in the fact that there has to be a revelation from God to enlighten man as to what sin is and how deep it lies. The natural man, the pagan, thinks thus: "O well, I admit that I have not understood everything in heaven and earth; if there is to be a revelation, let it inform us about the heavenly; but that there should be a revelation to explain what sin is, that is the most preposterous thing of all. I don't pretend to be a perfect man, far from it, but I know and I am willing to concede how far I am from perfection -- ought I not then to know what sin is?" But Christianity makes answer, "No, that is what you know least about, how far you are from perfection, and what sin is!" Behold, in this sense, in a Christian sense, sin doubtless is ignorance, it is ignorance of what sin is.

The definition of sin which was given in the preceding chapter therefore still needs to be completed: sin is, after having been informed by a revelation from God what sin is, then before God in despair not to will to be oneself, or before God in despair to will to be oneself.

3. Sin Is Not a Negation but a Position

For the truth of this affirmation the orthodox dogmatic as a whole has constantly contended, and it has rejected as pantheistic every definition of sin which makes it something negative -- weakness, sensuality, finiteness, ignorance, etc. Orthodoxy has perceived very rightly that

here is where the battle has to be fought, or (to recall the foregoing) that it is here the end must be made fast, that here is the place to put up resistance. Orthodoxy has rightly perceived that, if sin is defined negatively, all of Christianity totters. Therefore, orthodoxy insists that there must be a revelation from God in order to teach fallen men what sin is, a revelation which, quite consistently, must be believed, since it is a dogma. And naturally paradox, faith, dogma, these three determinants, form an alliance and accord which is the firmest support and bulwark against pagan wisdom.

So it is with orthodoxy. By a strange misunderstanding, a so-called speculative dogmatic, which certainly - has suspicious dealings with philosophy, has entertained the notion that it is able to comprehend this definition of sin as a position. But if this is true, then sin is a negation. The secret of all comprehending is that the very act of comprehension is higher than every position which it posits. The concept posits a position, but the fact that it is comprehended means precisely that it is negated. The speculative dogmatic, being itself aware of this to a certain degree, has known no other way to help itself but by the maneuver, not very seemly in a philosophic science, of throwing out a detachment of asseverations at the point where a movement is being made. One asseverates, each time more solemnly than the last, and with more and more oaths and curses, that sin is a position, that to say that it is merely a negation is pantheism and rationalism, and God knows what all, but altogether something which the speculative dogmatic renunciates and abhors -- and then one goes on to comprehend what it means that sin is a position. That is to say that after all it is a position only up to a certain degree, not any more so than that one can after all comprehend it.

And the same duplicity of speculation is manifested also at another point, which is, however, related to the same subject. The interpretation of sin, or the way sin is defined, is decisive for the interpretation of repentance. Then since this thing of negating a negation is so speculative, there is nothing else to be done, repentance must be a negation of the negation -- and so sin becomes the negation.

However, it is certainly very much to be desired that a sober thinker would for once explain how far this purely logical process, which recalls the grammatical rule that two negatives make an affirmative, and the mathematical rule that two minuses are a plus -- how far, I say, this logical process is valid in the world of reality, in the world of qualities; whether after all the qualities are not subject to a different dialectic; whether in this case "transition" does not play a different rôle. Sub specie aetemi, aeterno modo, etc. the element of time is lacking in which things can be spaced out, hence everything is, and there is no transition at all. In this abstract medium to posit is eo ipso the same thing as to cancel or "resolve." But to regard reality in the same way is pretty close to madness. One can say also in abstracto that the perfect tense follows the imperfect. But if in the world of reality a man were to infer that it followed by itself and followed at once, that a work he had not completed (the imperfect) became complete (the perfect) -- he surely would be crazy. But so it is too with the so-called "position" of sin when the medium in which it is posited is pure thinking; that medium is far too unstable to insure that this assertion that sin is a position can be taken seriously.

However, all such questions are aside from the issue which immediately concerns me here. I am merely keeping a steady hold upon the Christian dogma that sin is a position -- not, however, as though it could be comprehended, but as a paradox which must be believed. To my way of thinking, this is the correct thing. If only one can get it made manifest that all attempts at comprehending are selfcontradictory, then the thing assumes the correct position, and then it becomes clear that it must be left to faith whether one will believe or not.

I can well comprehend (this being not too divine a matter to be comprehended) that one who just simply has to comprehend, and only can think of such matters as offer themselves to comprehension, may find this material very scanty. But in case the whole of Christianity hinges upon this, that it must be believed, not comprehended, that it either must be believed or one must be offended at it -- is it then so meritorious to be determined to comprehend it? Is it meritorious, or is it not rather insolence or thoughtlessness, to will to comprehend that which is not willing to be comprehended? When a King takes the notion of wishing to be entirely incognito, to be treated in all respects as a simple man, is it then, just because in general it seems to men a greater distinction to do him royal homage, is it then the correct thing to do it? Or is it not precisely to assert oneself and one's own way of thinking directly in opposition to the King's will? Is it not to do as one willfully prefers to do, instead of deferring to the King's will? Or would it, I wonder, give pleasure to the King in proportion as such a man was more ingenious in displaying toward him the proper reverence of a subject when the King does not wish to be treated in that way -- that is to say, the more ingenious such a man might be in acting contrary to the King's will?

So let others admire and extol him who claims to be able to comprehend Christianity -- I regard it as a plain ethical duty, which perhaps demands no little self-denial in such speculative times when all "the others" are busy about comprehending -- I regard it then as a plain duty to admit that one neither can nor shall comprehend it. Just this, however, is doubtless what the age, what Christendom, needs, namely, a little Socratic ignorance in relation to Christianity -- but I say emphatically Socratic ignorance. Let us never forget (yet after all how many are there that ever have known it or thought of it?) -- let us never forget that the ignorance of Socrates was a kind of godly fear and divine worship, that his ignorance was the Greek rendering of the Jewish perception that the fear of God is the beginning of wisdom. Let us never forget that precisely out of reverence for the Deity he was ignorant, that, so far as a pagan could be, he kept watch as a judge on the border between God/and man, watching out to see that the deep gulf of qualitative distinction be firmly fixed between them, between God/and man, that God/and man may not in a way, philosophice, poetice, etc., coalesce into one. Lo, for this reason Socrates was the ignorant man, and for this reason the Deity recognized - him as the most knowing. -- But Christianity teaches that everything Christian exists only for faith; for this reason precisely it wills to be a Socratic, a Godfearing ignorance, which by ignorance defends faith against speculation, keeping watch to see that the deep gulf of qualitative distinction between God/and man may be firmly fixed, as it is in the paradox and in faith, lest God/and man, still more dreadfully than ever it occurred in paganism, might in a way, philosophice, poetice, etc., coalesce into one . . . in the System.

Only from one side can there be any question here of illuminating the fact that sin is a position. In the foregoing description of despair attention was constantly directed to an ascending scale. The expression for the scale was in part potentiation of consciousness of the self, in part potentiation as from passive suffering to conscious action. Both expressions in combination are in turn the expression for the fact that despair does not come from without but from within. And in the same degree despair is more and more positive [ponerende]. But according to the definition of sin we have formulated, a constituent of sin is the self as infinitely potentiated by the conception of God, and thus in turn it is the greatest possible consciousness of sin as a deed. This is the expression for the fact that sin is a position; the positive factor in it is precisely this, that it is before God.

Moreover, the determination of sin as a position involves also, in an entirely different sense, the possibility of offense, the paradox. For the paradox results from the doctrine of the atonement. First Christianity goes ahead and establishes sin so securely as a position that the human understanding never can comprehend it; and then it is the same Christian doctrine which in turn undertakes to do away with this position so completely that the human understanding never can comprehend it. Speculation, which chatters itself away from the paradoxes, lops a little bit off at both ends, and so it goes easier: it does not make sin so entirely positive -- and in spite of this it cannot get it through its head that sin should be entirely forgotten. But Christianity, which is the first discoverer of the paradoxes, is in this case also as paradoxical as possible; it works directly against itself when it establishes sin so securely as a position that it seems a perfect impossibility to do away with it again -- and then it is precisely Christianity which, by the atonement, would do away with it so completely that it is as though drowned in the sea.

Appendix to I:

But Then in a Certain Sense Does Not Sin Become a Great Rarity?

(The Moral)

It was remarked in Part First that the more intense despair becomes, the more rare it is in the world. But now, as we have seen, sin is that despair which has been still further potentiated and qualitatively potentiated, and so this surely must be exceedingly rare! Marvelous objection! Christianity has concluded all under sin; we have endeavored to represent the Christian position as rigorously as possible -- and from this results the strange conclusion that sin is not to be found at all in paganism, but only in Judaism and Christianity, and there again only very rarely!

And yet this is (but only in one sense) perfectly correct. "After having been informed by a revelation from God what sin is, then before God in despair not to will to be oneself, or before God in despair to will to be oneself," is to sin -- and certainly it is rare for a man to be so developed, so transparent to himself, that this can fit his case. But what logically follows from this? Yea, one may well take heed of this, for here there is a peculiar dialectical turn. From the fact that a man is not in a more intense despair it did not follow that he is not in despair. On the contrary, it was proved precisely that most men, by far the majority of men, are in despair, despair in a lower form. There is no merit in being in despair in a higher degree. Aesthetically it is an advantage, for aesthetically one has regard merely to strength; but ethically the more intense kind of despair is further from salvation than is the lower.

And so it is also in the case of sin. The lives of most men, being determined by a dialectic of indifference, are so remote from the good (faith) that they are almost too spiritless to be called sin, yes, almost too spiritless to be called despair.

To be in the strictest sense a sinner is again very far from being meritorious. But then on the other hand how on earth can one expect to find an essential consciousness of sin (and after all that is what Christianity wants) in a life which is so retarded by triviality, by a chattering imitation of "the others," that one hardly can call it sin, that it is too spiritless to be so called, and fit only, as the Scripture says, to be "spewed out"?

But this is not the end of the matter, for the dialectic of sin merely catches one in another way. For how does it come about that a man's life becomes so spiritless that it is as if Christianity could not be brought into relation to it, as when a jack-screw (and like a jack-screw is the uplifting power of Christianity) cannot be employed because there is no solid ground but only moss and bog? Is this something that befalls a man? No, it is man's own fault. No man is born with spiritlessness, and however many there be who in death bring with them this as the only acquisition of their lives -- this is not the fault of life.

But it must be said, and as outspokenly as possible, that the so-called Christendom (in which after a sort all men are Christians in a way, so that there are just as many, precisely as many Christians as there are men) -- it must be said that not only is it a wretched edition of Christianity, full of misprints disturbing to the sense, and of senseless omissions and additions, but that it has abusively taken Christianity's name in vain. In a small country there are born hardly three poets in every generation, but of priests there are a plenty, many more than can get appointments. With regard to a poet people speak of his having a call; but as for becoming a priest, it seems enough to the generality of men (and that means of Christians) that one has taken an examination. And yet, alas, a true priest is even more rare than a true poet, and the word "call" originally was used in a religious sense. But with respect to being a poet people still retain a notion that it is something, and that there is something in it that a man is called. On the other hand, to be a priest is in the eyes of the generality of men (and so also of Christians) a thing bereft of every uplifting conception, lacking the least trace of the mysterious, in puns naturalibus [i.e., without mincing words] it is a career. "Call" means a benefice; people talk about getting a call; but about having a call -- O yes, they talk about being "called" for trumps.

And, alas, the fate of this word in Christendom is like a motto for Christianity as a whole. The misfortune is not that Christian truth is never uttered (just as it is not the misfortune that there are not priests enough), but that it is uttered in such a way that at last the generality of men attach to it no significance whatever (just as the generality of men attach to being a priest no other significance than that which goes with the week-day occupations of a merchant, attorney, bookbinder, veterinary, etc.), so that the highest things make no impression at all, but sound out and are heard as something which somehow, God knows how, has become use and wont, like so many other things. What wonder then that certain people, instead of finding their own conduct indefensible, find it incumbent upon them to defend Christianity.

After all, a priest surely ought to be a believer. And think what a believer is! A believer is surely a lover, yea, of all lovers the most in love. With respect to enthusiasm a lover is after all only a stripling in comparison with a believer. Think now of a lover. He would be capable, would he not, day in and day out, as long as it was day and well into the night, of talking about his love. But dost thou believe it could occur to him, dost thou believe it would be possible for him, dost thou not believe that it would be an abomination to him, to talk in such a way as to try to prove by three reasons that there is after all something in this thing of being in love? -- pretty much as when the parson proves by three reasons that it is profitable to pray, so that this thing of prayer has sunk so low in price that there must be three reasons alleged to bring it a little bit into repute. Or as when the parson (and this is the same thing, only still more laughable) proves by three reasons that to pray is a bliss surpassing all understanding. Oh, priceless anticlimax! The fact that something surpasses all understanding is proved by three . . . reasons, which, whatever else they may be good for, surely do not surpass the understanding, but precisely on the contrary make it evident to the understanding that this bliss does not surpass the understanding; for, after all, reasons certainly lie within the compass of the understanding. No, for that which surpasses the understanding, and for him who believes in it, the three reasons signify no more than three bottles or three red deer! -- And now further. Dost thou believe it would occur to a lover to put up a defense for his love, that is, to admit that to him it was not the absolute, unconditionally the absolute, but that he thinks this thought of love along with objections against it, and from this proceeds the defense; that is to say, dost thou believe that he could or would concede that he was not in love, denounce himself as not being a lover? And in case a man were to propose to a lover to talk thus, dost thou not believe that he would regard that man as mad? And in case, besides being in love, he was something of an observer, dost thou not believe that he would suspect that the man who made to him this proposal had never known what it is to be in love, or would like to get him to betray and deny his love . . . by defending it? -- Is it not evident that it could never occur to one who really is in love to want to prove it by three reasons or to defend it? For in fact he himself is that which is more than all reasons and more than every defense -- he is a lover. And he who does this is not in love, he merely gives himself out [udgiver] to be that, and unfortunately -- or fortunately -- he does it so stupidly that he merely denounces [angiver] himself as one who is not in love.

But this is just the way Christianity is talked about . . . by believing priests. They either "defend" Christianity, or they translate it into "reasons" -- if they are not at the same time dabbling in "comprehending" it speculatively. This is what is called preaching, and it is regarded in Christendom as already a big thing that such preaching is done and that some hear it. And it is precisely for this reason that Christendom (here is the proof of it) is so far from being what it calls itself that the lives of most men are, Christianly understood, too spiritless even to be called in a strictly Christian sense sin.

Chapter 2: Continuation of Sin

Every state or condition in sin is new sin, or, as it might be more exactly expressed and as it will be expressed in the following, the state of being in sin is the new sin, is emphatically the sin. This seems perhaps to the sinner an exaggeration; he at the most recognizes every actual sin as a new sin. But eternity which keeps his accounts must register the state of being in sin as a new sin. It has only two rubrics, and "everything which is not of faith is sin"; every unrepented sin is a new sin, and every moment it is unrepented is new sin. But how rare is the man who possesses continuity with respect to his consciousness of himself! Generally men are only momentarily conscious, conscious in the great decisions, but the daily things are not computed at all; such men are spirit (if this word may be applied to them) once a week for one hour -- of course that is a pretty bestial way of being spirit. Eternity, however, is essential continuity and requires this of man, or requires that he shall be conscious of himself as spirit and shall have faith. The sinner on the other hand is so thoroughly in the power of sin that he has no conception of its totalitarian character, or that he is in the byway of perdition. He takes into account only each individual new sin by which he acquires new headway onward along the path of perdition, just as if the previous instant he were not going with the speed of the previous sins along that same path. So natural has sin become to him, or sin has so become his second nature, that he finds the daily continuance quite a matter of course, and it is only when by a new sin he acquires as it were new headway that for an instant he is made aware. By perdition he is blinded to the fact that his life, instead of possessing the essential continuity of the eternal by being before God in faith, has the continuity of sin.

But, "The continuity of sin!" Is not sin precisely the discontinuous? Lo, here we have again the notion that sin is merely a negation to which one can acquire no title, as one can acquire no title to stolen property, a negation, an impotent attempt to give itself consistency, which nevertheless, suffering as it does from the torture of impotence in the defiance of despair, it is not able to do. Yes, so it is speculatively; but Christianly sin is (and this has to be believed, it is indeed the paradox which no man can comprehend) -- sin is a position which out of itself develops a more and more positive [ponerende] continuity.

And the law for the growth of this continuity is moreover different from the law which applies to a debt or to a negation. For a debt does not grow because **it** is not paid, it grows every time it is added to. But sin grows every instant one does not get out of it. It is as far as possible from being true that the sinner is right in only regarding every new sin as an increase of sin -- so far from being true that, Christianly understood, the state of remaining in sin is really a greater sin. We have even a proverb which says that to sin is human, but to remain in sin is devilish. But Christianly this proverb must be understood in a rather different sense. The merely desultory way of conceiving the case, which has regard only to the new sin and passes over the intermediate state, the interval between the particular sins, is just as superficial a way of conceiving it as it would be to assume that the railway train moved only when the locomotive puffed. No, this puffing and the onrush which succeeds it is really not the thing that has to be considered, but rather the even momentum with which the locomotive proceeds and which occasions the puffing. And so it is with sin. The state of remaining in sin is in the deepest sense sin, the particular sins are not the continuation of sin, but they are the expression for the continuation of sin; in the particular new sins the momentum of sin merely becomes more observable.

The state of being in sin is a worse sin than the particular sins, it is the sin emphatically, and thus understood it is true that the state of remaining in sin is the continuation of sin, is a new sin. Generally one understands this differently, one understands that the one sin gives birth to new sin. But this has a far deeper ground for the fact that the state of being in sin is new sin. Psychologically it is a masterly stroke of Shakespeare to let Macbeth say (Act iii, Scene 2), "Sündentsprossne Werke erlangen nur durch Süinde Kraft und Stärke" That is to say, sin is within itself a consistency, and in this consistency of evil within itself it possesses a certain power. But one never reaches such a point of view when one considers merely the particular sins.

Doubtless most men live with far too little consciousness of themselves to have a conception of what consistency is; that is to say, they do not exist qua spirit. Their lives (either with a certain childish and lovable naïveté or in sheer banality) consist in some act or another, some occurrence, this or that; and then they do something good, then in turn something wrong, and then it begins all over again; now they are in despair, for an afternoon, perhaps for three weeks, but then they are jovial again, and then again they are a whole day in despair. They take a hand in the game of life as it were, but they never have the experience of staking all upon one throw, never attain the conception of an infinite self-consistency. Therefore among themselves their talk is always about the particular, particular deeds, particular sins.

Every existence which is under the rubric of spirit (even if it is such only on its own responsibility and at its own peril) has essentially consistency within itself, and consistency in something higher, at least in an idea. But again such an existence fears infinitely every inconsistency, because it has an infinite conception of what the consequence may be, that because of it one might be wrenched out of the totality in which one has one's life. The least inconsistency is a prodigious loss, for with that a man in fact loses consistency; that same instant the charm is perhaps broken, the mysterious power which bound all powers in harmony is enfeebled, the spring loses its tension, the whole machinery is a chaos where the forces fight in rebellion against one another, to the injury of the self, and therein there is no accord with oneself, no momentum, no impetus. The prodigious machine which in consistency was so compliant with its iron strength, so pliable with all its power, is in disorder; and the more excellent the machine was, all the more frightful is the confusion. -- The believer, who reposes in and has his strength in the consistency of the good, has an infinite fear of even the least sin, for he stands to lose infinitely. The immediate men -- the childlike or the childish -- have no totality to lose, they constantly lose and win only the particular thing and in the particular instance.

But as with the believer, so it is also with his counterpart, the demoniac man, with respect to the consistency of sin in itself. As the drunkard steadily keeps up the intoxication from day to day, for fear of the languor which would ensue from arresting it, and the possible consequences if for one day he were to remain entirely sober -- so it is with the demoniac. Yea, just as the good man, if one were to approach him temptingly, picturing sin in one or another alluring form, would bid him, "tempt me not," so one has instances of exactly the same thing on the part of the demoniac. Face to face with one who is stronger than he in the good, the demoniac, when one would picture to him the good in its blissful sublimity, might beg for himself, beg him with tears in his eyes, that he would not talk to him, would not, as he expresses it, make him weak. Just because the demoniac is consistent in himself and in the consistency of evil, just for this cause he also has a totality to lose. A single instant outside of his consistency, one single dietetic imprudence, one single glance aside, one instant when the whole thing, or at least a part thereof, is seen and understood in a different way -- and with that, he would never more be himself, he says. That is, he has given up the good in despair, it could not help him anyway, he says, but it well might disturb him, make it impossible for him ever again to acquire the full momentum of consistency, make him weak. Only in the continuation of sin he is himself, only in that does he live and have an impression of himself. 'What does this mean? It means that the state of being in sin is that which, in the depth to which he has sunk, holds him together, impiously strengthening him by consistency; it is not the particular new sin which (crazy as it sounds to say it) helps him, but the particular new sin is merely the expression for the state of being in sin which properly is the sin.

By "the continuation in sin," which is the theme we now have to deal with, we are to think not so much of the particular new sins as of the state of being in sin, which in turn becomes the potentiation of sin in itself, an abiding in the state of sin with consciousness thereof, so that the law for the movement in potentiation is, here as everywhere, in the inward direction, in more and more intense consciousness.

1. The Sin of Despairing over One's Sin

Sin is despair, the potentiation of this is the new sin of despairing over one's sin. It can easily be seen moreover that this is characterized as potentiation. It is not a new sin in the sense of repetition, as in the case of a man who once stole $100 and another time steals $1,000. No, it is not a question of particular acts of sin; the state of sin is sin, and this is potentiated in a new consciousness.

Despairing over one's sin is the expression for the fact that sin has become or would become consistent in itself. It will have nothing to do with the good, will not be weak enough to harken once in a while to another sort of talk. No, it will hear only itself, have to do only with itself, shut itself in with itself, yea, enclose itself within one enclosure more and by despair over its sin secure itself against every assault of the good or every aspiration after it. It is conscious of having cut the bridge behind it and so of being inaccessible to the good as the good is to it, so that though in a weak moment it were to will the good, this would nevertheless be impossible. Sin itself is detachment from the good, but despair over sin is a second detachment. This of course tortures out of sin its utmost demoniac powers, bestowing upon it the ungodly hardiness or obduracy which must constantly regard everything which is of the nature of repentance and everything which is of the nature of grace not only as empty and meaningless but as its foe, as the thing which most of all it has to guard against, quite in the same way as the good guards itself against temptation. So understood, it is rightly said by Mephistopheles in Faust that nothing is more miserable than a devil who despairs; for by despairing must here be understood unwillingness to hear anything about repentance and grace. To indicate the character of this potentiation from sin to despair over sin one might say that the former is the breach with the good, the latter is the breach with repentance.

Despair over sin is an attempt to maintain oneself by sinking still deeper. As one who ascends in a balloon rises by casting weights from him, so does the despairing man sink by casting from him the good (for the weight of the good is uplift), he sinks, doubtless he thinks he is rising -- he does indeed become lighter. Sin itself is the struggle of despair; but then when strength is exhausted there must needs be a new potentiation, a new demoniacal introversion, and this is despair over one's sin. This is a step in advance, an ascent in the demoniacal, but of course it means sinking deeper in sin. It is an attempt to impart to sin as a positive power firmness and interest, by the fact that now it is eternally decided that one will hear nothing about repentance, nothing about grace. Nevertheless despair over sin is conscious of its own emptiness, conscious of the fact that it has nothing whatever to live on, not even a lofty conception of one's own self.

Psychologically it is a masterly line Macbeth utters after the murder when he is in despair over his sin (Act ii, Scene 3):

For, from this instant,

There's nothing serious in mortality:

All is but toys: renown and grace is dead.

The masterly double stroke is in the last words, "renown and grace." By sin, that is to say, by despairing over his sin, he has lost every relation to grace -- and to himself at the same time. His selfish self culminates in ambition. Now he has indeed become king, and yet, by despairing over his sin, and about the reality of repentance, about grace, he has also lost himself, be cannot even maintain himself in his own eyes, and he is precisely as far from being able to enjoy his own self in ambition as he is from grasping grace.

In real life (in so far as despair over sin actually occurs in life -- but there occurs at all events something they call such) people generally have a mistaken notion of despair over sin, presumably because in the world one generally has to do with levity, thoughtlessness and pure prattle, and therefore becomes quite solemn and reverently lifts the hat before every expression of something deeper. Either in confused obscurity about oneself and one's significance, or with a trace of hypocrisy, or by the help of cunning and sophistry which is present in all despair, despair over sin is not indisposed to bestow upon itself the appearance of something good. So it is supposed to be an expression for a deep nature which thus takes its sin so much to heart. I will adduce an example. When a man who has been addicted to one sin or another, but then for a long while has withstood temptation and conquered -- if he has a relapse and again succumbs to temptation, the dejection which ensues is by no means always sorrow over sin. It may be something else, for the matter of that it may be exasperation against providence, as if it were providence which had allowed him to fall into temptation, as if it ought not to have been so hard on him, since for a long while he had victoriously withstood temptation. But at any rate it is womanish without more ado to regard this sorrow as good, not to be in the least observant of the duplicity there is in all passionateness, which in turn has this ominous consequence that at times the passionate man understands afterwards, almost to the point of frenzy, that he has said exactly the opposite of that which he meant to say. Such a man asseverated with stronger and stronger expressions how much this relapse tortures and torments him, how it brings him to despair, "I can never forgive myself for it," he says. And all this is supposed to be the expression for how much good there dwells within him, what a deep nature he is. In this representation I intentionally introduced the catchword, "I can never forgive myself for it," precisely the word which is commonly used in such a connection. And precisely by this catchword one can orient oneself dialectically. He can never forgive himself for it -- but now in case God would forgive him for it, he might well have the kindness to forgive himself. No, his despair over sin, and all the more, the more it storms in the passion of expression, whereby without being aware of it in the least he informs against himself when he "never can forgive himself" that he could sin thus (for this sort of talk is pretty nearly the opposite of penitent contrition which prays God for forgiveness) -- this despair is far from being a characteristic of the good, rather it is a more intensive characterization of sin, the intensity of which is a deeper sinking into sin. The fact is that during the time he victoriously withstood temptation he was in his own eyes better than he actually was, he was proud of himself. It is now in the interest of pride that the past should be something entirely left behind. But in the relapse the past suddenly becomes again entirely present. This reminder his pride cannot endure, and hence the deep distress etc. But the direction of this distress is evidently away from God, manifesting a hidden self-love and pride -- instead of humbly beginning by thanking God humbly for helping him so long to withstand temptation, acknowledging before God and before himself that this after all is much more than he had deserved, and so humbling himself under the remembrance of what he had been.

In this instance as usual the explanation given in the old works of edification is so profound, so understanding, so instructive. They teach that God sometimes permits the believer to stumble and fall into one temptation or another -- precisely to humble him and thereby confirm him the more in the good; the contrast between the relapse and the perhaps considerable progress in the good is so humiliating, the identity with himself so painful. The better a man is, the more dangerous, in case he does not make the right turn, is even the least little bit of impatience. He may perhaps for sorrow sink into the darkest melancholy -- and a fool of a pastor may not be far from admiring his deep soul and the power of good which is in him. . . as though this were the good. And his wife, yea, she feels herself deeply humbled in comparison with such an earnest and holy man who can thus sorrow for his sin. Perhaps his talk is still more deceptive, he perhaps does not say, I can never forgive myself for it (as if before he had forgiven himself for his sins -- a blasphemy), no, he talks about God never forgiving him for it. And, alas, this is only a mystification. His sorrow, his concern, his despair, is selfish (like the dread of sin which at times almost frightens a man into sin) because it is self-love which would like to be proud of itself, like to be without sin -- and consolation is what he is least in need of, wherefore also the prodigious quantity of consoling thoughts the physicians of the soul prescribe only make the sickness worse.

2. The Sin of Despairing of (Mark the distinction between despairing over one's sin, and despairing of the forgiveness of sins.) the Forgiveness of Sins (Offense)

The potentiation in consciousness of the self is in this instance knowledge of Christ, being a self face to face with Christ. First there came (in Part First) ignorance of having an eternal self; then knowledge of having a self wherein there is after all something eternal.

Thereupon (as a transition to Part Second) it was shown that this distinction is referable to the self which has a human conception of itself or whose goal is man. The contrast to this was a self face to face with God, and this was taken as the basis of the definition of sin.

Now comes a self face to face with Christ -- a self which nevertheless in despair will not be itself, or in despair will be itself. For despair of the forgiveness of sins must be related to one or the other formula of despair; that of weakness, or that of defiance; that of weakness which being offended does not dare to believe, or that of defiance which being offended will not believe. Only in this case (since here it is not a question about being oneself simply, but about being oneself qua sinner, consequently oneself as characterized by one's imperfection) weakness and defiance are the converse of what they ordinarily are. Ordinarily weakness is: in despair not to will to be oneself. Here this is defiance; for here it is clearly defiance not to will to be the man one is, a sinner, and for this reason to will to dispense with the forgiveness of sins. Ordinarily defiance is: in despair to will to be oneself. Here this is weakness: in despair to will to be oneself, a sinner, in such wise that there is no forgiveness.

A self face to face with Christ is a self potentiated by the prodigious concession of God, potentiated by the prodigious emphasis which falls upon it for the fact that God also for the sake of this self let Himself to be born, became man, suffered, died. As was said in the foregoing, "the more conception of God, the more self," so here it is true that the more conception of Christ, the more self. A self is qualitatively what its measure is. That Christ is the measure is on God's part attested as the expression for the immense reality a self-possesses; for it is true for the first time in Christ that God is man's goal and measure, or measure and goal. -- But the more self, the more intense the sin.

There is also another side from which the potentiation in sin can be shown. In the first instance we considered that sin was despair, its potentiation was despair over sin. But now God offers reconciliation in the forgiveness of sins. Yet the sinner despairs, and despair acquires a still deeper expression. It now relates itself after a sort to God, but precisely thereby it is still further away, still more deeply sunken in sin. When the sinner despairs of the forgiveness of sins it is almost as if he were directly picking a quarrel with God, it sounds in fact like a rejoinder when he says, "No, there is not any forgiveness of sins, it is an impossibility"; this looks like a hand-to-hand scuffle. But yet a man must remove himself to a qualitative distance from God in order to be able to say this and in order that it may be heard, and in order to fight cominus he must be eminus; so strangely constructed in an acoustic sense is the world of spirit, so strangely are the relationships of distance arranged. A man must be as far as possible removed from God for that "No" to be heard, while yet in a way he wants to pick a quarrel with God. The greatest possible nearness to God, actually treading on His toes, means to be far off. In order to behave forwardly toward God one must retire far backward; if one is nearer, one cannot be forward, and if one is forward, this signifies eo ipso that one is far off. O human impotence in the face of God! When one behaves forwardly toward a man of high station, one may perhaps as a punishment be cast far away from him; but to behave forwardly toward God one must retire backward far from Him.

In real life the sin of despairing of the forgiveness of sins is generally misunderstood, especially now that they have done away with the ethical, so that one seldom or never hears a sound ethical word. Aesthetic-metaphysically it is honored as a sign of a deep nature that one despairs of the forgiveness of sins, pretty much as if one were to regard it as a sign of a deep nature in a child that it is naughty. On the whole it is unbelievable what confusion has invaded the religious sphere since in man's relationship to God there has been abolished the "Thou shalt," which is the only regulative principle. This "Thou shalt" ought to be a part of every definition of the religious; instead of which people have employed fantastically conceptions of God as an ingredient in human self-importance, so as to be self-important over against God. As in political life one becomes important by belonging to the Opposition, and in the last resort may well wish that there should be a government so that one might at least have something to oppose; so in the last resort one does not wish to abolish God -- if merely with a view to becoming still more self-important by being the Opposition. And all that which in the old days was regarded with horror as the expression of impious insubordination has now become spirited, the sign of a deep nature. "Thou shalt believe," that is what was said in the old days. as soberly as possible and in so many words -- now it is spirited and the sign of a deep nature not to be able to do so. "Thou shalt believe in the forgiveness of sins," was what they said, and as the only commentary to this text it was said, "It will go ill with thee if thou canst not, for what one shall do, one can do" -- now it is spirited and the sign of a deeper nature not to be able to believe it. Splendid result attained by Christendom! If not a word about Christianity were heard, men would not be so conceited (as paganism never has been at any time); but by the help of the fact that Christian conceptions are unchristianly floating in the air they are employed in the interest of this most potentiated impertinence, in so far as they are not misused in another and equally shameless way. For it surely is very epigrammatic that swearing was after all not customary in paganism but on the other hand is properly at home in Christendom; that paganism generally uttered the name of God with great solemnity, with a certain horror, with a dread of the mysterious, whereas in Christendom the name of God is surely the word which occurs most frequently in daily speech and is absolutely the word to which one attaches the least meaning and uses most carelessly, because this poor revealed God (who was so imprudent and unwise as to become revealed instead of keeping Himself hidden as superior persons always do) has become a personage all too well known by the whole population, to whom one renders an exceedingly great service by going once in a while to church, where one is praised for it by the parson, who on God's behalf thanks one for the honor of the visit, confers upon one the title of pious, and on the other hand taunts a bit those who never do God the honor of going to church.

The sin of despairing of the forgiveness of sins is offense. The Jews were quite right in being offended at Christ because He would forgive sins. It requires a singularly high degree of dullness (that is to say, the sort ordinarily found in Christendom) in case a man is not a believer (and if he is, then he believes that Christ is God) not to be offended at the fact that a man would forgive sins. And in the next place it requires an equally singular degree of dullness not to be offended at the assertion that sin can be forgiven. This is for the human understanding the most impossible thing. Not that I would extol it as a sign of genius that one is unable to believe this, for it shall be believed.

In paganism of course this sin did not exist. If the pagan might have the true conception of sin (but even this he could not have because he lacked the conception of God), he could not get further than to despair over his sin. Yea, what is more (and herein lies all the concession one can make to human understanding and human thinking), one might praise the pagan who really managed to despair, not over the world, not over himself in general, but over his sin.(One will observe that despair over sin is here dialectically conceived in the direction toward faith. That there is this dialectical possibility must never be forgotten, even though this work only deals with despair as sin. This dialectical possibility is due to the fact that despair is also the first factor in faith. On the other hand, when the direction is away from faith, away from the God-relationship, despair over sin is the new sin. In the life of spirit everything is dialectical. Offense is thus, as a possibility annulled, a factor in faith; but offense with a direction away from faith is sin. One can reproach a man for not even being offended at Christianity. When one speaks thus, one speaks as being offended as something good, and on the other hand one may say that to be offended is sin.) Humanly speaking, both depths of understanding and ethical definitions are requisite for this. No man as such can get further, and seldom does one get so far. But Christianly everything is altered, for thou shalt believe in the forgiveness of sins.

And where does Christendom find itself with reference to the forgiveness of sins? Indeed, the situation of Christendom is really despair over the forgiveness of sins. This, however, must be understood in the sense that Christendom is so backward that it is not even manifest that the situation is such. People have not even reached the consciousness of sin, they know only the kind of sin which paganism also knew, and they live on happily in pagan security. But by the fact that they live in Christendom they go further than paganism, they go on to imagine that this security is . . . consciousness of the forgiveness of sins. Indeed, how can it be otherwise in Christendom? In this the parsons confirm the congregation.

The fundamental misfortune of Christendom is really Christianity, the fact that the doctrine of the God-Man (the Christian understanding of which, be it noted, is secured by the paradox and the possibility of offense) is taken in vain, the qualitative distinction between God and man is pantheistically abolished -- first speculatively with an air of superiority, then vulgarly in the streets and alleys. Never anywhere has any doctrine on earth brought God and man so near together as has Christianity; neither could anyone else do it, only God Himself can, every human invention remains after all a dream, an uncertain imagination. Neither has any doctrine ever so carefully defended itself against the most shocking of all blasphemies, that after God had taken this step it then should be taken in vain, as though God and man coalesced in one and the same thing -- never has any doctrine ever defended itself against this as Christianity has, which defends itself by the help of the offense. Woe unto the slack orators, woe unto the loose thinkers, and woe, woe unto all the adherents who have learnt from them and extolled them!

If order is to be maintained in existence -- and that after all is what God wills, for He is not a God of confusion -- first and foremost it must be remembered that every man is an individual man, is himself conscious of being an individual man. If once men are permitted to coalesce into what Aristotle calls "the multitude," a characteristic of beasts, this abstraction (instead of being regarded as less than nothing, as in fact it is, less than the lowliest individual man) will be regarded as something, and no long time will elapse before this abstraction becomes God. And then, why then in fact it corresponds philosophice with the God-Man. Then as people in the various nations have learnt that the multitude overawes the King and the daily papers overawe the Privy Council, so then at last they discover that the summa summarum of all men overawes God. This then is called the doctrine of the God Man or the doctrine that God and men are idem per idem [identical]. Naturally several of the philosophers who took part in spreading this doctrine of the preponderance of the generations of mankind over the individual now turn away in disgust when their doctrine has sunk so low that the mob is God. But these philosophers forget that after all this was their doctrine, they overlook the fact that it was not more true when the superior men accepted it, when the élite of the superior class or an elect circle of philosophers was the Incarnation.

This means that the doctrine of the God-Man has made Christendom impudent. It almost appears as if God had been too weak. It is as though it had come to pass with Him as with the good-natured man who makes too great a concession and is rewarded by ingratitude. It was God who discovered the doctrine of the God-Man, and now Christendom has got the thing turned topsy-turvy and imputes to God consanguinity, so that the concession God has made means pretty much what in these times it means when a king grants a freer constitution -- and one knows well enough what that means, "He pretty well had to." It is as though God had got Himself into an embarrassing situation; it is as though the shrewd man were in the right if he were to say to God, "It is Thine own fault. Why hast Thou put Thyself upon such familiar terms with man? It never would have occurred to anyone, never have entered into any man's heart, that there might be likeness between God and man. It was Thou Thyself that had this proclaimed, now Thou art reaping the fruits."

Yet Christianity has secured itself from the very beginning. It begins with the doctrine of sin. The category of sin is the category of the individual. Speculatively sin cannot be thought at all. The individual man is subsumed under the concept; one cannot think an individual man but only the concept man. -- Hence it is that Speculation at once reaches the doctrine of the preponderance of the generations over the individual; for it is not to be expected that Speculation should recognize the impotence of the concept in relation to reality. -- But as one cannot think an individual man, so neither can one think an individual sinner; one can think sin (then it becomes negative), but not an individual sinner. Just for this reason, however, there can be no seriousness about sin when it is merely thought. For seriousness is precisely the fact that thou and I are sinners. Seriousness is not sin in general, but the emphasis of seriousness falls upon the sinner who is an individual. In relation to "the individual man" Speculation, if it is consistent, must think very scornfully of what it is to be an individual or that it is something which cannot be thought. If it would do anything in this line, it must say to the individual, "Is that anything to waste time on? Above all try to forget it, to be an individual man is not to be anything -- think, and then thou art the whole of humanity, cogito ergo sum." This, however, might perhaps be a lie, and the individual might be the highest. Yet suppose it is so. But to be entirely consistent Speculation must also say, "The thing of being an individual sinner, that's not to be anything, it is subsumed under the concept, waste no time on it etc." And then what further? Is one perhaps to think sin instead of being an individual sinner? -- just as one was exhorted to think the concept of man instead of being the individual man. And then what further? Does a man become himself "sin" by thinking sin? Cogito ergo sum. A capital proposal! However, one does not even in this case need to be afraid of becoming sin . . . the pure sin, for sin cannot be thought. This after all Speculation itself might concede, since sin is in fact a falling away from the concept. But not to dispute any longer e concessis, the principal difficulty is another. Speculation does not take heed of the fact that in relation to sin the ethical has its place, which employs an emphasis which is the converse of that of Speculation and accomplishes the opposite development; for the ethical does not abstract from reality but goes deeper into reality, operating essentially by the aid of the category of the individual, which is the category overlooked and despised by Speculation. Sin is a characteristic of the individual; it is frivolity and a new sin to act as if it were nothing to be an individual sinner. Here Christianity is in place. It marks a cross before Speculation. It is as impossible for Speculation to get out of this difficulty as for a sailing vessel to sail directly against a contrary wind. The seriousness of sin is its reality in the individual, whether it be thou or I. Speculatively one has to look away from the individual. So, it is only frivolously one can talk speculatively about sin. The dialectic of sin is directly contrary to that of Speculation.

Here Christianity begins with the doctrine of sin, and therefore with the individual.(The doctrine of the sin of the human race has often been misused because it has not been noticed that sin, common though it is to all, does not gather men together in a common concept, into a society or a partnership ("any more than out in the churchyard the multitude of the dead constitute a society"), but it splits men into individuals and holds every individual fast as a sinner -- a splitting which in another sense is both in correspondence with and teleologically in the direction of the perfection of existence. This men have not observed, and so they have let the fallen race become once for all good again in Christ. And so in turn they have saddled God with an abstraction which, as an abstraction, presumes to claim kinship with Him. But this is a false pretext which only makes men insolent. For if the individual is to feel himself akin to God (and this is the doctrine of Christianity), the whole weight of this falls upon him in fear and trembling, and he must discover (if it were not an old discovery) the possibility of offense. But if the individual is to attain this glory through an abstraction, the thing becomes too easy, and essentially it is taken in vain. The individual does not in this case get the prodigious weight of God, which by humiliation presses down as deeply as it uplifts; the individual imagines that he possesses everything as a matter of course by participating in this abstraction. Being a man is not like being an animal, where the specimen is always less than the species. Man is distinguished from other animals not only by the advantages which are commonly enumerated, but qualitatively by the fact that the individual is more than the species. And this characteristic is again dialectical, it means that the individual is a sinner, but then again that it is perfection to be the individual.(The doctrine of the sin of the human race has often been misused because it has not been noticed that sin, common though it is to all, does not gather men together in a common concept, into a society or a partnership ("any more than out in the churchyard the multitude of the dead constitute a society"), but it splits men into individuals and holds every individual fast as a sinner -- a splitting which in another sense is both in correspondence with and teleologically in the direction of the perfection of existence. This men have not observed, and so they have let the fallen race become once for all good again in Christ. And so in turn they have saddled God with an abstraction which, as an abstraction, presumes to claim kinship with Him. But this is a false pretext which only makes men insolent. For if the individual is to feel himself akin to God (and this is the doctrine of Christianity), the whole weight of this falls upon him in fear and trembling, and he must discover (if it were not an old discovery) the possibility of offense. But if the individual is to attain this glory through an abstraction, the thing becomes too easy, and essentially it is taken in vain. The individual does not in this case get the prodigious weight of God, which by humiliation presses down as deeply as it uplifts; the individual imagines that he possesses everything as a matter of course by participating in this abstraction. Being a man is not like being an animal, where the specimen is always less than the species. Man is distinguished from other animals not only by the advantages which are commonly enumerated, but qualitatively by the fact that the individual is more than the species. And this characteristic is again dialectical, it means that the individual is a sinner, but then again that it is perfection to be the individual.) For it is Christianity to be sure which has taught this about the God-Man, about the likeness between God and man, but Christianity is a great hater of wanton and impertinent forwardness. By the help of the doctrine of sin and of the individual sinner God and Christ have been secured once for all, and far better than any king, against the nation, the people, the crowd, etc., item against every demand for a freer constitution. All these abstractions are before God nonexistent, before God in Christ there live only individual men (sinners) -- yet God can well oversee the whole, He can care for the sparrows too. God is wholly a friend of order, and to that end He is Himself present at every point, in every instant, He is omnipresent -- which is specified in the text-books as one of the titles by which God is called, which men once in a while think about a little but surely never try to think every instant. His concept is not like that of man under which the individual is subsumed as a thing which cannot be absorbed by the concept, His concept comprises everything, and in another sense, He has no concept. God does not help Himself by an abbreviation, He comprehends (comprehendit) reality itself, all the individuals; for Him the individual is not subsumed under the concept.

The doctrine of sin, the doctrine that we are sinners, thou and I, which absolutely disperses the "crowd," fixes then the qualitative distinction between God and man more deeply than ever it was fixed anywhere -- for again this God alone can do, sin is in fact before God etc. In no respect is a man so different from God as in the fact that he is a sinner, as every man is, and is a sinner "before God," whereby indeed the opposites are held together in a double sense: they are held together (continentur), not allowed to separate from one another; but by being thus held together the differences display themselves all the more strikingly, as when one speaks of holding colors together, opposita juxta se posita magis illucescunt. Sin is the only thing universally predicated of man which cannot in any way, either via negationis or via eminentia, be affirmed of God. It may be affirmed of God that He is not finite as man is, and so, via negationis, that He is infinite; but to affirm of God that He is not a sinner is blasphemy. As a sinner man is separated from God by a yawning qualitative abyss. And obviously God is separated from man by the same yawning qualitative abyss when He forgives sins. In case it were possible by a converse kind of accommodation to transfer the divine attributes to a human being, in one respect man will never in all eternity come to resemble God, namely, in forgiving sins.

Here then lies the utmost concentration of the offense, which precisely that doctrine has found necessary which teaches the likeness between God and man.

But offense is the most decisive determinant of subjectivity, of the individual man, the most decisive it is possible to think of. Doubtless to think of offense without thinking the offended man is not so impossible as to think of the music of the flute without thinking the flute-player; but after all even thought must admit that offense even more than love is an unreal concept which only becomes real when there is an individual who is offended.

So then offense is related to the individual. And therewith Christianity begins, by making every man an individual, an individual sinner; and now everything that heaven and earth can manage to raise up by way of the possibility of offense (God alone disposing of it) is concentrated in one place -- and that is Christianity. Then it says to every individual, "Thou shalt believe," i.e. thou shalt either be offended or thou shalt believe. Not one word more. There is nothing more to add. "Now I have spoken," says God, "in eternity we shall speak together again. In the meanwhile thou canst do what thou wilt, but the Judgment is to come."

What, a judgment! Why, we men have learned, indeed experience teaches, that when there is a mutiny aboard ship or in an army, the guilty are so numerous that the punishment cannot be applied; and when it is a question of the public, "the highly respected cultured public," then not only is there no crime, but, according to the newspapers, upon which one can rely as upon the Gospel or divine revelation, this is the will of God. Why is this? The reason for it is that the concept of judgment corresponds to the individual, one does not pronounce a judgment en masse; one can put the people to death en masse, play the hose on them en masse, flatter them en masse, in fine can treat the people in many ways like beasts, but to hold judgment over the people as beasts one cannot do, for one cannot hold judgment over beasts; even though ever so many are judged, if there is to be any seriousness and truth in the judgment, it is each individual who is judged.(Lo, for this reason God is "the Judge" because before him there is no crowd but only individuals.) Now when the guilty are so numerous it is not humanly possible to do this, therefore one must give the whole thing up, one perceives that there can be no question of any judgment, they are too numerous to be judged, one cannot make them or in any way manage to make them individuals, so one must give up holding judgment.

And since now in our enlightened age when people find all anthropomorphic and anthropathic conceptions of God improper, yet do not find it improper to think of God as a judge in likeness of an ordinary civil judge or solicitor general who cannot get at the rights of such a prolix affair -- they conclude then that it will be exactly so in eternity. Therefore, only let us hold together and secure ourselves by seeing to it that the parson preachifies in this way. And if there should be an individual who ventured to talk differently, an individual who was foolish enough to make his own life anxious and responsible in fear and trembling, and should then want also to worry others -- then let us secure ourselves by regarding him as mad, or, if need be, by putting him to death. If only there are many of us engaged in it, it is not wrong, what the many do is the will of God. To this wisdom, as we know by experience -- for we are not inexperienced youths, we do not throw out ill-considered words, we talk as men of experience -- all men hitherto have submitted, kings and emperors and their excellencies. By the aid of this wisdom all our cattle have been bred up -- and, by Jove, God shall also have to submit to it. The thing to do is to become many, a whole lot of us, if we do that, then we are secured against the judgment of eternity.

Yes, doubtless they are secured if it was only in eternity they became individuals. But they were and are before God constantly individuals. A man seated in a glass case is not put to such embarrassment as is a man in his transparency before God. This is the factor of conscience. By the aid of conscience things are so arranged that the judicial report follows at once upon every fault, and that the guilty one himself must write it. But it is written with sympathetic ink and only becomes thoroughly clear when in eternity it is held up to the light, while eternity holds audit over the consciences. Substantially everyone arrives in eternity bringing with him and delivering the most accurate account of every least insignificance which he has committed or has left undone. Therefore, to hold judgment in eternity is a thing a child could manage; there is really nothing for a third person to do, everything, even to the most insignificant word is counted and in order. The case of the guilty man who journeys through life to eternity is like that of the murderer who with the speed of the railway train fled from the place where he perpetrated his crime. Alas, just under the railway coach where he sat ran the electric telegraph with its signal and the order for his apprehension at the next station. When he reached the station and alighted from the coach he was arrested. In a way he had himself brought the denunciation with him.

So then despair of the forgiveness of sins is offense. And offense is the potentiation of sin. Generally, one hardly thinks of this as sin at all; it is likely that people hardly account offense a sin, and of that therefore they do not talk, but rather of sins, among which offense has no place. Still less do they interpret offense as the potentiation of sin. This is due to the fact that they do not Christianly construct the opposition sin/ faith, but sin/virtue.

3. The Sin of Abandoning Christianity Modo Ponendo, of Declaring It Falsehood

This is sin against the Holy Ghost. The self is here most despairingly potentiated; it not merely casts away from itself the whole of Christianity, but it makes it a lie and a falsehood. What a prodigiously despairing conception of itself that self must have!

The potentiation of sin is clearly shown when it is apprehended as a war between man and God where the tactics are changed; the potentiation ascends from the defensive to the offensive. Sin is despair: here one fights by evading. Then came despair over one's sin: here one still is fighting by evasion or by fortifying oneself in the position to which one has retired, but constantly pedem referens [foot backwards]. Now the tactic is changed: notwithstanding that sin becomes more and more absorbed in itself, and so withdraws, yet in another sense it comes nearer, becomes more and more decisively itself. Despair of the forgiveness of sins is a definite position directly in the face of the offer of God's compassion; sin is now not entirely in flight, not merely on the defensive. But the sin of abandoning Christianity as a falsehood and a lie is offensive warfare. All the foregoing forms of despair conceded in a way that the adversary is the stronger, but now sin is aggressive.

Sin against the Holy Ghost is the positive form of offense.

The doctrine of Christianity is the doctrine of the God-Man, of kinship between God and men, but in such a way, be it noted, that the possibility of offense is, if I may dare to express it thus, the guarantee whereby God makes sure that man cannot come too near to Him. The possibility of offense is the dialectical factor in everything Christian. Take that away, and then Christianity is not simply paganism but something so fantastic that paganism might well declare it bosh. To be so near to God as Christianity teaches that man can come to Him, and dare come to Him, and shall come to Him in Christ, has never entered into any man's head. If this then is to be understood bluntly, just as a matter of course, without the least reservation, to be taken quite unconcernedly and flippantly -- then, if paganism's poetic fiction about the gods might be called human craziness, Christianity might be the invention of a crazy god; such a doctrine could only occur to a god who had lost his wits -- so a man must judge who had kept his wits. The incarnate God, if man wanted to be as it were a chum of His, would be an apt counterpart to Prince Henry in Shakespeare.

God and man are two qualities between which there is an infinite qualitative difference. Every doctrine which overlooks this difference is, humanly speaking, crazy; understood in a godly sense, it is blasphemy. In paganism man made God a man (the Man-God); in Christianity God makes Himself man (the God-Man) -- but in the infinite love of His compassionate grace He made nevertheless one stipulation, He can do no other. This precisely is the sorrow in Christ: "He can do no other"; He can humble Himself, take the form of a servant, suffer and die for man, invite all to come unto Him, sacrifice every day of His life and every hour of the day, and sacrifice His life -- but the possibility of the offense He cannot take away. Oh, unique work of love! Oh, unfathomable sorrow of love! that God Himself cannot, as in another sense He does not will, cannot will it, but, even if He would, He could not make it impossible that this work of love might not turn out to be for a person exactly the opposite, to be the extremist misery! For the greatest possible human misery, greater even than sin, is to be offended in Christ and remain offended. And Christ cannot, "Love" cannot render this impossible. Lo, for this reason He says, "Blessed is he who shall not be offended in me." More He cannot do. So then He may (that is possible), He may by His love have the effect of making a man more miserable than ever in any other way he could become. Oh, unfathomable contradiction in love! But for all that, in love, He cannot find the heart to leave unfinished the work of love. Alas, if then this were to make a man more miserable than ever in any other way he could become!

Let us talk of this quite humanly. Ah, wretched is the man who never has felt the compelling urge of love to sacrifice everything out of love, and who accordingly has not been able to do it! But then when he discovered that precisely this sacrifice of his out of love might possibly occasion the other, the loved one, the greatest unhappiness -- what then? Then either love within him lost its resilience, from being a life of power collapsed into the introverted rumination of a sad sentiment, he was a deserter to love, he did not venture to perform this work of love, himself sinking down, not under this work, but under the weight of this possibility. For just as a weight is infinitely heavier when it is attached to the end of a rod and the man who lifts it has to hold the opposite end, so every work becomes infinitely harder when it becomes dialectic, so that what love prompts one to do for the beloved, care for the beloved seems again in another sense to dissuade from doing. -- Or else love conquered, and he ventured to do this work out of love. Oh, but in the joyfulness of love (as love always is joyful, especially when it sacrifices all) there was nevertheless a deep sorrow -- for this sad result indeed was possible! Behold, he therefore brought to completion this work of love, he offered the sacrifice (in which for his part he exulted), but not without tears. Over this -- what shall I call it? -- historical painting of inward life there hovered that dark possibility. And yet, if this had not hovered over it, his work would not have been that of true love -- O my friend, what hast thou maybe attempted to do in life? Tax thy brain, tear off every covering and lay bare the viscera of feeling in thy breast, surmount every barrier which separates thee from him of whom thou readest, and then read Shakespeare -- and thou shalt shrink from the collisions. But Shakespeare himself seems to have shrunk back from the genuinely religions collisions. Perhaps these can only be expressed in the language of the gods. And this language no man can speak; for, as a Greek already has said so beautifully, "From men man learns to speak, from the gods to keep silent."

That there is an infinite difference of quality between God and man is the possibility of offense which cannot be taken away. Out of love God becomes man; He says, "Look what it is to be a man"; but He adds, "O take heed, for at the same time I am God -- blessed is he who shall not be offended in me. As man He assumes the lowly form of a servant. He expresses what it is to be a lowly man, to the intent that no one shall think himself excluded, or think that it is human prestige or prestige among men which brings one nearer to God. No, he is the lowly man. "Look hither," He says, "and learn what it is to be a man; O but take heed, for at the same time I am God -- blessed is he who shall not be offended in me." Or conversely, "I and the Father are one, and yet I am this particular lowly man, poor, forsaken, delivered into the hands of men -- blessed is he who shall not be offended in me. I, this lowly man, am He who maketh the deaf to hear, the blind to see, the lame to walk, the leper to be cleansed, the dead to rise up -- blessed is he who shall not be offended in me."

Under accountability to the highest seat of authority I therefore make bold to say that these words, "blessed is he who shall not be offended in me," belong essentially to the preaching about Christ, if not in the same way as the words of institution at the Holy Communion, yet at least like the words, "let every man examine himself." They are Christ's own words, and they must (especially in Christendom) be again and again enjoined, repeated, addressed to every man severally. Everywhere(And such is now the case almost everywhere in Christendom, which, as it seems, either entirely ignores the fact that Christ Himself it is who so frequently and with such heartfelt emphasis warned against offense, even at the end of His life, and even when He addressed His faithful Apostles who had followed Him from the beginning and for His sake had forsaken all -- or maybe silently regards this as an extravagant apprehension on the part of Christ, inasmuch as the experience of thousands and thousands proves that one can have faith in Christ without having noticed the least trace of the possibility of offense. But this might be a mistake which surely will be made evident when the possibility of offense shall judge Christendom) where these words do not resound, or at least wherever the statement of Christianity is not at every point permeated by this thought -- there Christianity is blasphemy. For without a bodyguard, without servants who might prepare His way and make men attentive to who it was that came, Christ walked here upon earth in the lowly form of a servant. But the possibility of offense (O how great a sorrow this was to Him in His love!) defended Him and defends Him, fixes a yawning abyss between Him and the man who was closest to Him and stood nearest.

For he who is not offended worships in faith. But to worship (which is the expression of faith) is to express the consciousness that the infinite yawning abyss of quality is fixed between them. For in faith again the possibility of offense Is the dialectical factor.(Here is a little task for acute observers. In case one assumes that all the many parsons here and in foreign lands who deliver and write sermons are believing Christians, how can it be explained that one never hears or reads a prayer which in our time especially is so pertinent: "God in heaven, I thank Thee that Thou hast not required it of man that he should comprehend Christianity; for if that were required, I should be of all men the most miserable. The more I seek to comprehend it, the more incomprehensible it appears to me, and the more I discover merely the possibility of offense. Therefore I thank Thee that Thou dost only require faith, and I pray Thee to increase it more and more." This prayer would from the point of view of orthodoxy be entirely correct, and, assuming that it is true in the man who prays, it at the same time would be correct as irony upon Speculation as a whole. But is faith I wonder to be found on earth?)

But the sort of offense here in question is modo ponendo, it affirms of Christianity that it is a falsehood and a lie, and therefore affirms the same of Christ.

To illustrate this sort of offense it is best to pass in review the various forms of offense which are fundamentally related to the paradox (Christ), and then with every definition to come back to the Christian conception, for every such definition is related to Christ, has Christ in mente.

The lowest form of offense, that which, humanly speaking, is the least guilty, is to let the whole question about Christ remain undecided and to judge in this fashion: "I do not presume to pass any judgment; I do not believe, but I pass no judgment." That this is a form of offense escapes the attention of most men. The fact is that people have clean forgotten the Christian "thou shalt." Therefore, it is that they do not perceive that this is offense, this thing of treating Christ as a matter of indifference. The fact that Christ is preached to thee signifies that thou shalt have an opinion about Christ. The judgment that He is, or that He exists, or that He has existed, is the decision for the whole of existence. If Christ is preached to thee, it is offense to say, "I will have no opinion about it."

This however must be understood with a certain qualification in these times, inasmuch as Christianity is so poorly preached as it now is. There doubtless are living thousands of men who have heard Christ preached and have never heard a word about this "shall." But he who has heard it and says, "I will have no opinion about it," is offended. For he denies the divinity of Christ when he denies that it has a right to require a man to have an opinion. It is of no avail for such a man to say, "I do not affirm anything about Christ, either yes or no"; for then one has only to ask, "Hast thou then no opinion as to whether thou shalt have an opinion about this or not?", and if he replies, "Well, yes," he has trapped himself; and if he replies, "No," then Christianity condemns him all the same, requiring that he shall have an opinion about Christianity and also about Christ, that no one shall presume to treat Christ as a curiosity. When God lets Himself be born and becomes man, this is not an idle notion of His, something that occurs to Him as a way of undertaking something to put an end after all to the boredom which people have been impudent enough to say must be associated with being God -- it is not for the interest of an adventure. No, when God does this, it is the seriousness of existence. And the seriousness in this seriousness is that everyone shall have an opinion about it. When a king visits a provincial town, he regards it as an affront if without sufficient excuse an office-bearer in the town fails to do him homage. But what I wonder would he judge if one were to ignore entirely the fact that the King was in town, were to behave as a private person who on such an occasion "doesn't care a fig for His Majesty and the royal law"? And so it is also when it pleases God to become man -- that then it pleases a man (and what the office-bearer is to the King, that is every man before God) to say of it, "Well, that's something about which I don't wish to have any opinion." So, it is one speaks superciliously of that upon which one essentially looks down -- and so one superciliously looks down upon God.

The next form of offense is the negative but passive form. It feels to be sure that it is not able to ignore Christianity, it is not capable of letting all that about Christ remain in doubt, and then being for the rest busy about life. But neither does it believe; it continues to stare at one and the same point, the paradox. To that extent it honors Christianity after all, it gives expression to the conviction that the question, "What think ye of Christ?", is the most decisive question. Such an offended man lives on like a shadow; his life is consumed because in his inmost soul he is constantly preoccupied with this decision. And thus, he attests (as the suffering of unhappy love attests the reality of love) -- he attests what a reality Christianity possesses.

The last form of offense is that about which we are speaking in this chapter, the positive form. It declares that Christianity is a falsehood and a lie, it denies Christ (that He existed and That He is what He claimed to be) either docetically or rationalistically, so that Christ either does not become a particular man except apparently, or He becomes only a particular man, so that He either becomes docetically, poetry and mythology which make no claim to reality, or rationalistically, a reality which makes no claim to be divine. In this denial of Christ as the paradox there is naturally implied the denial of everything Christian: sin, the forgiveness of sins, etc.

This form of offense is sin against the Holy Ghost. As the Jews said of Christ that He cast out devils by the help of the devil, so does this form of offense make of Christ an invention of the devil.

This offense is the highest potentiation of sin, which is a fact people generally overlook inasmuch as they do not Christianly construct the opposition sin/faith.

On the other hand, this opposition is affirmed in the whole of this work, which straightway in the first section (I.A) constructed the formula for the situation where no offense at all is to be found: "By relating itself to its own self and by willing to be itself, the self is grounded transparently in the Power which constituted it." And this formula again, as has often been noted, is the definition of faith.

PURITY OF HEART IS TO WILL ONE THING

. Preface

Although this little book (it can be called an occasional address, yet without having the occasion which produces the speaker and gives him authority, or the occasion which produces the reader and makes him eager to learn) is like a fantasy, like a dream by day as it confronts the relationships of actuality: yet it is not without assurance and not without hope of accomplishing its object. It is in search of that solitary "individual," to whom it wholly abandons itself, by whom it wishes to be received as if it had arisen within his own heart; that solitary "individual" whom with joy and gratitude I call my reader; that solitary "individual" who reads willingly and slowly, who reads over and over again, and who reads aloud -- for his own sake. If it finds him, then in the distance of the separation the understanding is perfect, if he retains for himself both the distance and the understanding in the inwardness of appropriation.

When a woman makes an altar cloth, so far as she is able, she makes every flower as lovely as the graceful flowers of the field, as far as she is able, every star as sparkling as the glistening stars of the night. She withholds nothing, but uses the most precious things she possesses. She sells off every other claim upon her life that she may purchase the most uninterrupted and favorable time of the day and night for her one and only, for her beloved work. But when the cloth is finished and put to its sacred use: then she is deeply distressed if someone should make the mistake of looking at her art, instead of at the meaning of the cloth; or make the mistake of looking at a defect, instead of at the meaning of the cloth. For she could not work the sacred meaning into the cloth itself, nor could she sew it on the cloth as though it were one more ornament. This meaning really lies in the beholder and in the beholder's understanding, if he, in the endless distance of the separation, above himself and above his own self, has completely forgotten the needlewoman and what was hers to do. It was allowable, it was proper, it was duty, it was a precious duty, it was the highest happiness of all for the needlewoman to do everything in order to accomplish what was hers to do; but it was a trespass against God, an insulting misunderstanding of the poor needlewoman, when someone looked wrongly and saw what was only there, not to attract attention to itself, but rather so that its omission would not distract by drawing attention to itself. S.K.

Chapter 1: Introduction: Man, and the Eternal

Father in heaven! What is a man without Thee! What is all that he knows, vast accumulation though it be, but a chipped fragment if he does not know Thee! What is all his striving, could it even encompass a world, but a half-finished work if he does not know Thee: Thee the One, who art one thing and who art all! So may Thou give to the intellect, wisdom to comprehend that one thing; to the heart, sincerity to receive this understanding; to the will, purity that wills only one thing. In prosperity may Thou grant perseverance to will one thing; amid distractions, collectedness to will one thing; in suffering, patience to will one thing. Oh, Thou that giveth both the beginning and the completion, may Thou early, at the dawn of day, give to the young man the resolution to will one thing. As the day wanes, may Thou give to the old man a renewed remembrance of his first resolution, that the first may be like the last, the last like the first, in possession of a life that has willed only one thing. Alas, but this has indeed not come to pass. Something has come in between. The separation of sin lies in between. Each day, and day after day something is being placed in between: delay, blockage, interruption, delusion, corruption. So, in this time of repentance may Thou give the courage once again to will one thing. True, it is an interruption of our ordinary tasks; we do lay down our work as though it were a day of rest, when the penitent (and it is only in a time of repentance that the heavy-laden worker may be quiet in the confession of sin) is alone before Thee in self-accusation. This is indeed an interruption. But it is an interruption that searches back into its very beginnings that it might bind up anew that which sin has separated, that in its grief it might atone for lost time, that in its anxiety it might bring to completion that which lies before it. Oh, thou that givest both the beginning and the completion, give Thou victory in the day of need so that what neither a man's burning wish nor his determined resolution may attain to, may be granted unto him in the sorrowing of repentance: to will only one thing.

"To everything there is a season," says Solomon.(Ecclesiastes 3:1) And in these words he voices the experience of the past and of that which lies behind us. For when an old man relives his life, he lives it only by dwelling upon his memories; and when wisdom in an old man has outgrown the immediate impressions of life, the past viewed from the quiet of memory is something different from the present in all its bustle. The time of work and of strain, of merrymaking and of dancing is over. Life requires nothing more of the old man and he claims nothing more of it. By being present, one thing is no nearer to him than another. Expectation, decision, repentance in regard to a thing do not affect his judgment. By being a part of the past, these distinctions all become meaningless, for that which is completely past has no present to which it may attach itself. Oh, the desolation of old age, if to be an old man means this: means that at any given moment a living person could look at life as if he himself did not exist, as if life were merely a past event that held no more present tasks for him as a living person, as if he, as a living person, and life were cut off from each other within life, so that life was past and gone, and he had become a stranger to it. Oh, tragic wisdom, if it were of everything human that Solomon spoke, and if the speech must ever end in the same manner, insisting that everything has its time, in the well-known words: "What profit hath he that worketh in that wherein he laboureth" (Ecclesiastes 3:9)? Perhaps the meaning would have been clearer if Solomon had said, "There was a time for all, all had its time," in order to show that, as an old man, he is speaking of the past and that in fact he is not speaking to someone but is talking to himself. For the person who talks about human life, which changes with the years, must be careful to state his own age to his listeners. And that wisdom which is related to such a changeable and temporal element in a man must, as with every frailty, be treated with caution in order that it shall not work harm.

Only the Eternal is always appropriate and always present, is always true. Only the Eternal applies to each human being, whatever his age may be. The changeable exists, and when its time has passed it is changed. Therefore any statement about it is subject to change. That which may be wisdom when spoken by an old man about past events may be folly in the mouth of a youth or of a grown man when spoken of the present. The youth would not be able to understand it and the grown man would not want to understand it. Even one who is a little advanced in age may fully agree with Solomon in saying, "There is a time to dance from sheer joy." And yet how can he agree with him? For his dancing time is past, and therefore he speaks of it as of something past. And it does not matter whether, in that day when both youth and the longing to dance were his, he grieved at its being denied him, or whether in joyous abandon he yielded to the invitation to dance: one who is a little advanced in age will still say quietly, "There is a time to dance." But for the youth, to be allowed to hurry off to the dance and to sit shut in at home are two such different things that it does not occur to him to consider them on the same level and to say, "There is a time for the one and a time for the other." A man is changed in the course of the years, and each time some portion of life lies behind him he tends to talk of its varied content as if it were all on the same level. But it does not follow from this that he has become any wiser. For by this, one has only said that he has changed. Perhaps even now there is something that makes him restless in the same way that the dance disturbs the youth, something that absorbs his attention in the same way that a toy absorbs a child. It is in this manner that a man changes, over the years. Old age is the final change. The old man speaks in the same vein of it all, of all the changeable that is now past.

But is this all of the story? Has all been heard that may be said about being a man, and about man's temporal life? The most important and decisive thing of all is certainly left out. For the talk about the natural changes of human life over the years, together with what externally happened there, is not in essence any different from talking of plant or of animal life. The animal also changes with the years. When it is older it has other desires than it had at an earlier age. At certain times it, too, has its happiness in life, and at other times it must endure hardship. Yes, when late autumn comes, even the flower can speak the wisdom of the years and say with truthfulness, "All has its time, there is 'a time to be born and a time to die'; there is a time to jest lightheartedly in the spring breeze, and a time to break under the autumn storm; there is a time to burst forth into blossom, beside the running water, beloved by the stream, and a time to wither and be forgotten; a time to be sought out for one's beauty, and a time to be unnoticed in one's wretchedness; there is a time to be nursed with care, and a time to be cast out with contempt; there is a time to delight in the warmth of the morning sun and a time to perish in the night's cold. All has its time; 'what profit hath he that worketh in that wherein he laboureth?'

Yes, the animal, too, when it has lived its time may speak the wisdom of the years and say with truth, "All has its time. There is a time to leap with joy, and a time to drag oneself along the earth; there is a time to waken early, and a time to sleep long; there is a time to run with the herd, and a time to go apart to die; there is a time to build nests with one's beloved, and there is a time to sit alone on the roof; there is a time to soar freely among the clouds, and a time to sink heavily to the earth. All has its time; 'what profit hath he that worketh in that wherein he laboureth?' " And, in case you should say to the flower. "Is there, then, nothing more to tell?" then it will answer you, "No, when the flower is dead, the story is over." Otherwise the story must have been different from the beginning and been different as it went along, not merely becoming different at the end. For let us assume that the flower concluded its story in another fashion and added, "The story is not over, for when I am dead, I am immortal." Would this not be a strange story? If the flower were really immortal then immortality must be just that which prevented it from dying, and therefore immortality must have been present in each instant of its life. And the story of its life must once again have been wholly different in order to express continually immortality's difference from all the changeableness and the different kinds of variations of the perishable. Immortality cannot be a final alteration that crept in, so to speak, at the moment of death as the final stage. On the contrary, it is a changelessness that is not altered by the passage of the years. Therefore, to the old man's words that "all has its time," the wise Solomon adds, "God made all things beautiful in his time; also he hath set eternity within man's heart" (Ecclesiastes 3: 11). (Kierkegaard often takes some liberty with his quotations paraphrasing what he takes them essentially to mean. "He hath made everything beautiful in his time: also he hath set the world in their heart from the beginning to the end.") Thus says the sage. For the talk about change, and the varied way of talking about change is indeed confusing, even when it comes from the mouth of an old man. Only the Eternal is constructive. The wisdom of the years is confusing. Only the wisdom of eternity is edifying.

If there is, then, something eternal in a man, it must be able to exist and to be grasped within every change. Nor can it be wisdom to say, indiscriminately, that this something eternal has its time like the perishable, that it makes its circle like the wind that never gets further; that it has its course like the river that never fills up the sea. Nor can it be wisdom to talk of this eternal element in the same vein as if one were speaking of the past, as if it is past and past in the sense that it can never, not even in repentance, relate itself to a present person but only to an absent one. For repentance is precisely the relation between something past and someone that has his life in the present time. It was unwise of the youth to wish to talk in the same terms of the pleasure of dancing and of its opposite. For this clear act of folly betrayed that the youth, in his youth, would like to have outgrown youth. But as for the Eternal, the time never comes when a man has grown away from it, or has become older -- than the Eternal.

If there is, then, something eternal in a man the discussion of it must have a different ring. It must be said that there is something that shall always have its time. something that a man shall always do, just as one Apostle says that we should always give thanks to God. (For example: 2 Thessalonians 1:3.) For that which has its time must properly be looked upon as an associate and an equal with other temporal things that in their turn shall pass away. But the Eternal is that which is set over all, The Eternal will not have its time, but will fashion time to its own desire, and then give its consent that the temporal should also be given its time. So the Scripture says, "The one shall be done, the other shall not be neglected."(Matthew 23:23. See note 2. The precise text is: "These ought ye to have done and not to leave the other undone.") But that which shall not be neglected is just that which cannot come into consideration until that is done which ought to be done. In like fashion with the Eternal. If the wisdom of life should ever alter that which. concerns the eternal in a man to the point of changing it into something temporal, then this would be folly whether it be spoken by an old man or by a youth. For m relation to the Eternal, age gives no justification for speaking absurdly, and youth does not exclude one from being able to grasp what is true. Should someone explain that the fear of God, in the sense of that felt in this world of time, should belong to childhood and therefore disappear with the years as does childhood itself, or should be like a happy state of mind that cannot be maintained, but only remembered; should someone explain that penitence comes like the weakness of old age, with the wasting away of strength, when the senses are blunted, when sleep no longer strengthens but weakens; then this would be Impiety and folly. Yes, to be sure, it is a fact that there was a man who with the years forgot his childish fear of God, was swindled out of the best, and was taken in by that which was most insolent. Yes, to be sure, it is a fact that there was a man whom repentance first overtook in the painfulness of old age, when he no longer had the strength to sin, so that the repentance not only came late, but the despair of late repentance became the final stage. But this is no story of an event that calls for an ingenious explanation or that would even of itself explain life. When it happens, it is a horrible thing. And even if a man should become a thousand years old, he would not have become so old that he dares speak otherwise of it than the youth -- with fear and trembling. For in relation to the Eternal, a man ages neither in the sense of time nor in the sense of an accumulation of past events. No, when an old person has outgrown the childish and the youthful, ordinary language calls this, maturity and a gain. But willfully ever to have outgrown the Eternal is spoken of as falling away from God and as perdition; and only the life of the ungodly "shall be as the snail that melts, as it goes" (Psalm 58:8).

Chapter 2: Remorse, Repentance, Confession: Eternity's Emissaries to Man

There is, then, something which should at all times be done. There is something which in no temporal sense shall have its time. Alas, and when this is not done, when it is omitted, or when just the opposite is done, then once again, there is something (Or more correctly it is the same thing, that reappears, changed, but not changed in its essence) which should at all times be done. There is something which in no temporal sense shall have its time. There must be repentance and remorse.

One dare not say of repentance and remorse that it has its time; that there is a time to be carefree and a time to be prostrated in repentance. Such talk would be: to the anxious urgency of repentance -- unpardonably slow; to the grieving after God -- sacrilege; to what should be done this very day, in this instant, in this moment of danger -- senseless delay. For there is indeed danger. There is a danger that is called delusion. It is unable to check itself. It goes on and on: then it is called perdition. But there is a concerned guide, a knowing one, who attracts the attention of the wanderer, who calls out to him that he should take care. That guide is remorse. He is not so quick of foot as the indulgent imagination, which is the servant of desire. He is not so strongly built as the victorious intention. He comes on slowly afterwards. He grieves. But he is a sincere and faithful friend. If that guide's voice is never heard, then it is just because one is wandering along the way of perdition. For when the sick man who is wasting away from consumption believes himself to be in the best of health, his disease is at the most terrible point. If there were some one who early in life steeled his mind against all remorse and who actually carried it out, nevertheless remorse would come again if he were willing to repent even of this decision. So wonderful a power is remorse, so sincere is its friendship that to escape it entirely is the most terrible thing of all. A man can wish to slink away from many things in life, and he may even succeed, so that life's favored one can say in the last moment, "I slipped away from all the cares under which other men suffered." But if such a person wishes to bluster out of, to defy, or to slink away from remorse, alas, which is indeed the most terrible to say of him, that he failed, or -- that he succeeded?

A Providence watches over each man's wandering through life. It provides him with two guides. The one calls him forward. The other calls him back. They are, however, not in opposition to each other, these two guides, nor do they leave the wanderer standing there in doubt, confused by the double call. Rather the two are in eternal understanding with each other. For the one beckons forward to the Good, the other calls man back from evil. Nor are they blind guides. Just for that reason there are two of them. For in order to make the journey secure, they must look both forward and backward. Alas, there was perhaps many a one who went astray through not understanding how to continue a good beginning. For his course was along a false way, and he pressed on so continuously that remorse could not call him back onto the old way. There was perhaps someone who went astray because, in the exhaustion of repentance, he could go no further, so that the guide could not help him to find the way forward. When a long procession is about to move, a call is heard first from the one who is furthest forward. But he waits until the last has answered. The two guides call out to a man early and late, and when he listens to their call, then he finds his way, then he can know where he is, on the way. Because these two calls designate the place and show the way. Of these two, the call of remorse is perhaps the best. For the eager traveler who travels lightly along the way does not, in this fashion, learn to know it as well as a wayfarer with a heavy burden. The one who merely strives to get on does not learn to know the way as well as the remorseful man. The eager traveler hurries forward to the new, to the novel, and, indeed, away from experience. But the remorseful one, who comes behind, laboriously gathers up experience.

The two guides call out to a man early and late. And yet, no, for when remorse calls to a man it is always late. The call to find the way again by seeking out God in the confession of sins is always at the eleventh hour. Whether you are young or old, whether you have sinned much or little, whether you have offended much or neglected much, the guilt makes this call come at the eleventh hour. The inner agitation of the heart understands what remorse insists upon, that the eleventh hour has come. For in the sense of time, the old man's age is the eleventh hour; and the instant of death, the final moment in the eleventh hour. The indolent youth speaks of a long life that lies before him. The indolent old man hopes that his death is still a long way off. But repentance and remorse belong to the eternal in a man. And in this way each time that repentance comprehends guilt it understands that the eleventh hour has come: that hour which human indolence knows well enough exists and will come, when it is talked about in generalities, but not when it actually applies to the indolent one himself. For even the old man thinks that there is some time left and the indolent youth deceives himself when he thinks that difference in age is the determining factor in regard to the nearness of the eleventh hour. See, then, how good and how necessary it is that there are two guides. For whether it be the lightly armed desire of youth which it is presumed will press forward to victory, or whether it be the mature man s determination that will fight its way through life, they both count on having a long time at their disposal. They presuppose, in the plans for their efforts, a generation or at least a number of years, and therefore they waste a great deal of time and on that account the whole thing so readily ends in delusion.

But repentance and remorse know how to make use of time in fear and trembling. When remorse awakens concern, whether it be in the youth, or in the old man, it awakens it always at the eleventh hour. It does not have much time at its disposal, for it is at the eleventh hour. It is not deceived by a false notion of a long life, for it is at the eleventh hour. And in the eleventh hour one understands life in a wholly different way than in the days of youth or in the busy time of manhood or in the final moment of old age. He who repents at any other hour of the day repents in the temporal sense. He fortifies himself by a false and hasty conception of the insignificance of his guilt. He braces himself with a false and hasty notion of life's length. His remorse is not in true inwardness of spirit. Oh, eleventh hour, wherever thou art present, how all is changed! How still everything is, as if it were the midnight hour; how sober, as if it were the hour of death; how lonely, as if it were among the tombs; how solemn, as if it were within eternity. Oh, heavy hour of labor (although labor is at rest), when the account is rendered, yet there is no accuser there; when all is called by its own name, yet there is nothing said; when each improper word must be repeated, in the light of eternity! Oh, costly bargain, where remorse must pay so dearly for what seemed in the eyes of lightheartedness and busyness and proud struggling and impatient passion and the judgment of the world to be reckoned as nothing! Oh, eleventh hour, how terrible if Thou shouldst remain, how much more terrible than if death should continue through a whole life!

So repentance must have its time if all is not to be confused. For there are two guides. The one beckons forward. The other calls back. But repentance shall not have its time in a temporal sense. It will not belong to a certain section of life as fun and play belong to childhood, or as the excitement of love belongs to youth. It will not come and disappear as a whim or as a surprise. No, remorse should be an action with a collected mind, so that it may be spoken of to the edification of the hearer and so that new life may be born of it, so that it does not become an event whose sorrowful heritage is a feeling of sadness. In a setting of freedom, bearing the impress of eternity, repentance should have its time, yes, even its time of preparation. For in proportion to what should be done there, the time of collection and preparation is not a drawnout affair. On the contrary there is a sense of reverence, a holy fear, a humility, that that which is to be done in the pure sincerity of this act of repentance may not become vain and overhasty. That a man wishes to prepare himself is no torpid delay. On the contrary, it is an intense agitation of heart that is already in alliance with what is to be done there. From the point of view of the Eternal, repentance must come instantaneously, indeed there is not even time to utter the words. But man is in the temporal dimension and moves along in time. Thus the Eternal and the temporal seek to make themselves intelligible to each other. Just as the temporal does not wish for delay simply in order to withdraw itself, but, conscious of its weakness, asks time to prepare itself; so the Eternal yields not because it gives up its claim, but in order by tender treatment to give frail man a little time.

The Eternal with its "obey at once" must not become a sudden shock which merely confuses the temporal. It should, on the contrary, be of assistance to the temporal throughout life. As the superior in relation to its mental inferior, or as an older person in relation to a child, can press its claim to such an extreme that it ends by actually weakening the mind of the mentally inferior or the child, so also the Eternal can in the imagination of an excitable person make an attempt to push the temporal into madness. Hut the grieving of repentance after God and the heartfelt anxiety must not, above all, be confused with impatience. Experience teaches that the right moment to repent is not always the one that is immediately present. For repentance in this precipitate moment when labored thoughts and various passions are acutely active or at least are strained by this unburdening may so easily be mistaken about that which is really to be repented. It can so easily be confused with its opposite, with the momentary feeling of contrition, that is, with impatience. It can so easily be confused with a painful agonizing sorrow after the world, that is, with impatience; with a desperate feeling of grief in itself, that is, with impatience. But impatience, no matter how long it continues to rage, never becomes repentance. However clouded, then, the mind becomes, the sobs of impatience no matter how violent they are, never become sobs of repentance. The tears of impatience lack the blessed fruitfulness. They are like empty clouds that bear no water, or like convulsive puffs of wind. On the other hand, if a man assumed an even heavier guilt, but at the same time improved and year after year went steadily forward in the good, it is certain that from year to year, as he advanced in the good, he would with greater intensity repent of his guilt, the guilt which year by year in a temporal sense he would be leaving further and further behind. For it is indeed the case that guilt must be alive for a man if he is honestly to repent. But just for that reason, precipitate repentance is false and is never to be sought after. For it may not be the inner anxiety of heart but only the momentary feeling that presents the guilt so actively. This kind of repentance is selfish, a matter of the senses, sensually powerful for the moment, excited in expression, impatient in the most diverse exaggerations -- and, just on this account, is not real repentance. Sudden repentance would drink down all the bitterness of sorrow in a single draught and then hurry on. It wants to get away from guilt. It wants to banish all recollection of it, fortifying itself by imagining that it does this in order not to be held back in the pursuit of the Good. It is its wish that guilt, after a time, might be wholly forgotten. And once again, this is impatience. Perhaps a later sudden repentance may make it apparent that the former sudden repentance lacked true inwardness.

It is told that there was once a man who through his misdeeds deserved the punishment which the law meted out to him. After he had suffered for his wrong acts he went back into ordinary society, improved. Then he went to a strange land, where he was not known, and where he became known for his worthy conduct. All was forgotten. Then one day there appeared a fugitive that recognized the distinguished person as his equal back in those miserable days.

This was a terrifying memory to meet. A deathlike fear shook him each time this man passed. Although silent, this memory shouted in a high voice until through the voice of this vile fugitive it took on words. Then suddenly despair seized this man, who seemed to have been saved. And it seized him just because repentance was forgotten, because the improvement toward society was not the resigning of himself to God, so that in the humility of repentance he might remember what he had been. For in the temporal, and sensual, and social sense, repentance is in fact something that comes and goes during the years. But in the eternal sense, it is a silent daily anxiety. It is eternally false, that guilt is changed by the passage of a century. To assert anything of this sort is to confuse the Eternal with what the Eternal is least like -- with human forgetfulness.

If anyone in a brazen and impious mood should pronounce absolution from the Good, on the ground that all is lost, then this is sacrilege and this will only add to the guilt by piling up more and more fresh guilt. Now let us indeed consider this. Guilt is not increased for the reason that it seems more and more tragic to the improved individual. It is not a gain that guilt should be wholly forgotten. On the contrary, it is loss and perdition. But it is a gain to win an inner intensity of heart through a deeper and deeper inner sorrowing over guilt. It is not a gain to notice, because of a man's forgetfulness, that he is growing older. But it is a gain to notice that a man has grown older by the deeper and deeper penetration into his heart of the transformation wrought by remorse. One should be able to tell the age of a tree from its bark; in truth one can also tell a man's age in the Good by the intensity of his repentance. There is a battle of despair that struggles -- with the consequences. The enemy attacks constantly from behind, and yet the fighter shall continue to advance. When this is so, the repentance is still young and weak. There is a suffering of repentance, that is not impatient in bearing the punishment, but yet each moment cringes under it. When this is so, the repentance is still young and weak. There is a silent, sleepless sorrow at the picturing of what has been wasted. It does not despair, but in its daily grieving, it is always restless. When this is so, the repentance is still young and weak. There is a laborious moving forward in the Good that is like the gait of one whose feet are without skin. He is willing enough, he will gladly walk swiftly, but he has suffered a loss of courage. The pains make his going uncertain and agonizing. When this is so, the repentance is still young and weak.

But when, in spite of this, more confident steps are made along the way, when punishment itself becomes a blessing, when consequences even become redemptive, when progress in the Good is apparent; then is there a milder but deep sorrow that remembers the guilt. It has wearied out and overcome what could deceive and confuse the sight. Therefore it does not see falsely, but sees only the one sorrowful thing. This is the older, the strong and the powerful repentance. When it is a matter of the senses, it is true that they deteriorate and decline in the course of the years. Of a dancer one must say that her time is past when her youth is gone. But it is otherwise with a penitent. And it must be said of repentance that, if it is forgotten, then its strength was only an immaturity; but the longer and the more deeply one treasures it, the better it becomes. For guilt looks most terrifying the nearer at hand one sees it. But repentance is most acceptable to God, the further away repentance views the guilt, along the way of the Good.

So, then, repentance should not merely have its time, but even its time of preparation.

Although it should be a silent daily concern, it should also be able to collect itself and be well prepared for the solemn occasion. One such an occasion is the office of Confession, the holy act for which preparation should be made in advance. As a man changes his raiment for a feast, so is a man changed in his heart who prepares himself for the holy act of confession. It is indeed like a changing of raiment to lay off manyness, in order rightly to center down upon one thing; to interrupt the busy course of activity, in order to put on the quiet of contemplation and be at one with oneself. And this being at one with oneself is the simple festival garment of the feast that is the condition of admittance. The manyness, one may see with a dispersed mind, see something of it, see it in passing, see it with half-closed eyes, with a divided mind, see it and indeed not see **it.** In the rush of busyness, one may be anxious over many things, begin many things, do many things at once, and only half do them all. Hut one cannot confess without this at-oneness with oneself. He that is not truly at one with himself during the hour of the office of Confession is merely dispersed. If he remains silent, he is not collected; if he speaks, it is only in a chatty vein, not in confession.

But he that in truth becomes at one with himself, he is in the silence. And this is indeed like a changing of raiment: to strip oneself of all that is as full of noise as it is empty, in order to be hidden in the silence, to become open. This silence is the simple festivity of the holy act of confession. For at dancing and festive occasions worldly judgment holds that the more musicians, the better. But when we are thinking of divine things, the deeper the stillness the better. When the wanderer comes away from the much-traveled noisy highway into places of quiet, then it seems to him (for stillness is impressive) as if he must examine himself, as if he must speak out what lies hidden in the depths of his soul. It seems to him, according to the poets' explanation, as if something inexpressible thrusts itself forward from his innermost being, the unspeakable, for which indeed language has no vessel of expression. Even the longing is not the unspeakable itself. It is only a hastening after it. But what silence means, what the surroundings will say in this stillness, is just the unspeakable.

Now the surprise expressed by the trees, if it can be said that the trees looked down in surprise upon the wanderer, explains nothing. And the wood's echo makes very clear indeed that it explains nothing. No, as an impregnable fortress throws back the attack of the enemy, so the echo throws back the voice, no matter how loudly the wanderer shouts. And the clouds hang as they please, and dream only of themselves. Whether seeming to be in restful revery, or enjoying voluptuous soft movements; whether in their transparence running swiftly off, driven by the wind, or gathering in a dark mass to battle with the wind, at least they do not trouble themselves over the wanderer.

And the sea, like a wise man, is sufficient unto itself. Whether it lies like a child and amuses itself with its soft ripples as a child that plays with its mouth, or at noon lies like a drowsy thinker in carefree enjoyment and allows its gaze to wander over all, or in the night ponders deeply over its own being; whether in order to see what is going on, it cunningly conceals itself as though it no longer existed, or whether it rages in its own passion the sea has a deep ground, it knows well enough what it knows. That which has that deep ground always knows this; but there is no sharing of this knowledge.

And what a puzzling arrangement the army of stars presents! Yet there seems to be an agreement between them that they shall arrange themselves in this fashion. But the stars are so far away that they cannot see the wanderer. It is only the wanderer who can see the stars, hence there may come no agreement between him and the stars. So this melancholy of poetical longing is grounded in a deep misunderstanding, because the lonely wanderer is everywhere surrounded in nature by that which does not understand him, even though it always seems as if an understanding must be arrived at.

Now the unspeakable is like the murmuring of a brook. If you go buried in your own thoughts, if you are busy, then you do not notice it at all in passing. You are not aware that this murmuring exists. But if you stand still, then you discover it. And if you have discovered it, then you must stand still. And when you stand still, then it persuades you. And when it has persuaded you, then you must stoop and listen attentively to it. And when you have stooped to listen to it, then it captures you. And when it has captured you, then you cannot break away from it, then you are overpowered. Infatuated, you sink down at its side. At each moment it is as if in the next moment it must offer an explanation. But the brook goes on murmuring, and the wanderer at its side grows older.

It is otherwise with one who confesses. The stillness also impresses him, yet not in the melancholy mood of misunderstanding, but rather with the seriousness of eternity. He is not, like the wanderer, uncertain about how he came upon the still places. Nor is he like the poet who wishes to seek out loneliness and its mood. No, to confess is a holy act, for which purpose, the mind is collected in preparation. That which environs you knows well enough what this stillness means and that it calls for earnestness. It knows that it is its wish to be understood. It knows that fresh guilt is incurred if it be misunderstood. And the One that is present at this confession is an omniscient One. He knows and remembers all that this man has ever confided to Him, or that this man has ever withdrawn from His confidence. He is an omniscient One that again at the final moment of this man's life will remember this hour, will remember what this man confided to Him and what this man withdrew from His confidence. He is an omniscient One who knows every thought from a distance, who knows plainly the very path of each thought, even when it eludes a man's own consciousness. He is an omniscient One "who seeth in secret," with whom a man speaks even in silence, so that no one shall venture to deceive Him either by talk, or by silence, as in this world where one man can conceal much from the other now by being silent, and again even more by talking.

The person making the confession is not like a servant that gives account to his lord for the management which is given over to him because the lord could not manage all or be present in all places. The all-knowing One was present at each instant for which reckoning shall be made in the account. The account of what is done is not made for the lord's sake but for the servant's sake, who must even render account of how he used the very moment of rendering the account. Nor is the person confessing like one that confides in a friend to whom sooner or later he reveals things that the friend did not previously know. The all-knowing One does not get to know something about the maker of the confession, rather the maker of confession gets to know about himself. Therefore, do not raise the objection against the confession that there is no point in confiding to the all-knowing One that which He already knows. Reply first to the question whether it is not conferring a benefit when a man gets to know something about himself which he did not know before. A hasty explanation could assert that to pray is a useless act, because a man's prayer does not alter the unalterable. But would this be desirable in the long run? Could not fickle man easily come to regret that he had gotten God changed? The true explanation is therefore at the same time the one most to be desired. The prayer does not change God, but it changes the one who offers it. It is the same with the substance of what is spoken. Not God, but you, the maker of the confession, get to know something by your act of confession.

Much that you are able to keep hidden in darkness, you first get to know by your opening it to the knowledge of the all-knowing One. Even the most atrocious misdeeds are committed, even blood is spilt, and many times it must in truth be said of the guilty one: he knew not what he did. Perhaps he died, without ever in repentance really getting to know what it was he had done. For does passion ever properly know what it does? Does not passion's insidious temptation and its apparent excuse center in that deceptive ignorance about itself because, in the instant, it has forgotten the Eternal? For if passion continues in a man, it changes his life into nothing but instants and as passion cunningly serves its deluded master, it gradually gains the ascendancy until the master serves it like a blind serf!

For when hate, and anger, and revenge, and despondency, and melancholy, and despair, and fear of the future, and reliance on the world, and trust in oneself, and pride that infuses itself even into sympathy, and envy that even mingles itself with friendship, and that inclination that may have changed but not for the better: when these dwell m a man -- when was it without the deceptive excuse of ignorance? And when a man remained ignorant of them, was it not precisely because he at the same time remained ignorant of the fact that there is an all-knowing One.

Yes, there is an ignorance which no one needs be troubled over if he was deprived either of the opportunity or the capacity to learn. But there is an ignorance about one's own life that is equally tragic for the learned and for the simple, for both are bound by the same responsibility. This ignorance is called self-deceit. There is an ignorance that by degrees, as more and more is learned, gradually changes into knowledge. But there is only one thing that can remove that other ignorance which is self-deception. And to be ignorant of the fact that there is one thing and only one thing, and that only one thing is necessary, is still to be in self-deception.

The ignorant one may have been ignorant of much. He can increase his knowledge, and still there is much that he does not know. But if the self-deluded one speaks of quantity, and of variety, then he is still in self-deception, still deeply ensnared by and in the grip of multiplicity. The ignorant man can gradually acquire wisdom and knowledge, but the self-deluded one if he won "the one thing needful" would have won purity of heart.

Chapter 3: Barriers to Willing One Thing: Variety and Great Moments Are Not One Thing

So let us, then, upon the occasion of a time of Confession speak about this sentence: PURITY OF HEART IS TO WILL ONE THING as we base our meditation on the Apostle James' words in his Epistle, Chapter 4, verse 8:

"*Draw nigh to God and he will draw nigh to you. Cleanse your hands, ye sinners; and purify your hearts ye double-minded.*" For only the pure in heart can see God, and therefore, draw nigh to Him; and only by God's drawing nigh to them can they maintain this purity. And he who in truth wills only one thing can will only the Good, and he who only wills one thing when he wills the Good can only will the Good in truth.

. . . . .

Let us speak of this, but let us first put out of our minds the occasion of the office of Confession in order to come to an agreement on an understanding of this verse, and on what the apostolic word of admonition "purify your hearts ye double-minded" is condemning, namely, *double-mindedness.* Then at the close of the talk we may return more specifically to a treatment of the occasion.

. . . . .

I. If it is to be Possible, that a Man Can Will Only One Thing, Then He Must Will the Good.

To will only one thing: but will this not inevitably become a long-drawn-out talk? If one should consider this matter properly must he not first consider, one by one, each goal in life that a man could conceivably set up for himself, mentioning separately all of the many things that a man might will? And not only this; since each of these considerations readily becomes too abstract in character, is he not obliged as the next step to attempt to will, one after the other, each of these goals in order to find out what is the single thing he is to will, if it is a matter of willing only one thing? Yes, if someone should begin in this fashion, then he would never come to an end. Or more accurately, how could he ever arrive at the end since at the outset he took the wrong way and then continued to go on further and further along this false way? It is only by a painful route that this way leads to the Good, namely, when the wanderer turns around and goes back. For as the Good is only a single thing, so all ways lead to the Good, even the false ones: when the repentant one follows the same way back. Oh, Thou the unfathomable trustworthiness of the Good! 'Wherever a man may be in the world, whichever road he travels, when he wills one thing, he is on a road that leads him to Thee! Here such a

far-flung enumeration would only work harm. Instead of wasting many moments on naming the vast multitude of goals or squandering life's costly years in personal experiments upon them, can the talk do as life ought to do -- with a commendable brevity stick to the point?

In a certain sense nothing can be spoken of so briefly as the Good, when it is well described. For the Good without condition and without qualification, without preface and without compromise is, absolutely the only thing that a man may and should will, and is only one thing. Oh, blessed brevity, oh, blessed simplicity, that seizes swiftly what cleverness, tired out in the service of vanity, may grasp but slowly! That which a simple soul, in the happy impulse of a pious heart, feels no need of understanding m an elaborate way, since he simply seizes the Good immediately, is grasped by the clever one only at the cost of much time and much grief. The way this one thing is willed is not such that: one man wills one thing but that which he wills is not the Good; another wills one thing nor is what he wills the Good; a third wills one thing and what he wills *is* the Good. No, it is not done in that way. The person who wills one thing that is not the Good, he does not truly will one thing. It is a delusion, an illusion, a deception, a self-deception that he wills only one thing. For in his innermost being he is, he is bound to be, double-minded. Therefore the Apostle says, "Purify your hearts ye doubleminded," that is, purify your hearts of double-mindedness; in other words, let your heart in truth will only one thing, for therein is the heart's purity.

And again it is of this same purity of heart that the Apostle is speaking when he says, "If someone lacks wisdom, then let him pray... but in faith, not like a double-minded man" (James 1:5,6, 8). For purity of heart is the very wisdom that is acquired through prayer. A man of prayer does not pore over learned books for he is the wise man "whose eyes are opened" -- when he kneels down (Numbers 24:16).

In a word, then, there is a man whose mind remains piously ignorant of the multitude of things, for the Good is one thing. The more difficult part of the talk is directed to the man whose mind in its double-mindedness has made the doubtful acquaintance of the multitude of things, and of knowledge. If it is certain that a man in truth wills one thing, then he wills the Good, for this alone can be willed in this manner. But both of these assertions speak of identical things, or they speak of different things. The one assertion plainly designates the name of the Good, declaring it to be that one thing. The other assertion cunningly conceals this name. It appears almost as if it spoke of something else. But just on that account it forces its way, searchingly, into a man's innermost being. And no matter how much he may protest, or defy, or boast that he wills only one thing, it searches him through and through in order to show the double-mindedness in him if the one thing he wills is not the Good.

For in truth there was a man on earth who seemed to will only one thing. It was unnecessary for him to insist upon it. Even if he had been silent about it, there were witnesses enough against him who testified how inhumanly he steeled his mind, how nothing touched him, neither tenderness, nor innocence, nor misery; how his blinded soul had eyes for nothing, and how the senses in him had only eyes for the one thing that he willed. And yet it was certainly a delusion, a terrible delusion, that he willed one thing. For pleasure and honor and riches and power and all that this world has to offer only appear to be one thing. It is not, nor does it remain one thing, while everything else is in change or while he himself is in change. It is not in all circumstances the same. On the contrary, it is subject to continual alteration. Hence even if this man named but one thing whether it be pleasure, or honor or riches, actually he did not will one thing. Neither can he be said to will one thing when that one thing which he wills is not in itself one: is in itself a multitude of things, a dispersion, the toy of changeableness, and the prey of corruption! In the time of pleasure see how he longed for one gratification after another. Variety was his watchword. Is variety, then, to will one thing that shall ever remain the same? On the contrary, it is to will one thing that must never be the same. It is to will a multitude of things. And a person who wills in this fashion is not only double-minded but is at odds with himself. For such a man wills first one thing and then immediately wills the opposite, because the oneness of pleasure is a snare and a delusion. It is the diversity of pleasures that he wills. So when the man of whom we are speaking had gratified himself up to the point of disgust, he became weary and sated. Even ıf he still desired one thing -- what was it that he desired? He desired new pleasures; his enfeebled soul raged so that no ingenuity was sufficient to discover something new -- something new! It was change he cried out for as pleasure served him, change! change! And it was change that he cried out for as he came to pleasure's limit, as his servants were worn out -- change! change!

Now it is to be understood that there are also changes in life that can prove to a man whether he wills one thing. There is the change of the perishable nature when the sensual man must step aside, when dancing and the tumult of the whirling senses are over, when all becomes soberly quiet. That is the change of death. If, for once, the perishable nature should seem to forget to close in, if it should seem as if the sensual one had succeeded in slipping by: death does not forget. The sensual one will not slip past death, who has dominion over what belongs to the earth and who will change into nothing the one thing which the sensual person desires.

And last of all, there is the change of eternity, which changes all. Then only the Good remains and it remains the blessed possession of the man that has willed only one thing. But that rich man whom no misery could touch, that rich man who even in eternity to his own damnation must continue to will one thing, ask him now whether he really wills one thing. So, too, with honor and riches and power. For in the time of strength as he aspired to honor, did he really discover some limit, or was that not simply the striver's restless passion to climb higher and higher? Did he find some rest amid his sleeplessness in which he sought to capture honor and to hold it fast? Did he find some refreshment in the cold fire of his passion? And if he really won honor's highest prize, then is earthly honor in itself one thing? Or in its diversity when the thousands and thousands braid the wreath, is honor to be likened to the gorgeous carpet of the field -- created by a single hand? No, like worldly contempt, worldly honor is a whirlpool, a play of confused forces, an illusory moment in the flux of opinions. It is a sense-deception, as when a swarm of insects at a distance seem to the eye like one body; a sense-deception, as when the noise of the many at a distance seems to the ear like a single voice.

Even if honor were unanimous it would still be meaningless, and the more so, the more thousands that create the unanimity. And the greater the multitude that created unanimity, the sooner will it show itself to be meaningless. And indeed it was this unanimity of the thousands that he desired. It was not the approbation of the good men. They are soon counted. No, it was rather the approbation of the thousands. Is, then, this desire for counting, is this to will one thing? To count and count until it suffices, to count and count until a mistake is made; is this to will one thing? Whoever, therefore, wills this honor or fears this contempt, whether or not he is said to will one thing in his innermost being, is not merely doubleminded but thousand-minded, and at variance with himself. So is his life when he must grovel -- in order to attain honor; when he must flatter his enemies -- in order to attain honor; when he must woo the favor of those he despises -- in order to attain honor; when he must betray the one whom he respects -- in order to attain honor. For to attain honor means to despise oneself after one has attained the pinnacle of honor -- and yet to tremble before any change. Change, yes, where does change rage more unchecked than here? What desertion is more swift and sudden, like a mistake in foolery, like a hit by a blind man, when the seeker for honor has not even time to take off the garb of honor before insult seizes him in it? Change, the final change, the absolute certainty among the range of unpredictables: no matter how loud the thunder of honor may sound over his grave, even if it could be heard over the whole earth, there is one who cannot hear it: the dead man, he who died with honor, the single thing he had desired. But also in dying he lost the honor, for it remains outside, it marches home again, it dies away like an echo. Change, the true change, when eternity exists: I should like to know if honor's crown is offered to the much-honored one there! And yet eternity is more lust than the earth and the world; for in eternity there is a crown of honor laid aside for each of those that have in truth willed only one thing. So also with riches and power and the world that passes away and the lust thereof. The one who has willed either of them, even if he only willed one thing, must, to his own agony, continue to will it when it has passed, and learn by the agony of contradiction that it is not one thing. But the one who in truth willed one thing and therefore willed the Good, even if he be sacrificed for it, why should he not go on willing the same in eternity, the same thing that he was willing to die for? Why should he not will the same, when it has triumphed in eternity?

To will one thing, therefore, cannot mean to will that which only appears to be one thing. The fact is that the worldly goal is not one thing in its essence because it is unreal. Its so-called unity is actually nothing but emptiness which is hidden beneath the manyness. In the shortlived moment of delusion the worldly goal is therefore a multitude of things, and thus not one thing. So far is it from a state of being and remaining one thing, that in the next moment it changes itself into its opposite. Carried to its extreme limit, what is pleasure other than disgust? What is earthly honor at its dizzy pinnacle other than contempt f or existence? What are riches, the highest superabundance of riches, other than poverty? For no matter how much all the earth's gold hidden in covetousness may amount to, is it not infinitely less than the smallest mite hidden in the contentment of the poor! What is worldly omnipotence other than dependence? What slave in chains is as unfree as a tyrant! No, the worldly goal is not one thing. Diverse as it is, in life it is changed into its opposite, in death into nothing, in eternity into damnation: for the one who has willed this goal. Only the Good is one thing in its essence and the same in each of its expressions. Take love as an illustration. The one who truly loves does not love once and for all. Nor does he use a part of his love, and then again another part. For to change it into small coins is not to use it rightly. No, he loves with all of his love. It is wholly present in each expression. He continues to give it away as a whole, and yet he keeps it intact as a whole, in his heart. Wonderful riches! When the miser has gathered all the world's gold in sordidness -- then he has become poor. When the lover gives away his whole love, he keeps it entire -- in the purity of the heart. Shall a man in truth will one thing, then this one thing that he wills must be such that it remains unaltered in all changes, so that by willing it he can win immutability. If it changes continually, then he himself becomes changeable, double-minded, and unstable. And this continual change is nothing else than impurity.

Now, willing one thing does not mean to commit the grave mistake of a brazen, unholy enthusiasm, namely, to will the big, no matter whether it be good or bad. Also, one who wills in this fashion no matter how desperately he does it, is indeed double-minded. Is not despair simply double-mindedness? For what is despairing other than to have two wills? For whether the weakling despairs over not being able to wrench himself away from the bad, or whether the brazen one despairs over not being able to tear himself completely away from the Good: they are both double-minded, they both have two wills. Neither of them honestly wills one thing, however desperately they may seem to will it. Whether it was a woman whom desire brought to desperation, or whether it was a man who despaired in defiance; whether a man despaired because he got his will, or despaired because he did not get his will: each one in despairing has two wills, one that he fruitlessly tries wholly to follow and one that he fruitlessly tries wholly to avoid. In this fashion has God, better than any king, insured himself against every rebellion. For it has indeed happened that a king has been dethroned by a rebellion. But each rebel against God, in the last instance, is himself reduced to despair. Despair is the limit -- There and no further!" Despair is the limit. Here are met the cowardly timorous ill-temper of self-love, and the proud defiant presumption of the mind -- here they are met in equal impotence.

Only too soon personal experience and the experience of others teaches how far most men's lives are from being what a man's life ought to be. All have great moments. They see themselves in the magic mirror of possibility which hope holds before them while the wish flatters them. But they swiftly forget this sight in the daily round of things. Or perhaps they talk enthusiastic words, "for the tongue is a little member and boasteth great things."(James 3:5.)But talk takes the name of enthusiasm in vain by proclaiming loudly from the housetop what it should work out in silence. And in the midst of the trivial details of life these enthusiastic words are quickly forgotten. It is forgotten that such a thing was said of this man. It is forgotten that it was he himself who said it. Now and then, perhaps, memory wakens with horror, and remorse seems to promise new strength. But, alas, this, too, lasts only for a goodsized moment. All of them have intentions, plans, resolutions for life, yes, for eternity. But the intention soon loses its youthful strength and fades away. The resolution is not firmly grounded and is unable to withstand opposition. It totters before circumstances and is altered by them. Memory, too, has a way of failing, until by common practice and habit they learn to draw sympathy from one another. If someone proclaims the slender comfort that excuses yield, instead of realizing how treacherous is such sympathy, they finally come to regard it as edifying, because it encourages and strengthens indolence. Now there are men who find it edifying that the demand to will one thing be asserted in all its sublimity, in all its severity, so that it may press its claim into the innermost fastness of the soul. Others find it edifying, that a wretched compromise should be made between God, the claim, and the language used. There are men who find it edifying if only someone will challenge them. But there are also the sleepy souls who regard it as not only pleasing, but even edifying, to be lulled to sleep.

This is indeed a lamentable fact; but there is a wisdom which is not from above, but is earthly and fleshly and devilish. It has discovered this common human weakness and indolence; it wants to be helpful. It perceives that all depends upon the will and so it proclaims loudly, "Unless it wills one thing, a man's life is sure to become one of wretched mediocrity, of pitiful misery. He must will one thing regardless of whether it be good or bad. He must will one thing for therein lies a man's greatness." Yet it is not difficult to see through this powerful error. As to the working out of salvation, the holy Scripture teaches that sin is the corruption of man. Salvation, therefore, lies only in the purity with which a man wills the Good. That very earthly and devilish cleverness distorts this into a temptation to perdition; weakness is a man's misfortune; strength the sole salvation: "When the unclean spirit is gone out of a man, he walketh through dry and empty places but finds no rest. Then he turns back again and now he brings with him" that unclean cleverness, the wisdom of the desert and the empty places, that unclean cleverness -- that now drives out the spirit of indolence and of mediocrity "so that the last stage becomes worse than the first."(Matthew 12:43, 45.) How shall one describe the nature of such a man? It is said of a singer that by overscreeching he can crack his voice. In like fashion, such a man s nature by overscreeching itself and the voice of conscience, has cracked. It is said of a man who stands dizzily upon a high place, that all things run together before his eyes. Such a man has made himself giddy in the infinite, where those things which are forever separate run together into one thing, so that only the vast remains.

It is this dryness and emptiness that always gives birth to giddiness. But no matter how desperately such a man may seem to will one thing, he is double-minded. If he, the self-willed one, had his way, then there would be only this one thing: he would be the only one that was not double-minded, he the only one that had cast off every chain, he the only one that was free. But the slave of sin is not yet free; nor has he cast off the chain, "because he scoffs at it."(Compare Börne, Collected Works, Vol. II, p. 126: "All are not free who scoff at their chains.")He is in bonds, and therefore double-minded, and for once he may not have his own way. There is a power that binds him. He cannot tear himself loose from it. Nay, he cannot even wholly will it. For this power, too, is denied him. If you, my listener, should see such a man, although it is unlikely, for without a doubt weakness and mediocrity are the more common, if you should meet him in what he himself would call a weak moment, but which, alas, you would have to call a better moment; if you should meet him when he had found no rest in the desert, when the giddiness passes away for a moment and he feels an agonizing longing for the Good; if you should meet him when, shaken in his innermost being, and not without sadness, he was thinking of that man of single purpose who even in all his frailty still wills the Good: then you would discover that he had two wills, and you would discover his painful double-mindedness.

Desperate as he was, he thought: lost is lost. But he could not help turning around once more in his longing for the Good. How terribly embittered he had become against this very longing, a longing that reveals that, just as a man m all his defiance has not power enough wholly to loose himself from the Good, because it is the stronger, so he has not even the power wholly to will it.

Perhaps you may even have heard that desperate one say, "Some good went down with me." When a man meets his death by drowning, as he sinks, without being quite dead he comes to the surface again. At last a bubble comes out of his mouth. When this has happened, then he sinks, dead. That bubble was the last breath, the last supply of air, that could make him lighter than the sea. So with that remark. In that remark the last hope of salvation expired. In that remark he gave himself up. Was there still concealed in this thought a hope of salvation? Hidden in the soul, was there still in this thought a possible link with salvation? When a remark is pronounced in confidence to another man (oh, terrible misuse of confidence, even if the desperate one only misused it against himself!), when this word is heard, then he sinks forever.

Alas, it is horrible to see a man rush toward his own destruction. It is horrible to see him dance on the rim of the abyss without any intimation of it. But this clarity about himself and about his own destruction is even more horrible. It is horrible to see a man seek comfort by hurling himself into the whirlpool of despair. But this coolness is still more horrible: that, in the anxiety of death, a man should not cry out for help, "I am going under, save me"; but that he should quietly choose to be a witness to his own destruction! Oh, most extreme vanity, not to wish to draw man's eyes to himself by beauty, by riches, by ability, by power, by honor, but to wish to get his attention by his own destruction, by choosing to say of himself what at most pity in all sadness may venture to say of such a person at his grave, "Yet, some good went down with him." Oh, horrible doubleness of mind in a man's destruction, to wish to draw a sort of advantage out of the fact that the Good remains the only thing that a man has not willed. For now the other will becomes apparent to him, even if it were so weak as to be but a feeble dallying in the moment of destruction, an attempt to be exceptional by means of his own destruction.

To will one thing cannot, then, mean to will what in its essence is not one thing, but only seems to be so by means of a horrible falsehood. Only through a lie is it one thing. Now just as he that only wills this one thing is a liar, so he that conjures up this one thing is the father of lies. That dryness and emptiness is not in truth one thing, but is in truth nothing at all. And it is destruction for the man that only wills that one. If, on the contrary, a man should in truth will only one thing, then this thing must, in the truth of its innermost being, be one thing. It must, by an eternal separation, cut off the heterogeneous from itself in order that it may in truth continue to be one and the same thing and thereby fashion that man who only wills one thing into conformity with itself.

In truth to will one thing, then, can only mean to will the Good, because every other object is not a unity; and the will that only wills that object, therefore, must become double-minded. For as the coveted object is, so becomes the coveter. Or would it be possible that a man by willing the evil could will one thing, provided that it was possible for a man so to harden himself as to will nothing but the evil? Is not this evil, like evil persons, in disagreement with itself, divided against itself? Take one such man, separate him from society, shut him up in solitary confinement. Is he not at odds with himself there, just as a poor union between persons of his sort is an association that is ridden with dissension? But a good man, even if he lived in an out-of-the-way corner of the world and never saw any human being, would be at one with himself and at one with all about him because he wills one thing, and because the Good is one thing. *Each one who in truth would will one thing must be led to will the Good,* even though now and then it happens that a man begins by willing one thing that is not in its deepest sense the Good although it may be something quite innocent; and then, little by little, he is changed really in truth to will one thing by willing the Good. Love, from time to time, has in this way helped a man along the right path. Faithfully he only willed one thing, his love. For it, he would live and die. For it, he would sacrifice all and in it alone he would have his eternal reward. Yet the act of being in love is still not in the deepest sense the Good. But it may possibly become for him a helpful educator, who will finally lead him by the possession of his beloved one or perhaps by her loss, in truth to will one thing and to will the Good. In this fashion a man is educated by many means; and true love is also an education toward the Good.

Perhaps there was a man whose enthusiasm reached out toward a definite cause. In his enthusiasm he desired only one thing. He would live and die for that cause. He would sacrifice all for that in which alone he would have his happiness, for love and enthusiasm are not satisfied with a divided heart. Yet his endeavor was perhaps still not in the deepest sense the Good. Thus enthusiasm became for him a teacher, whom he outgrew, but to whom also he owed much. For, as it is said, all ways lead to the Good, when a man in truth only wills one thing. And where there is some truth in the fact that he wills one thing, this is all for the best. But there is danger that the lover and the enthusiast may swerve out of the true course and aim perhaps for the impressive instead of being led to the Good. The Good is certainly also in truth the impressive, but the impressive is not always the Good. And one can bid for a woman's favor by willing something when it is merely impressive. This can flatter the girl's pride and she can repay it with her adoration. But God in heaven is not as a young girl's folly. He does not reward the impressive with admiration. The reward of the good man is to be allowed to worship in truth.

Chapter 4: Barriers to Willing One Thing: The Reward Disease

II. If it be Possible for a Man Really in Truth to Will One Thing, Then He Must Will the Good in Truth.

A. If it be Possible for a Man to Will the Good in Truth, Then he Must be at One With Himself in Willing to Renounce All Double-Mindedness.

Therefore, if it be possible for a man to will one thing, then he must will the Good, for only the Good is one. Thus if it becomes a fact that he wills one thing, he must will the Good in truth.

Oh, that one might be able, at this point, to speak rightly! For at this point what the talk is concerned with is the life that most men lead: they desire the Good, and yet the world is still so filled with double-mindedness. Here, too, the speaker has his own life, his own frailties, his own share of doubleness of mind. Oh, that the talk might not seem to wish to judge or accuse others. For to wish to judge others instead of one's self would also be double-mindedness. Oh, that the talk might not seem to press demands that are binding upon others but that exempt the speaker, as if he had only the task of talking. For this, too, is double-mindedness, just as it is hidden pride to wish to offer comfort to others but not to be willing to let oneself be comforted. No matter how adroitly, by means of a sad or cheerful mood, he knows how in sympathy to console others, if at the same time he believes that for himself there is no consolation, this is hidden pride and so double-mindedness. Oh, that one might wound no one except to his healing; that the talk might embitter no one and yet be the truth, that the talk along with truth might be sufficiently penetrating to reveal that which is hidden! Oh, that the talk might wipe out double-mindedness and win hearts for the Good! Yet not by persuasion. For this also readily becomes double-minded, to wish to enjoy the pleasure of persuading, to treasure the longing for it, to quiet oneself by it -- and thereby forget what is to be done. Oh, that the talk might repel the listeners from the speaker and attract them only to the Good!

I. *In the first place a statement must be made which is easy to grasp: that the man who desires the Good for the sake of the reward does not will one thing, but is double-minded.*

The Good is one thing; the reward is another that may be present and may be absent for the time being, or until the very last. When he, then, wills the Good for the sake of the reward, he does not will one thing but two. It is now certain that he will not in this way make much progress along the pathway of the Good. For in truth it is as if a man, instead of naturally using both eyes to see one thing, should use one eye to see one side and the other eye to see the other side. This does not succeed. It only confuses sight. However, we are not speaking about this here, except to note that it is double-mindedness. In ancient times this problem was also frequently an object of consideration. There were shameless teachers of impudence(Compare Thrasymachus in Plato's Republic I. 16, 20.) who thought it right to do wrong on a large scale and then to make it appear as if one willed the Good. In this way they thought one had a double advantage: the pitiful advantage of being able to do wrong, to be able to get one own way, to let one's passions rage, and the hypocritical advantage of seeming to be good. But in ancient times there was also a simple sage, whose simplicity became a snare for the impudent ones' sophistry. He taught that in order really to be certain that it was the Good that man willed, one ought even to shun seeming good, presumably in order that the reward should not become tempting. For so different is the Good and the reward, when the reward is separately striven after, that the Good is the ennobling and the sanctifying; the reward is the tempting. But the tempting is never the Good. This reward, that we are talking about here, is the world's reward. For the reward which God for eternity has joined with the Good has nothing bad. in it. It is also quite certain. Neither things present nor things to come, nor height nor depth, can separate it from the Good.(Compare Romans 8:38, 39.) Angels cannot will such separation and all the devils are not strong enough to accomplish it. But if the world itself is not Good in its innermost being; if, as the Scripture says, it still "lieth in wickedness,"(I John 5:19) or if it is far from being as one for whom it is a rare exception not to will the Good; if this be so, then earthly reward is of a doubtful character. And hence it is all the more likely that the world will reward what it takes for the Good, what to a certain degree resembles the Good, what, as those impudent ones taught, has the Good's appearance - and those impudent ones were not lacking in intimate knowledge of the world. Hence reward is indeed that which tempts.

The question is not difficult. If a man loves a girl for the sake of her money, who will call him a lover? He does not love the girl, but the money. He is not a lover but a money-seeker. But if a man said, "It is the girl I love and she has money," and he should ask us for our judgment, for we have no particular call to judge, then a good answer would be, "It is a difficult matter with this money. Money may have a great influence, one can easily be deceived, and it is very difficult to know oneself." If he were really very intent on this matter he could even wish that the money were not there, just to test his love. For a true lover would say, "The girl has only one fault, she has money."

And what now may the girl say! If she said, "The advantage I wish to have is that it is I that have made him rich," I wonder if she could be called a real lover? For she did not really love him, but the money. If, on the contrary, the two in their love agreed to do a good act with this money which was a hindrance to them, then it would be made possible for them to desire love alone. Let us hope that no one would set about to disturb the innocent fancy of this beautiful thought by telling us, "What life will surely teach that pair!" Alas, there is a wretched knowledge, a shabby acquaintance with the real, that is not merely wretched and shabby but also on all occasions puts on an important front. As though that knowledge were anything but infamy in any person who in a cowardly and traitorous and envious and empty puffed-up manner dares to make such a comment! As if that knowledge were other than contemptible double-mindedness that both wills and does not will, and therefore will only lie, lie about the Good, and lie about the man who is good. Yes, what was once said of memory is applicable to that sort of knowledge, namely, that one might prefer to learn the art of forgetting.(Cf. Themistocles in Cicero's *de Oratore* II. 74, 299.) Indeed it is easy enough for one to become schooled in that sort of knowledge. It may be learned readily enough from all the wretched ones, so that one might rather wish and pray, that there was an art that one could learn that would teach him to remain ignorant of such knowledge.

Now about desiring the girl without the money. Let us consider the Good, where all is on a more perfect plane, where earnestness and truth are the innocent fancy of beautiful thought. To will the Good for the sake of reward is double-mindedness. To will one thing is, therefore, to will the Good without considering the reward. In truth to will one thing is to will the Good, but not, therefore, to desire reward in the world. The reward can of course come without a man's willing it. Even though it is in the outward realms, the reward may come from God. But when a man considers that all reward in the outer realm can become what the world's reward always is -- a temptation for him, then he must guard himself even against true reward just in order rightly to be able to will the Good. Oh, that he might not forget, that this, even such a desire to guard himself, may once more be a temptation to pride.

But if it be true of the reward for Good in the world, that the reward the world gives is so dangerous, then the Good has almost an edifying quality here in this world (even if this edification is somewhat softened in the blessed smile of eternity). For here the man who in truth wills the Good, by willing one thing, is very rarely led into the difficulty of being tempted by reward. Now, that the Good has its own reward is indeed forever certain. There is nothing so certain. It is not even more certain that God exists, for that is one and the same thing. But here on earth, Good is often temporarily rewarded by ingratitude, by lack of appreciation, by poverty, by contempt, by many sufferings, and now and then by death. It is not this reward to which we refer when we say that the Good has its reward. Yet this is the reward that comes in the external world and that comes first of all. And it is precisely this reward which the man is anxious about, who wills the Good for the sake of the reward. For he has no time to wait, no time, no years, no life to give away -- for an eternity. Hence that reward which comes in the external world is so far from being desirable, that, on the contrary, it is both valuable and encouraging when it does not come in the outer world, so that the double-mindedness in the inner realm may perish, and so that the reward in heaven may be all the greater.

To will the Good for the sake of the reward is, as it were, a symbol of double-mindedness. And a double-minded man according to the Apostle James' words is, "unsteady in all his ways." Nor does he accomplish anything. For a double-minded man, says the same Apostle, may not expect to receive that for which he prays. Even if such a double-minded one, who wills the Good for the sake of the reward, may puff himself up, appear defiant, and fancy that he has won his goal, even if many blind ones foolishly think the same; yet let us not deceive each other, my listener, or allow a sense-deception to do so. It is quite possible that he will win good things, that are called reward. Still he does not get them as reward, at least not in truth, if it be true that to will the Good in truth is recognizable by one's willing it without reward. Oh, Thou the Good's wonderful at-oneness with thyself that protects thee from being deceived! When, for the sake of the reward, a double-minded person only pretends to will the Good, and he seems to get the reward, nevertheless he does not get it. For that which he gets, he does not get as reward -- for the Good. So far is he from getting it as reward that rather at the very moment that he receives the Good, he discovers that the reward has vanished.

Look at the girl who has money. A false lover can perhaps deceive her, so that it appears as if he loved her, although what he really loves is the money. She may joyfully, perhaps even gratefully, continue to live in the fantasy that she is loved. But no one can deceive the Good, nay, not in all eternity! Not in all eternity! Yes, it is just there that one has the least chance of deceiving it. Perhaps here on earth it can be accomplished; not that the Good is deceived, but men may be deceived by the likeness of the Good. Such does not escape the attention of the Good. From time to time it focuses its wrath on such a man and reveals his deception. But often the Good lets the deceiver go his way because the Good knows, in itself, that it is the stronger. Only a weak and effeminate man demands immediate justification, demands immediate success in the outer world, just because he is weak, and therefore must have an outward proof -- that he is the strongest. The one who is really strong and is really the more powerful, quietly concedes a domain to the weakling and readily allows him to give the impression of being the stronger. So with the Good, when it tolerates such a deceiver, it is as if it said to him secretly, "Yes, enjoy yourself with your false appearance, but remember, we two, we shall talk together again."

The double-minded one stands at a parting of the ways. Two visions appear: the Good and the reward. It is not in his power to bring them into agreement, for they are fundamentally different from each other. Only that reward which God for all eternity adds to the Good in the inner realm, only that is in truth homogeneous with the Good. So he stands pondering and reflecting. If he is wholly absorbed in his pondering, then he continues to stand -- a symbol of double-mindedness. But suppose he should tear himself free from the deliberation and should now go forward. Along which way? Ah, do not ask him about that. Perhaps he is able to answer learned questions and to betray extensive knowledge. But one thing he cannot do, one and only one thing he is not able to do: he cannot answer the question about which of the two ways he is taking. By repeated thoughtful pondering in an attempt to see the heterogeneous together, he has somewhat confused his sight. He believes he has found that there is a third way and that it is this third way along which he is going. This third way has no name. For it does not really exist, and so it is obvious that he, if he is sincere, cannot say which way he is taking. If he is sincere, for otherwise he would indeed declare that he is going along the way of the Good, it may even be important to convince men of that -- in order that they may honor him. For honor belongs to the reward which he is seeking after. The third way is the secret which he keeps to himself. And now how does he go along this third way which is narrower than any rope-dancer's rope, for it simply does not exist? Does he go steadily and firmly like one that has a definite goal before his eyes; like one that scarcely looks at anything around him in order not to be disturbed; like one that looks for one thing alone -- for the goal? No, only a person upon the path of the Good walks in this fashion with only the Good before his eyes.

Does he, then, go like the one that is hunting for every sensation along the broad way of pleasure? No, that he does not do. Does he go like a carefree youth who lightheartedly lets his gaze wander over everything about him on his way? Alas, he is too old for that. How does he go, then? He walks so slowly under the circumstances, because of the difficulty of the way. He feels his way forward with his foot and as he finally plants his foot and takes a step, he immediately looks about at the clouds, notes the way the wind blows, and whether the smoke goes straight up from the chimney. It is, namely, the reward -- earth's reward -- that he is looking for. And that reward is like the clouds and like the wind and like the smoke of the chimney. And so he asks his way continually. He gives minute attention to the faces of the passing people in order to learn how the reward stands, what the prices are, what demands the time and the people would place upon the Good if they were to give the reward.

What is he really after? Nay, do not ask him about that. Perhaps he would be able to answer every other question with the exception of that one about the way. But this question he cannot answer in definite terms, if he is to answer it sincerely, for the reason that the answer is all too readily at hand: that he wills the Good and detests vice -- when vice seems to be loathsome; that he wills the approbation of good people -- when they are in the majority and possess the power; that he will benefit the good cause -- when it is so good as to confer some advantage upon him. Yet in sincerity he dares not say definitely what he wills. He dares not say loudly and decisively with the full voice of conviction that he wills the Good. He utters it with the dull caution of double-mindedness. For he knows well enough that the Good and the reward are not rationed out together. Let us assume, that by such a careless utterance the Good and the reward came into conflict, and let us assume that he be considered as willing the Good in this manner. Now suppose that the reward is missing, which has previously happened in this world. What would he do then? Would he will the Good and even be willing to forego the appearance of willing the Good? No, definitely not. Does he, then, will the reward? Yes, but he will not plainly admit it. Does he, then, will the Good? Yes, now and then, perhaps, for decency's sake, as it is called. He pretends, therefore, to will the Good -- for the sake of honor and reward. As a matter of fact he does occasionally will the Good -- to save his face.

This is what happens to the man who hankers after a reward. He is so double-minded that one hardly knows whether to laugh or to weep over him, if one does not know that all doublemindedness is destruction. But if one knows this, he knows well enough what to do, especially when he has his own share of this double-mindedness.

Now this matter of willing the Good for the sake of reward may take a somewhat different form. Perhaps there was a man who really in all sincerity willed the Good. Humbly before God, and quickened in his enthusiasm, he cheerfully understood when the world and when men worked against him. He cheerfully understood that this opposition was the reward, and that there was nothing further to be said about it. Strengthened by God, bracing himself only by his confidence, he almost never desired to be rewarded in any other way by this world. But then he became weary. He clutched after the reward in the narrower sense, and after an easier understanding of the reward. For in general the closer the understanding lies to misunderstanding, the easier it becomes. He could not bear with the Eternal. He could not endure the opposition of the world and of the people. So first he claimed the reward, under the interpretation that there ought to be an agreement between the Good and the world. Finally, he demanded the reward alone. In this fashion he slipped backwards. Oh, sad end to a good beginning! Oh, Thou the Good's stern zeal for thyself, that Thou perhaps permit-test him to get the reward in the world, just when Thou hast rejected him; that Thou lettest him get the reward of the world, while he has ungratefully forgotten what a blessedness it is to have Thy reward, while earth withholds her reward from him!

Or he did not begin so high, but simply with willing the Good in truth. Without knowledge of the world, without having conceived in his heart the possibility of what may happen to a man, he piously hoped that the Good would not withhold its reward. Now understood in the light of eternity, this is an eternal and sacred truth. But in the sense of temporal existence, it is foolish and fruitless cleverness. So he went out into the school of experience, for we all go to school as long as we live. Life's school is for adults and therefore is somewhat more stern than the children's school, where the attentive and industrious ones come to the fore among those of the same age. So life took him into its stern school. But he resisted. He reduced his demands. He did not wish to deceive the Good. Alas, neither would that help. He believed that as long as he clung to the Good, he possessed a claim upon life. Now it seemed to him as though the Good alone had claims upon him. At this his courage slackened. He looked about him where so many others helped themselves to the reward. The tempter began to frighten him into a feeling of faintheartedness as to why he did not wish to be like the others and as to why he insisted upon running after the vagaries of imagination instead of laying hold of that which is certain. Then his mind was changed. In life it happened to him just as in school it might happen to the superior pupil if there were no teacher. The mediocre would gain the dominance and gain power to seduce the superior pupils, because the good pupil had no teacher in whom to seek protection. And in life there is no visible teacher who encourages the good pupil, for we are all pupils. If the good pupil keeps on, he must find the encouragement in himself. This he did not find. His courage was shattered. Perhaps he did not find what he now sought in the world. And so he went down, he the deceived one, whom the world deceived as to the reward, when he willed the Good and whom the world betrayed most terribly, when it got him to forsake the Good.

Chapter 5: Barriers to willing One Thing: Willing Out of Fear of Punishment

2. Next, it must be said that the man who only wills the Good out of fear of punishment does not will one thing. He is double-minded.

The other aspect of the reward-centered man is willing the good only out of fear of punishment. For in essence, this is the same as to will the Good for the sake of the reward, to the extent that avoiding an evil is an advantage of the same sort as that of attaining a benefit. The Good is one thing. Punishment is something else. Therefore the double-minded person does not desire one thing when he desires the Good under the condition that he shall avoid punishment. The condition lays its finger upon just the double-mindedness. If that condition were not there, he would not fear the punishment, for punishment is indeed not what a man should fear. He should fear to do wrong. But if he has done wrong, then he must, if he really wills one thing and sincerely wills the Good, desire to be punished, that the punishment may heal him just as medicine heals the sick. If one who is sick fears the bitterness of the medicine, or fears "to let himself be cut and cauterized by the physician," then what he really fears is -- to get well, even though in delirium he swears most positively that this is not the case, and that, on the contrary, he all too eagerly longs for his health. As for this assurance, the more zealously it is made, the more clearly is its double-mindedness revealed: that he desires his health and yet does not will it, although he has it in his power. To desire what one cannot carry out is not such double-mindedness because the hindrance is not within the control of the one who desires it. Hut when the person who desires is himself the obstacle that keeps himself from getting his desire fulfilled, not by giving it up, for then he would be at one with himself, but both by not willing and yet by willing to continue to desire: then the doublemindedness is clear -- if it can be made clear -- or at least the fact is clear that it is doublemindedness. If what a man fears is not the mistake itself, but the reproach at being caught in the mistake, then that fear so far from helping him out of the error may even lead him into that which is still more ruinous, even if apart from this he had made no mistake.

So, too, with one who wishes to do good out of fear of punishment, if indeed it can be done in that fashion, if it is not as when the fear-ridden person turns his whole life into nothing but illness, out of fear of becoming ill. Fear of the punishment is so far from helping him to do the Good in truth, that it ruins him, just because punishment is a medicine. But everyone, even a child knows that nothing is so dangerous as a medicine -- when it is used in the wrong way. Even if it does not end in death, it may bring on critical illness. And spiritually understood there is a ruinous illness, namely, not to fear what a man should fear: the sacredness of modesty, God in the heavens, the command of duty, the voice of conscience, the accountability to eternity. In order to be insured against or of being saved from this illness, it is profitable to a man that he should punish himself, "that he beat his breast and chastise his heart." It is still more fruitful that he be punished in order that the punishment may keep him awake and sober, for in whatever way this may be more precisely understood, it will be to his profit and his advantage; yes, truly to his advantage, if he voluntarily allows himself to be punished.

But then, in a spiritual sense, there is another illness, a still more destructive one: to fear what a man should not and ought not to fear. The first illness is defiance and obstinacy and willfulness. The second is cowardice and servility and hypocrisy. And this last is terrible just because it is an illness where the physician sees to his horror that the sick person has used the medicine -- in the wrong way. It may indeed seem that the one that wills the Good out of fear of punishment may still not be called ill, for he really wills the Good. For surely punishment is not an illness? Yet he is none the less ill and his illness is just this: the confusing of the illness and the medicine. It might seem that the one who wills the Good out of fear of punishment cannot be said to have used the medicine, and therefore cannot be said to have used it wrongly. For he indeed wills the Good. He wishes to be healthy -- out of his fear of having to use the medicine. But spiritually understood, where illness is not in the material body as the fever is in the blood, and where medicine is not something external, like drops in a bottle, then fear means: to use and to have used, to have taken the medicine -- in the wrong way. This shows itself clearly in the terrible and fatal manifestations of that other illness.

It has been noted that fear of poverty suddenly makes the extravagant person miserly; but it is never observed that it makes him thrifty, and why not? Because the fear of the medicine lay in taking it in the wrong way. Indeed, fear of the body's infirmities has taught the voluptuary to observe moderation in debauchery (for the fear was to take the medicine in the wrong way) but it has never made him chaste. It taught him, instead of forgetting God in the whirlpool of vice (sad distraction of mind!), daily to mock God by moderation -- in debauchery (abominable discretion!). And indeed, fear of punishment has made the sinner into a hypocrite, who in hypocrisy's loathesome doubleness of mind pretended to love God (for the fear was to take the medicine in the wrong way), but it has never made him pure of heart. This is firmly established: that punishment is not illness, but medicine. Thus it may be a punishment for the frivolous person to be confined to a sick bed, but suppose in truth he understands it as punishment, then the illness, the fever or whatever other disorder it now may be, then it is a medicine. On the other hand, all double-mindedness that wills the Good only out of fear of punishment can always be known in the end, because it considers punishment as an illness. If double-mindedness, then, which one may inwardly pity, is an overtense anxiety, as when the horrified imagination of the sick person alters the effect of the medicine: then the mark is that punishment is confused with illness and one who suffers from it simply does not in truth desire to be released from the illness, but in falsity desires to be rid of the medicine.

Now which is the punishment that is to be feared; what, more precisely, is understood by it? When we reflect upon that, double-mindedness becomes more obvious. For one and the same illness may be regarded very differently and its danger varies according to the different wrong conceptions of punishment that are present. Someone may think that by punishment is meant what is now seldom mentioned -- the punishment of eternity. And it might seem that the person was not double-minded who wills the Good out of fear of that punishment, since he refers the punishment to eternity, therefore to the same place where the Good has its home. And yet, he does not will the Good, he wills it only out of fear of punishment. Therefore -- if there were no punishment! In that "if" lurks double-mindedness. If there were no punishment!! In that "if" hisses double-mindedness. If there were no punishment, or if indeed there was a man who could convince him that eternity's punishment was a fantasy; or if it became common practice to think in this fashion; or if he could travel to a foreign country where it was common practice; or if cowardly and hypocritical superstition could discover a cheap means of propitiation!!! Look at the double-mindedness! Note that it can just as easily seek its consolation in unbelief as in superstition. And if double-mindedness does not seek them out, then it is they that try to capture double-mindedness until the matter becomes obvious. If one were briefly to characterize double. mindedness by a single appropriate expression, what would be more characteristic than that -- "if," "in case that"! For when the will in a man gets command so that he keeps on willing the Good and in truth willing only that one thing, then there is no "in case that." But double-mindedness brings itself to a stop continually by its "in case that." It does not contain the impetus of eternity and does not have the infinite's open road before it. It passes itself and meets itself as it is coming to a stop. It is said that by the holy sign of the cross one can halt the evil Spirit, so that it cannot go on. In this fashion, double-mindedness brings itself to a halt by its pitiful sign, by its "in case that." For a moment it may seem as if double-mindedness did not exist. Double-mindedness can perhaps speak in such a fashion that it deceives. But when a man begins to act and there is double-mindedness in him, then he is plunged immediately into this paralyzing "in case that." It is true that a man may fill up the temporal order with his talk, but eternity will reveal the nature of his deeds. Only for him who wills the Good in truth, only for him can what is taught about the punishments of eternity be eternally true. The one that merely fears the punishment, for him it cannot remain eternally true, for there is nothing eternal in him, since the Eternal can only be in him if he wills the Good in truth. There is only one proof that the Eternal exists: faith in it.

Fear is a tottering proof, that proves that the fearful one does not believe or does so as when the devil believes, but trembles because he does not believe. Only one thing can help a man to will the Good in truth: the Good itself. Fear is a deceitful aid. It can embitter one's pleasure, make life laborious and miserable, make one old and decrepit; but it cannot help one to the Good since fear itself has a false conception of the Good -- and the Good does not allow itself to be deceived. Or does not this also belong to the true nature of the Good, this zeal for itself, that will not tolerate anyone else, any strange helper, any interference by some contentious one who might only create confusion. For, when the Good took up its place at the goal where the reward beckons or where the Good itself beckons to a man, the Good against its will would then be forced to see and to put up with the fact that there were two paths, and two men bent on them; the one be-cause he willed the Good in truth, and humbly but gladly followed its beckoning; the other because fear drove him thence. Spiritually understood, is it conceivable that two such different men could possibly be able to come to the same place! For in a spiritual sense, place is not something external, to which a slave might come against his will when the overseer uses his scourge. And the path is not something that does not matter whether one rides forwards or backwards. But the place and the path are within a man and just as the place is the blessed state of the striving soul, so the path is the striving soul's continual transformation. Nay, as the Good is only one thing, so it wishes also to be the only thing that aids a man. The Good suckles and nurses the infant, rears and nourishes the youth, strengthens the adult, supports the aged. The Good teaches the striving one. It helps him. But only in the way that the loving mother teaches a child to walk alone. The mother is far enough away from the child so that she cannot actually support the child, but she holds out her arms. She imitates the child's movements. If it totters she swiftly bends as if she would seize it -- so the child believes that it is not walking alone. The most loving mother can do no more, if it be truly intended that the child shall walk alone. And yet she does more; for her face, her face, yes, it is beckoning like the reward of the Good and like the encouragement of Eternal Blessedness. So the child walks alone, with eyes fixed upon the mother's face, not on the difficulties of the way; supporting himself by the arms that do not hold on to him, striving after refuge in the mother's embrace, hardly suspecting that in the same moment he is proving that he can do without her, for now the child is walking alone. Fear, on the other hand, is a dry nurse for the child: it has no milk; a bloodless corrector for the youth: it has no beckoning encouragement; a niggardly disease for the adult: it has no blessing; a horror for the aged: when fear has to admit that the long painful time of schooling did not bring Eternal Blessedness.

Fear also wishes to help a man. It desires to teach him to walk alone, but not as a loving mother does it. For it is fear itself that continually upsets the child. It desires to help him forward, but not as a loving mother's beckoning. For it is fear itself that weighs him down so that he cannot move from the spot. It desires to lead him to the goal, and yet it is the fear itself that makes the goal terrifying. It desires to help him to the Good, and yet that kind of learner never wins the favor of the Good. Nor does he ever become God's friend. For, as the Scriptures teach, not only thieves and robbers, but also the fearful may not enter into the kingdom of Heaven. The fearful one desires Heaven not for itself. He desires it only out of fear of punishment. Is not such a man double-minded even though he was not one of those who would appear wholly other than he was? Would not such a man be double-minded if you saw him in his dreams, when in sleep he has cast off the yoke of fear, when all is as he would really have it be, and he is as he really is, as he would be upon waking if fear did not exist? For it is said of old that one learns to know a man's soul by his dreams.(Plato's Republic IX. 572)

If by the word punishment, one thinks of eternity's punishment, it gives a false impression, as if indeed it were not double-mindedness to will the Good only out of fear of punishment. But yet this is double-mindedness. Even if it happened to be a good man who in the agony of fear preserved a certain slavish blamelessness out of fear of punishment: still he is double-minded. He does continually what he really would rather not do, or at least what he has no pleasure in doing, for this pleasure is only a low sensual pleasure, in fact of all sensual pleasures it is the lowest. It is the one whose miserable glory consists solely in avoiding something, hence the pleasure is not a pleasure in itself, but only by contrast. Nor does he attribute the punishment to God and to the Good. On the contrary, as he pictures it, the Good is one thing, the punishment is an entirely different matter. But in that case the Good is not one thing. Thus by his double-mindedness he brings about a strained relation between the Good and the punishment. He wishes that the punishment did not exist, and thereby he really wishes also that the Good did not exist, for otherwise he must have another relation to the Good than the one that he has through punishment. Now punishment does exist, and so he performs the Good out of fear of punishment. But the one that wills the Good in truth, understands that punishment only exists for the sake of the transgressors. He devoutly understands that punishment is like all other things which fall to the lot of one who loves God. It is a helping hand. The double-minded person shuns punishment as a suffering, a misfortune, an evil, and thereby detaches himself and his understanding from punishment, and wholly detaches punishment from the Good. This obstinacy is like the infantile notion of a child, who in his lack of judgment even sets up a cleft in the father's nature; for the child imagines that the father is the loving one, that punishment on the other hand is something that a bad man has invented. That the loving father himself should have invented the punishment out of love for the child would not become apparent to the child. So also with the relation between the Good and punishment. It is the Good who, out of love for the pupil, has invented punishment. We all go to school, only life's school is for adults. For this reason the punishment is of a more serious kind than in a children's school. It is less obvious, and therefore all the more serious; less immediate, and therefore all the more serious; less external, and therefore all the more serious. It does not follow blow for blow upon the mistake, and therefore all the more serious; one has not been spared because it may seem as if the punishment had been forgotten, hence it is all the more serious. Yet by this seriousness punishment does in truth press one toward the Good, if one really wills it. Doubleness of mind has no desire to do that. It continues to have an effeminate, sensuous conception of punishment, and an impotent will for the Good. It often happens with such a double-minded person, that the older he gets the more impoverished his life becomes: when his youth, in which there was something better than fear, is spent, and when fearfulness and cleverness conspire together in order to make him into a slave, if one wishes to put it so -- to the Good. It is so different with the one who wills the Good in truth. He is the only one who is free, made free by the Good. However, a man does not in truth will the Good if he only wills it out of fear of punishment, and hence is only in a state of slavery to the Good.

Yet double-mindedness seldom dwells on eternity's punishment. The punishment it fears is more often understood in an earthly and temporal sense. Of a man who only wills the Good out of fear of punishment, it is necessary to say with special emphasis, that he fears what a man should not and ought not to fear: loss of money, loss of reputation, misjudgment by others, neglect, the world's judgment, the ridicule of fools, the laughter of the frivolous, the cowardly whining of consideration, the inflated triviality of the moment, the fluttering mistforms of vapor. Yes, this double-minded man becomes as unsteady in all his ways as the one who willed the Good for the sake of the reward, because he is continually intent upon what is in flux, upon what is always changing, and he fears continually that which no man should fear. He fears that which has power to wound, maltreat, ruin, or strike dead the body, but which has no power whatever over the soul unless it obtains it through fear. Should a man love neither the earth, nor the pleasures of the eye, nor the pleasures of the flesh, nor a haughty life; should he covet neither what is the world's, the possession of money and prestige among men, then he shall fear neither what is the world's, neither the world nor men, neither poverty nor the expelling hand of persecution. If he fears these things, then he is the prey of double-mindedness, just as in this double-mindedness he is the slave of mankind.

Yes, there is a sense of shame, that is favorable to the Good. Woe to the man who casts it off! This sense of shame is a saving companion through life. Woe to the man that breaks with it! It is in the service of sanctification and of true freedom.

Woe to the man who is scandalized by it as if it were a compulsion! If a man goes alone through life, according to the word of the Scriptures(Genesis 2:18) that is not good, yet if he goes accompanied by that shame, oh, he shall become good and become one thing. And if the solitary one should stumble, if this sense of shame were still his companion, then we should not cry out as the book of Ecclesiastes does, "Woe to him that is alone," nor say of the solitary one, as does Ecclesiastes, "If he falls, who shall help him up."(Ecclesiastes 4:10.) For this sense of shame intends to serve him better than the best friend. It will help him better than all human sympathy which easily leads into double-mindedness -- not into willing one thing. There is no question but what a man usually acts more intelligently, shows more strength, and to all appearances more self-control, when under the scrutiny of others than when he believes himself to be unobserved. But the question is whether this intelligence, this strength, this self-control is real, or whether through the devotion of long-continued attention to it, it does not easily slip into the lie of simulation which kindles the unsteady blush of double-mindedness in his soul. Each one who is not more ashamed before himself than before all others, if he is placed in difficulty and much tried in life, will in one way or another end by becoming the slave of men. For to be more ashamed in the presence of others than when alone, what else is this than to be more ashamed of seeming than of being? And turned about, should not a man be more ashamed of what he is than of what he seems? For otherwise he cannot in truth will one thing, since by trying to appear well in the eyes of others he is only striving after a changing shimmer and its reflection in human favor.

The clever one, who fears the judgment of others and is ashamed before others -- if he is not ashamed most of all before himself, ah, perhaps his cunning might succeed in becoming undetectable, it might permit him to imagine that it was already unfathomable; and so, what then? This one who does not misuse his power because he fears the judgment of men and of being ashamed before men -- if he is not ashamed most of all before himself, ah, perhaps either he himself or some eye-servant might even succeed in imagining that it could be done so craftily that not even God could see through it; and so, what then? Indeed it is unnecessary for the talk to wait for what will happen, that is, to wait for the outcome of his doublemindedness. For the talk is only about the presence of double-mindedness in him, and that is already obvious. Whether it becomes obvious to men or not, double-mindedness is none the less present, and the double-minded person is to be pitied. For let us not forget that truth is right in saying of each one who is in untruth, that he is indeed to be pitied, even when he himself and all men think him fortunate. Because, in the sense of truth, it does not help a man that he does not know that he is to be pitied, for this is only a further misfortune. But the one that is most ashamed of himself when he is alone, is thereby strengthened in willing one thing. However crafty this cunning may have been, the inventor himself can still see through it. Let it, then, be hidden from all men, no matter how its hiddenness might be able to support him, yet he could not hide it from that inner companion, before whom he is most of all ashamed.

We do not mean to imply here, that a man has ever lived, even in the most corrupt age, for whom no person existed whose judgment he might and could well fear with a wholesome shame, a person whose judgment could be a guide to him in order to will the Good in truth. But if this shame before the honored person is in truth to become a source of benefit to the humble man, then there is an indispensable condition: that the person must be ashamed most of all before himself. Therefore one could rightly say that in truth it is most beneficial of all to a man to feel shame before one who is already dead. And if he feels this humiliation before a living person, then to feel it before him as if he were already dead, or (if it seems more to your liking, my listener, I will use another expression, that means the same thing, although it contains the explanation in an aesthetic form) : to feel ashamed before him as before a transfigured one. One already dead is just such a transfigured one. One who is living can indeed be mistaken, can be changed, can be stampeded in a moment and by the moment. If, in truth, he is a genuinely honorable person, he himself will, by way of warning, remind you of this in order that by your relationship with him you may not be led into that doublemindedness, which lies in being the follower of another. The living person may perhaps favor you too much -- perhaps too little. If you see him each day, your shame will perhaps lose something of its intensity or perhaps bring on itself an acute disease, so that you could wish to possess a magic means of deceiving the revered one, so that you wished to be able to ingratiate yourself with him or by any means to raise yourself up in his good graces, because his judgment has become for you the most important thing of all. How much danger and temptation to double-mindedness! It does not disappear until you conduct yourself with him, as with one who is dead. Withdraw from him -- but never forget him. That only leaves when you are separated from him as though by death, when in earthly or temporal fashion you do not come too near him, but only forever remember what he himself would have termed the best thing in his nature! A man cannot get round a transfigured one. Favor and persuasion and overhastiness belong to the moments of earthly life. The departed one does not notice these appearances, the transfigured one cannot understand them. He does not wish to understand them.

If you will not give them up, then you must give him up; then you must, if you dare, offend the transfigured one, break with him, yes, annihilate him. For when he is not the transfigured one, then he simply does not exist. With the living one, you may speak in another manner, because he also exists in the earthly sense, and if you get him changed a little -- alas, to what other end than to your own destruction and to his disparagement! It would be as if you still had him to hold to, you had his words, his audible approval, and in the union between you two perhaps it would escape you both that a change had taken place. But the transfigured one exists only as transfigured, not visibly to the earthly eye, not audibly to the earthly ear, only in the sacredly still silence of shame. He cannot be changed, not in the least particular, without its being instantly noted, and without all being lost, and without his vanishing. The transfigured one exists only as transfigured. He cannot be changed into anything better. He is the transfigured one. He cannot be altered. He is indeed a departed one. He remains true to himself, one and the same -- this glorified one! How, then, could it be possible for one to become double-minded who by feeling ashamed before such a one is strengthened in willing the Good! However, even the most upright man can nevertheless be surprised by many frailties and occasionally may go astray. But then he has a hope: that there exists a God, a just government of the universe, that by punishment will awaken him and lead him back. How different it is! He that wills the Good in truth even hopes for the punishment; but that man who in his double-mindedness only wills the Good out of fear of punishment is far from willing the Good in truth.

The double-minded person stands at a parting of the ways, where two visions appear: the Good and the terrifying figure of punishment. The two do not belong together in his eyes, for while punishment, which God in His wisdom has connected with every transgression, is a Good, there is no denying that it is such a Good only when it is gratefully received, not when it is simply feared as an evil. But the double-minded person rarely has this Divine punishment in mind. He thinks rather of the world's punishment. But the Good and the punishment the world metes out are not identical. Or has the world perhaps really become so perfect and so holy, that it is like God, and that what it rewards is the Good and what it punishes, the evil? Or would any person who believes that he has received at God's hand an intimation of the life according to which he desires to model his own life, could such a man really think of worshiping the world in this way? To be sure, one may hear -- especially in the places where men festively gather in order to deceive one another by many speeches -- one may hear magnificent words about how the world progresses, and about our age and about our century. But, my listener, would you dare, as a father (and I feel confident that you have a lofty conception of the meaning of this name, a responsible conception of the charge which it lays upon you) would you dare, as a father, to say to your child as you sent him out into the world, "Go, with your mind at ease, my child, pay attention to what the many approve and what the world rewards, for that is the Good, but what the world punishes, that is evil. It is no longer true as it used to be, that the judgment of the masses is like foam on water -- nonsense, though loudly proclaimed; blind, though sharply decisive; impossible to follow because it changes more swiftly than a woman changes color. Now, there is no longer any doubt about the outcome, the Good is immediately victorious. Now, the Good exacts no sacrifice, no selfdenial, for the world desires the Good. Now, the judgment of the masses is the judgment of the wise men, the solitary ones are the fools. Now, the earth is the kingdom of God, and Heaven is only a reflection of it. Now, the world is the highest certainty, the only one a man can build upon, the only one a man can swear by."

Surely, my listener, the speech need not ask you, for it vests assured in advance what your answer would be. But I would like to ask of the most ardent attender of those festivities: would you dare, if you should speak as a father to your own child, would you dare say any such thing? Or if it were the youth that, with all the earnest devotion of his soul, fixed his trusting gaze on you, assured that if, you said it, it must be so, and in gratitude, bound by a solemn vow to follow the guidance of your counsel through life; would you dare give him any such counsel? Or if you were witness to that lovable young man's beautiful enthusiasm when he read and heard of the great men who fought with a heavy destiny and suffered badly in the world, the glorious ones whom earth renounced because it was not worthy of them, would you dare, when no clamor caused your speech to wander but when the stillness of intimacy, of the lovable one's confidence, the in experience of the young man, all obliged you to tell the truth; at such a time would you dare lay your hand on your heart and say, "Such things no longer happen. Now the world has become enlightened and perfect. Now: to seek first after this world and its customs is identical with what was meant in former times by seeking first God's kingdom and His righteousness."

Alas, gradually as a man gets older, he grows accustomed to a great deal in life. Among other things, he gets in the habit of saying much that he has not properly reflected upon. Among contemporaries he gets into the way of hedging round what he says by so many presuppositions that that which is plain and elevating is almost forgotten. Now and then a word is let drop that expresses a plain and solid exasperation of long standing, "You know well enough what kind of world we live in." And at other times the world is praised to the point of idolatry, without either of these statements making any very deep impression on the one who speaks them. For the first does not arouse him. It does not frighten him into a condition of fear and trembling in which he resolves to save himself since the world is so bad. And the other does not strengthen the speaker into an eager desire for the Good by confidence in the perfection of the world. Alas, along with others in this life, he gets accustomed, amid the dull round of habit, almost to abandon himself as he plays about with mere words.

But when even the most tragic of life's spoiled children seriously admonishes a child, a youth, a maiden, he speaks with shame. There is at this point a beautiful reciprocity, for the youth approaches his elder with shame and the elder in admonishing the youth always speaks with shame. May God grant that all who have an opportunity to admonish youth may themselves derive some benefit from the shame which comes with the admonishment!

In the act of admonishing, and this deserves emphasis, the older person shall by no means set before the youth a horrifying picture of the world. To do so is never earnestness, but is only sickly imagination. But in the act of admonishing, he will shrink before the thought of leading the youth straight into the danger of double-mindedness by deceptively focusing his attention upon the punishment the world metes out. For in this, instead of impressing upon him a holy fear and shame before the Good, he is polluting the pure one by teaching him the fear of loss of money, loss of reputation, misjudgment by others, neglect, the world's judgment, the ridicule of fools, the laughter of the frivolous, the cowardly whining of consideration, the inflated triviality of the moment, the fluttering mist-forms of vapor. Alas, for many men these elevated thoughts are only too often like a gilding, that wears off in life's double-mindedness, which gnaws and gnaws. But even the man whom double-mindedness has eaten most bare, when he speaks admonishingly to a youth, is reminded that, out of shame, he dare say but one thing. In the act of admonishing even he will say (for it is no rare speaker that is here introduced to talk, and just on that account the praise of the Good is so much the more glorious because it does not require the approval of eloquence, for here it is well to note that it is one of life's most tragically spoiled children who speaks admonishingly to a youth) even he will say, "Do not be afraid, be slow to judge others, but attend closely to yourself, hold firmly to willing one thing, to willing the Good in truth, and thus, from now on, let this lead you wherever for now it will lead you -- because eternally it will lead you to victory. In this world let it lead you to prosperity or poverty, to honor or insult, to life or death: only do not let go this one thing. By its hand you may walk confidently even in danger. Even in danger of your life itself you may go as confidently as a child who clasps the mother's hand. Yes, even more confidently, for the child does not even know the danger." In the act of admonishing, therefore, a man should warn against fear of the world's punishment, which is doublemindedness.

Now and then someone speaks of "suffering punishment, when one does the Good." How is that possible? From whom shall that punishment come? Certainly not from God! Is it, then, from the world -- so that when in its wisdom the world is mistaken, it rewards the bad and punishes the Good? And yet no, it is not as that word "world" implies. The word does not mean what it says. It is improperly expressed. For the word "world" sounds great and terrifying, and yet it must obey the same law as the most insignificant and miserable man. But even if the world gathered all its strength, there is one thing it is not able to do, it can no more punish an innocent one than it can put a dead person to death.

To be sure the world has power. It can lay many a burden upon the innocent one. It can make his life sour and laborious for him. It can rob him of his life. But it cannot punish an innocent one. How wonderful, here is a limit, a limit that is invisible, like a line that is easy to overlook with the senses, but one that has the strength of eternity in resisting any infringement. This may be overlooked by the world whose attention is focused upon that which is big -- and the limit is insignificant, is for the present, a quiet-mannered nobody, but yet it is there. Perhaps it is completely hidden from the eyes of the world. For that, too, can be a part of the innocent one's suffering, that the world's injustice takes on the appearance of punishment -- in the world's eyes. But the limit is nevertheless there, and is in spite of all the strongest. And even if all the world rose up in tumult and even if everything were thrown into confusion: the limit is nevertheless there. And on the one side of it with the innocent ones is justice; and on the other side toward the world is an eternal impossibility of punishing an innocent one. Even if the world wishes to annihilate an innocent man and put him out of the way, it cannot put the limit out of the way, even though it be invisible. (Perhaps it is just on that account.) Even in the moment of his sacrificial death, the limit is there: then it stretches itself with the strength of eternity, then it cleaves itself with eternity's all-encompassing depth. The limit is there, and on the one side with the innocent ones is justice, and on the other side toward the world is an eternal impossibility of punishing an innocent one.

When the good man truly stands on the other side of the boundary line inside the fortification of eternity, he is strong, stronger than the whole world. He is strongest of all at the time when he seems to be overcome. But the impotent double-minded one has removed the boundary limit, because he only wills the Good out of fear of earth's punishment. If the world is not really the land of perfection, then by his double-mindedness he has surrendered himself to the power of mediocrity or pledged himself to the evil.

Chapter 6:Barriers to Willing One Thing: Egocentric Service of the Good

3. Furthermore it must be said that the man who wills the Good and wills its victory out of a self-centered willfulness does not will one thing. He is double-minded.

Suppose a man wills the Good simply in order that he may score the victory, then he wills the Good for the sake of the reward, and his double-mindedness is obvious, as the previous section of the talk has sought to point out. Actually he does not care to serve the Good, but to have the advantage of regarding it as a fruit of conquest. When, on the contrary, a man desires that the Good shall be victorious, when he will not call the outcome of the battle "victory," if he wins, but only when the Good is victorious: can he then, in any sense, be called and be double-minded? Yes, and yet if he be double-minded (for the decision as to the boundary line between the pure and the double-minded is here of a singular complexity), then his doublemindedness is more subtle and concealed, more presumptuous than that obvious and out- and out worldly sort. It is a powerful deception that seems nearest of all to approach the purity of heart that wills the Good in truth, even though it is at the other pole from it, just as the high place is from the deep chasm, just as heaven-storming pride is from humility's dwelling in the low places, just as if a pretentiously plausible approximation had been won by falsifying a line of separation that was eternally real. He does not will the Good for the sake of the reward. He wills that the Good shall triumph through him, that he shall be the instrument, he the chosen one. He does not desire to be rewarded by the world -- that he despises; nor by men -- that he looks down upon. And yet he does not wish to be an unprofitable servant. (Compare Luke 17:10.) The reward which he insists upon is a sense of pride and in that very demand is his violent double- mindedness. Yes, violent, for what else does he wish than to take the Good by storm, and by force to press himself and his service upon the Good! And if he will not give up this last presumptuousness, if he, in some way, does not desire what the Good wills, if he does not desire the Good's victory after the fashion that the Good wills it: then he is doubleminded. Even if he knows how to hide it from men, even if he hides it from himself, even if the true expression of the language seems for a moment to hide it by calling his condition of mind self-will, willfulness, for that sounds well, especially when it is strong enough to venture the most extreme things: does that seem to be double-mindedness? No, it does not seem to be double-mindedness, but it is.

In the eyes of this double-minded person the Good is one thing, its victory is another, and its victory through him may even be something else. Now it is indeed the case, that eternally the Good has always been victorious. But in time it is otherwise, temporally it may take a long time. The victory is slow, its uncertainty is a slow measure of length. Again, and again the faithful servant's life ends, and it seemed, at his death, as if he had accomplished nothing for the Good. And yet he was a faithful servant, who willed the Good in truth, and he was also loved by the Good, that prizes obedience more than the "fat of the ram." "Alas, why does time exist; if the Good eternally has always been victorious, why should it then creep slowly forward throughout the length of time or almost perish in time's slowness? Why should it fight laboriously through that which makes time the longest, through uncertainty? Why should the solitary 'individuals,'(See translator's introduction.) who sincerely will the Good, be so scattered, so separated, that they can scarcely call out to one another, scarcely catch sight of one another? Why should time hang like a weight upon them? Why should separation involve them in delay, when it is so swiftly accomplished in eternity? Why was an immortal spirit placed in the world and in time, just as the fish is drawn up out of the water and cast upon the beach?" Whoever talks in this questioning vein (and even if he say it amid groans, the utterance is the same), should be on his guard, for he scarcely knows by what spirit he is speaking. Alas, men often enough confuse impatience with humble, obedient enthusiasm; impatience even lends itself to this confusion. When a man is active early and late "for the sake of the Good," storming about noisily and restlessly, hurling himself into time, as a sick man throws himself down upon his bed, throwing off all consideration for himself, as a sick man throws off his clothes, scornful of the world's reward; when such a man makes a place among men, then the masses think what he himself imagines, that he is inspired. And yet he is at the other pole from that, for he is double-minded, and double-mindedness no more resembles inspiration than a whirlwind resembles the steadiness of the standing wind.

So it is with all impatience. It is a kind of ill-temper. Its root is already in the child, because the child will not take time for things. With the double-minded one, it is thus clear that time and eternity cannot rule in the same man. He cannot, he will not, understand the Good's Slowness; that out of mercy, the Good is slow; that out of love for free persons, it will not use force; that in its wisdom toward the frail ones, it shrinks from any deception. He cannot, he will not, humbly understand that the Good can get on without him. He is double-minded, he that with his enthusiasm could apparently become an apostle, but can quite as readily become a Judas, who treacherously wishes to hasten the victory of the Good. He is scandalized, he that by his enthusiasm seems to love the Good so highly. He is scandalized by its poverty, when it is clothed in the slowness of time. He is not devoted to the Good in service that may profit nothing. He only effervesces, and he that effervesces loves the moment. And he that loves the moment fears time, he fears that the course of time will reveal his doublemindedness, and he falsifies eternity; for otherwise eternity might still more effectively reveal his double-mindedness. He is a falsifier. For him eternity is the deceptive sensory illusion of the horizon; for him eternity is the bluish haze that limits time; for him eternity is the dazzling sleight-of-hand trick executed by the moment.

Such a double-minded person is perhaps hardly recognizable in this world, because his double-mindedness not evident inside the world. The world's reward and punishment do not serve as informers against him; for he has overcome the world, even if by a higher deception.

Hence his double-mindedness is first recognizable at the boundary where time and eternity touch upon each other. There it is clear and is always recognized by the all-knowing One. He will not be content with the blessed assurance which comforts beyond all measure: that eternally the Good has always been victorious; the blessed assurance which is a security that passeth all understanding; the blessed assurance that the unprofitable servant may have within himself at each moment, even when the time is the longest and he seems to have accomplished least of all, the blessed assurance which allows the unprofitable servant if he loses honor to speak more proudly than that royal word: All is lost save honor.(These words are attributed to Francis I as having been spoken after the battle of Pavia where he was taken prisoner.) the words And when even honor is lost to say: Nothing is lost, but all is gained.

But this double-minded person is not so easily recognizable on earth. He does not will the Good for the sake of reward, for then he would have become obvious in his aspiration or in his despair. He does not will the Good out of fear of punishment, for then he would have become obvious in his cowardice, in his shunning of punishment, or in his despair, when he was not able to avoid it. No, he wishes to sacrifice all, he fears nothing, only he will not sacrifice himself in daily self-forgetfulness. This he fears to do.

The double-minded man stands at a parting of the ways, and sees there two apparitions: the Good, and the Good in its victory, or even in its victory through him. This latter is presumptuousness, but even the first two apparitions are not wholly the same. In eternity they are the same, but not in time. And they must be kept apart. The Good so wills it. The Good puts on the slowness of time as a poor garment, and in keeping with this change of dress one who serves it must be clothed in the insignificant figure of the unprofitable servant. With the eye of his senses, he is not permitted to see the Good in victory. Only with the eye of faith can he strive after its eternal victory. Therein lies his double-mindedness. For as there is a double -- mindedness which divides up the nature of the Good which the Good has united for all eternity: so is his double -- mindedness of that sort that unites what the Good in time has set apart. The one double-minded person forgets the Eternal and on that account misuses time, the other misuses eternity.

Chapter 7: Barriers to Willing One Thing: Commitment to a Certain Degree

4. Before finally leaving the subject of double-mindedness for a similar examination of purity, the talk should at least touch upon that versatile form of double-mindedness: the doublemindedness of weakness as it appears in the common things of real life; upon the fact that the person who only wills the Good up to a certain degree is double-minded.

At bottom this is the way all double-mindedness expresses itself in relation to the Good, in that it wills the Good only up to a certain degree. But what has been set forth above, what of double-mindedness might perhaps be spoken of as its deceptive transactions in the "big," still had a certain semblance of unity, and of inner consistency, in so far as it was one single thing that was betrayed into one-sidedness, yet this one-sidedness, however strange it may seem, was precisely the double-mindedness in that one-sided person.

It is otherwise with the transactions of daily life, for they are not in the "big." It is rare in daily life, to see anyone who wills some perverse thing with fixed consistency and effort. The transactions of daily life are made in the little things so that double-mindedness presents a much greater diversity within the "individual."

A merchant who deals in only one kind of ware is a rare sight, and so is that doublemindedness which has a certain unreal unity. A merchant generally deals in different wares, and double-mindedness, too, is generally a number of different things. On that account the false road is harder to detect than that clear-cut one. Nay, the false roads cross each other and the right road in the most different ways and the "individual" shares in this crossing in an equally varied way. To be sure his life is distinguishable as falling within double-mindedness. But it is not easy to designate it any more closely, because within this double-mindedness, he is not at one with himself in anything definite, but is tossed about in vacillation by every breeze. For he learns and learns and yet never comes to a knowledge of truth.(Compare 2 Timothy 3:7) Or if he comes almost to it, then he quickly turns further and further away the more he learns of this confused and confusing instruction. In preference to the earlier doublemindedness, this has the Good on its side, in that it wills the Good, even though weakly; and in that it is without the obstinacy that marked the previously mentioned double-mindedness. But upon occasion weakness may be just as incurable.

This double-mindedness is difficult to speak of because it approximates both the one and the other, and because it alters itself continually, changing so swiftly that it may have transformed itself several times before the talk had hardly finished describing a single expression. It plays about gaily not only in all possible colors, but there is not even any law for this play of colors that blends colors and color relations in ever new confusion. Hence there is always something new under the sun -- and yet the old double-mindedness persists. Indeed what makes it even more difficult to speak of, is that in daily life, where it is right at home, double-mindedness, within limits, keeps comparatively to itself, so that a double-minded person, by being a little less double-minded than the others, claims distinction even though his degree of difference is quite within an essential sameness. Hence in the end it would seem as if that true eternal claim that demands purity of heart, by willing one thing, were done away with, as if it had been withdrawn from government, set away in retirement at such a distance from daily life that there simply could be no talk about it. For among the many-colored seething populace in the noise of the world from day to day and from year to year, there is no scrupulous check made as to whether a person wholly wills the Good if he has influence and might, runs a great business, is something in his own and in others' eyes. "What fright-fully niggardly pettiness," one thinks, "to be so scrupulous!" One does not consider that there is any presumptuousness in what one has spoken. Nay, one drops the clever remark in passing and hurries on, while the remark also hurries on from mouth to mouth amid the many colored seething populace. And in the rush of life, in trade and commerce from morning to night, there is no such scruple about whether a person wholly wills the Good, just so that in his business he is keen, not to say a "thief," just so that he saves and piles up money, just so that he has a good reputation and by good fortune manages to avoid slander (for whether he actually is guilty or not is here of little importance, for neither he nor the world has time to look into that. Slander is merely a danger as an obstacle to his business). "To what purpose such a delay in the midst of busyness?" And in the world, it is always busy. Yes, it is entirely true that this is the way things look in the world, the way they seem in the world, and the way they must seem within the deceptive horizon of the temporal order. But in eternity it will make a tremendous difference whether a person was scrupulous or not.

And yet eternity is not like a new world, so that one who had lived in time according to the ways of the time world and of the press of busyness, if he were to make a happy landing in eternity itself, could now try his luck in adopting the customs and practices of eternity. Alas, the temporal order and the press of busyness believe, that eternity is so far away. And yet not even the foremost professional theatrical producer has ever had all in such readiness for the stage and for the change of scenes, as eternity has all in readiness for time: all -- even to the least detail, even to the most insignificant word that is spoken; has all in readiness in each instant -- although eternity delays.

Oh, that this talk, far from detaining anyone who sincerely wills the Good, or calling anyone away from fruitful activity, might cause a busy man to pause. For this press of busyness is like a charm. And it is sad to observe how its power swells, how it reaches out seeking always to lay hold of ever-younger victims so that childhood or youth are scarcely allowed the quiet and the retirement in which the Eternal may unfold a divine growth. And suppose that busyness in its haste should make a concession, believing even in its superficial wisdom that there is something beneficial in having a busy man on hand who now and then hurriedly proclaims that higher reflection on life about willing the Good in truth. Alas, is this, then, the true relationship? Are almost all to be excused from that which every man should do for himself? But then for the sake of completeness is someone in the midst of busyness to be delegated the task of setting forth that higher claim -- that higher claim, which, if by some means it could be satisfied, even if in feebleness and in imperfection, would command a man's whole mind, his unrelenting industry, his best strength?

Thus in the midst of busyness, double-mindedness is to be found. Just as the echo dwells in the woods, as stillness dwells in the desert, so double-mindedness dwells in the press of busyness. That the one who wills the Good only to a certain degree, that he is double-minded, that he has a distracted mind, a divided heart, scarcely needs to be pointed out. But the reason may need to be explained and set forth, why, in the press of busyness, there is neither time nor quiet to win the transparency that is indispensable if a man is to come to understand himself in willing one thing or even for a preliminary understanding of himself in his confusion. Nay, the press of busyness into which one steadily enters further and further, and the noise in which the truth continually slips more and more into oblivion, and the mass of connections, stimuli, and hindrances, these make it ever more impossible for one to win any deeper knowledge of himself. It is true, that a mirror has the quality of enabling a man to see his image in it, but for this he must stand still. If he rushes hastily by, then he sees nothing. Suppose a man should go about with a mirror in his possession which he does not take out, how should such a man get to see himself? In this fashion the busy man hurries on, with the possibility of understanding himself in his possession. But the busy man keeps on running and it never dawns upon him that this possibility which he has in his possession is rapidly fading from his memory. And yet one hardly dares say this to one of these busy ones, for however rushed he otherwise may be, yet upon occasion he has plenty of time for a multitude of excuses by the use of which he becomes worse than he was before: excuses whose wisdom is about the same as when a sailor believes that it is the sea, not the ship, that is moving.

One hardly dares say this to him, for however rushed he otherwise may be, yet upon occasion when in the company of congenial spirits, he has ample time: "to rob the unripe fruit of ridicule of its wisdom," in order to poke fun at the speaker as one of life's incompetents, as a man whom the busy one in his cleverness ignores -- from the exalted viewpoint of his excuses. Then, too, the general approval is everywhere upon the side of the busy one -- everywhere, in the ever-increasing sum of the pressure of busyness, and in the swarming mass of excuses. For like a poisonous breath over the fields, like a mass of locusts over Egypt, so the swarm of excuses is a general plague, a ruinous infection among men, that eats off the sprouts of the Eternal. For with each one who is attacked, there is always just one more excuse for the next person. And while a person cannot, as a rule, prevent a sickness becoming more and more dangerous, more and more malignant, the more it attacks those around him, yet with excuses it is just the reverse. There the sickness seems to become milder and milder, the condition becomes more and more agreeable, the more persons there are attacked by it. And if we all agree that the wretched, stunted state of health of these excuses, is the highest of all, then there is no one to say anything to the contrary. Should there be an "individual" who could not feel easy about yielding, and who raised a strong objection to this widespread practice of excusing, alas, we have not yet heard all; for there is always one excuse held in reserve, that lies in wait at his door and demands of him, "What good does it do for a single individual to insist upon opposing this?" Hence once again with excuses it is even worse than with a virulent disease, for no one dies of a disease simply because others have died of it.

So the double-minded person, then, may have a feeling -- a living feeling for the Good. If someone should speak of the Good, especially if it were done in a poetical fashion, then he is quickly moved, easily stimulated to melt away in emotion. Suppose the world goes a little against him and then someone should tell him that God is love, that His love surpasses all understanding, encompassing in His Providence even the sparrow that may not fall to the earth without His willing it. If a person speaks in this way, especially in a poetical manner, he is gripped. He reaches after faith as after a desire, and with faith he clutches for the desired help. In the faith of this desire he then has a feeling for the Good. But perhaps the help is delayed. Instead of it a sufferer comes to him whom he can help. But this sufferer finds him impatient, forbidding. This sufferer must be content with the excuse, "that he 1 is not at the moment in the spirit or the mood to concern himself about the sufferings of others as he himself has troubles." And yet he imagines that he has faith, faith that there is a loving Providence who helps the sufferer, a Providence, who also uses men as his instruments. Possibly now the desired help comes. Again he quickly flares up with gratitude, basking in a soft conception of the loving Goodness of Providence. Now he thinks he has rightly grasped faith. Now it has been victorious in him over every doubt and every objection. Alas, and that other sufferer has been completely forgotten. What else is this condition if it is not doublemindedness! For suppose, after all, that there should be talk of objections to faith, of incidents and occurrences that seem as it were to cry out against the care of a loving Providence: then that other sufferer who with the excuse that by chance he was not in the mood was turned away sharply by the very one who could have helped him, that other sufferer is an even more powerful objection. But the double-minded one is wholly blind to the fact that at the very moment when he believes faith to have conquered in him, he has, precisely by his action, refuted this conviction. Or is this not double-mindedness that thinks to have a conviction while by his own action a man contradicts it? Is this not, in truth, the sole proof that a man has a conviction: that his own life actually expresses it? Is this not the sole certainty: that one's so-called conviction is not altered from moment to moment as a result of the different things that happen to one, things that momentarily alter a person and alter everything for a person so that today he has faith, and tomorrow he has lost it, and he gets it again day after tomorrow until something completely out of the ordinary happens, at which time he almost inevitably loses it, assuming that he has ever had it!

Suppose that there were two men: a double-minded man, who believes he has gained faith in a loving Providence, because he had himself experienced having been helped, even though he had hardheartedly sent away a sufferer whom he could have helped; and another man whose life, by devoted love, was an instrument in the hand of Providence, so that he helped many suffering ones, although the help he himself had wished continued to be denied him from year to year. Which of these two was in truth convinced that there is a loving Providence that cares for the suffering ones? Is it not a fair and a convincing conclusion: He that planted the ear, shall he not hear.(Psalms 94:9). But turn it around, and is the conclusion not equally fair and convincing: He whose life is sacrificing love shall he not trust that God is love? Yet in the press of busyness there is neither time nor quiet for the calm transparency which teaches equality, which teaches the willingness to pull in the same yoke with other men, that noble simplicity, that is in inner understanding with every man. There is neither time nor quiet to win such a conviction. Therefore, in the press of busyness even faith and hope and love and willing the Good become only loose words and double-mindedness. Or is it not doublemindedness to live without any conviction, or more rightly, to live in the constantly and continually changing fantasy that one has and that one has not a conviction!

In this fashion feeling deceives the busy one into double -- mindedness. Perhaps after the flaming up of the contrition of repentance, if this turns into emptiness, he had a conviction, at least so he believed, that there is a mercy that forgives sins. But even m the forgiveness he strongly denied any implication that he had been guilty of anything. Hence he had, so he thought, believed in a conviction that such a mercy exists, and yet in practice he denied its existence; in practice his attitude seemed designed to prove that it did not exist. Suppose that there were two men, that double-minded one, and then another man who would gladly forgive his debtor, if he himself might only find mercy. Which of these two was in truth convinced that such a mercy exists? The latter had indeed this proof that it exists, that he himself practices it, the former has no proof at all for himself, and only meets the contrary proof which he himself presents. Or the double-minded one perhaps had a feeling for right and wrong. It blazed strongly in him, especially if someone would describe in a poetical manner the zealous men, who by self-sacrifice in the service of truth, maintained righteousness and justice. Then some wrong happened to this man himself. And then it seemed to him as if there must appear some sign in heaven and upon earth since the world order could no more sleep than he until this wrong was put right again. And this was not self-love that inflamed him, but it was a feeling for justice, so he thought. And when he obtained his rights, no matter how much wrong it had cost those around him, then once again he praised the perfection of the world. Feeling had indeed carried him away, but also it had so enraptured him that he had forgotten the most important of all: to support righteousness and justice with self-sacrifice in the service of the truth. For which of these two is really convinced that justice exists in the world: the one that suffers wrong for doing the right, or the one that does wrong in order to obtain his right?

The immediate feeling is indeed -- primary. It is the *élan vital* out of which life flows, just as it is said that the heart is the source of life. But then this feeling must be "kept," understood in the sense that one says, "Keep thy heart with all diligence, for out of it are the issues of life."(Proverbs 4:23.) It must be cleansed of selfishness, kept from selfishness. It must not be delivered up to its own devices. On the other hand, that which will be kept must always put its trust in a higher power who will keep it; hence, even the loving mother begs God to keep her child.

In immediate feeling one man never understands another. As soon as something happens to himself, all things seem different to him. When he himself suffers he does not understand the suffering of another and neither is his own happiness the key to understand the happiness of another. The immediate feeling selfishly understands all in relation to itself, and is therefore in the discord of double-mindedness with all others. For only in the well-understood equality of sincerity can there be unity, and in selfish shortsightedness his conviction is continually being altered. If it is not altered it is an accident, since the cause of its exemption is only that by sheer chance his life was not touched by any change. But the stability of such a conviction is mere fantasy on the part of the one whom fate has pampered. Because a conviction is not firmly fixed when all press upon it equally and hold it firm. Rather, its true stability is revealed when everything is changed. It is rare indeed that a man's life is able to escape all changes, and in the changes the conviction based on immediate feeling is a fantasy, the momentary impression simply inflated into a consideration of the whole life.

Perhaps the double-minded one had a knowledge of the Good. In the moment of contemplation it stood out so distinctly before him, so clearly, that the Good, in truth, has all the advantage on its side, that the Good, in truth, is a gain both for this and for the future life. Yes, it lay on his heart, as though he must be able to convince the whole world of it. Perhaps it was not demanded of him that he should go out with his acquired conviction in order to convince others, but the testing that should try this newly won conviction nevertheless was not left out. Alas, I contemplation and the moment of contemplation, in spite of all their clarity, readily conceal a deception; because the moment of contemplation has something in common with the falsified eternity. It is a foreshortening that is necessary in order that the contemplation may take place. It must foreshorten time a good deal. Indeed it must actually call the senses and thoughts away from time in order that they may complete themselves in a spurious eternal well-roundedness. It is here as when an artist sketches a country. The sketch cannot be as big as the country, it must be in-finitely smaller; but on that account it also becomes all the easier for the observer to scan the outlines of that country. And yet it may well happen to the observer, if suddenly he were actually set down in that country where the many, many miles really exist and are valid, that he would be unable to recognize the country, or to make any sense of it, or as a traveler, to find his way about in it. So it will be with the double-minded person. His knowledge has indeed been a sense-deception. What was there, in air-tight fashion pressed together in the completeness of contemplation, shall now be stretched out at its full length. It is now no longer rounded off but is in motion. For life is like a poet, and on that account is different from the observer who always seeks to bring things to a conclusion. The poet pulls us into the very complex center of life.

Now the double-minded person stands there with contemplation's sketch. Time, that was ignored by contemplation, begins to assert its validity. And it is obvious that in all eternity, time has no right to deny that the Good has all the advantage on its side. But it has permission to stretch time out, and thereby to make somewhat more difficult what in contemplation is apparently so plainly understood. So the understanding does not, in this way, simply become less plain because it has become crooked and awry, but rather it has become less plain -- to go by. Now instead of keeping his contemplation to himself and holding himself to the contemplation in order to penetrate time with it in a direct but gradual manner, the doubleminded person lets time cut him off from contemplation. Is this not double-mindedness: to be in time without any contemplation, without any distinct thoughts, or to put it more exactly, to be within time deceived over and over again about having or having had an experience of contemplation! The moment of contemplation he had recklessly misunderstood as being earnest, and then as this earnestness really approached, he threw off contemplation, and misunderstood the moment of contemplation as a delusion, until he again becomes earnest in the moment of contemplation. Or perhaps the double-minded one himself admitted that he had done wrong, had acted badly, had gotten upon a false road. But then after reflection it became so evident, so attractive, that punishment really is like a medicine. It seemed to him that no physician had ever made his medicine so agreeable or inviting, as this reflection upon punishment had succeeded in rendering it. However, when the punishment came, momentarily, as a physician knows, it made the condition worse, in order that real health might break through. Then he became impatient. In reflection he had thought himself healed; thought how good it was, when it was all over. In this fashion the lazy man always has a disproportionate power of imagination. He thinks immediately how he will establish himself, and how fine it will be for him when now this and now that is done: he is less given to thinking -- that he should do this and that. And in reflection this looks very inviting, but when he must step out upon the road (for reflection is up above the road) then all is changed. Now instead of keeping the reflection and the estimate to himself, and conforming to them, he throws off reflection. He has lightly taken the reflection in vain, as if it were the healing quality of the medicine, and as the healing is about to begin, he light-mindedly misunderstands the reflection as a delusion. Is this not double-mindedness: to be ill, to put oneself under the physician's treatment, and yet not be willing to trust the physician, but arbitrarily to break off the treatment! Is this not double-mindedness, when the sick person is perhaps getting into the bath, where the heat increases, but now finding it suddenly too warm he springs out, regardless of all danger! Is it not double-mindedness, when he still has a remnant of deliberation left and with it an intimation that actually he is ill and so he begins to go through his cure all over again -- in the same fashion!

In the recognition, that contemplation and reflection are the distance of eternity away from time and actuality, there is indeed a truth: the knower can understand that truth, but he cannot understand himself. It is certain that without this recognition a man's life is more or less thoughtless. But it is also certain, that this recognition, because it is in a spurious eternity before the imagination, develops double-mindedness, if it is not slowly and honestly earned by the will's purity.

So the double-minded person may have had a will to the Good, for the one who is betrayed into double-mindedness by feeling, or by that distant recognition, he too has a will; but it received no power, and the germ of double-mindedness lay in the inner psychical disagreement. He also has a will to the Good. He is not without intentions or purposes, and resolutions and plans for himself, and not without plans of participation for others. But he has left something out: namely, he does not believe that the will in itself is, or indeed should be, the most solid of all, that it should be as hard as the sword that could hew stone, and yet be so soft that it could be wrapped around the body. He does not believe that it is the will by which a man should steady himself, yes, that when all fails, that it is the will that a man must hold to. He does not believe that the will is itself the mover, but rather that it should itself be mover, that in itself it is fluctuating and on that account should be supported, held firm, that it should be moved and supported by causes, considerations, advice of others, experiences, rules of life. If we, quite properly, should compare the will in man with the headway impetus of a ship in which he (the man) is carried forward: then he believes, on the contrary, that the will, instead of its propelling all, is itself something that should be tugged forward, that there are grounds, considerations, advice of others, experiences, rules of life, that go alongside of and push or pull the will forward as if the will could be compared to a barge -- yes, to a freight barge. But in the same stroke the will is made impotent, "up to a certain degree" discounted in relation to causes, considerations and advice, and in relation to how these react upon one another. He has turned everything around. What for each one, who with the impetus of eternity steers for a better world, would be a hindrance in life, he takes for an advantage in hastening forward, and what should be an advantage in hastening forward, he makes into a delay, or at least into something that is in itself neutral. Such a person must certainly remain in double-mindedness, upon the inland lake of double-mindedness, busy with trivialities, if, instead of charting a course out of all this delaying by means of the will to the Good, he only sails with the speed of the hindrance.

A man enters upon his life, hoping that all will go well for him and with good wishes for others. He steps out into the world's multiplicity, like one that comes from the country into the great noisy city, into the multiplicity where men engrossed in affairs hurry past one another, where each looks out for what belongs to him in the vast "back and forth," where everything is in passing, where it is as though at each instant one saw what he had learned borne out in practice, and in the same instant saw it refuted, without any cessation in the unrest of work, in multiplicity -- that all too vast a school of experience. For here one can experience everything possible, or that everything is possible, even what the inexperienced man would least believe, that the Good sits highest at the dinner table and crime next highest, or crime highest and the Good next highest -- in good company with each other. So this man stands there. He has in himself a susceptibility for the disease of double-mindedness. His feeling is purely immediate, his knowledge only strengthened through contemplation, his will not mature. Swiftly, alas, swiftly he is infected -- one more victim. This is nothing new, but an old story. As it has happened to him, so it has happened with the double-minded ones who have gone before him -- this in passing he now gives as his own excuse, for he has received the consecration of excuses.

Perhaps at this point a speaker, who was just as double- minded as that double-minded one, and therefore really only wishes to deceive, will describe the willing of the Good for us in an alluring fashion, yet, in an alluring fashion with the prospect of becoming something in the world. Perhaps he will close his description by saying that that double-minded person came to nothing in the world -- just to terrify us. But we do not wish to deceive. Still less do we wish to stir up terror, to frighten by a fraud, which is much like commending a falsehood. We wish only to say that, eternally understood, the double-minded one came to nothing. On the other hand, in the time order, in keeping with his ability and his indefatigable industry, he probably became a well-to-do man, a respected man -- or to a certain degree, a respected man, or at least what a man can become within the circumference of "to a certain degree." And by this it is not denied, that he could readily become the richest man in the world. For that, too, the condition of being the richest man, is only something "to a certain degree." Only the determinations of eternity are above "a certain degree." Like its truths, the time order with all that belongs to it is to a "certain degree"; only eternity and its truth is eternal. Therefore let us not deceive and say that in an earthly sense a man advances furthest in the time order by willing the Good in truth. Do not let the talk be as double-minded as the world is. No, in the time order a man advances furthest, in an earthly sense, by means of double-mindedness, and, it must be admitted, mainly by that double-mindedness that has about it a spurious gloss of unity and of inner coherence.

Behold! Honesty is the most enduring of all. It endures, too, at the time when the rich man becomes poor by his honesty. It still endures when the once rich but later poor man is dead and gone, and when the world has been destroyed and forgotten, and when there is neither poverty nor wealth nor money; or further still, when the once rich, but later poor man has long since forgotten the suffering of poverty, yet his honesty still endures. And yet suppose a man should believe that honesty is only related to money and to money values, that the same thing happens to it as to dishonesty, that it ends with the end of the order of money values. Yes, to be sure, honesty stands related to wealth, and poverty and money, but it also stands related to the Eternal. And it does not stand related in a double-minded fashion to money and to the Eternal, so as to aim at joining itself in a financial relationship -- to the Eternal. Because of this it endures. It does not "to a certain degree" endure the longest of all. It endures. That assertion is, therefore, no mere proverb. It is an eternal truth. It is the invention of eternity.

On the other hand, there is a proverb that says: One needs a little more than honesty to get through this world. But the questions to which these assertions are a reply differ I most widely. It is asked, what is it that endures; and it is asked, how may I pass through? He that merely asks, how may I pass through, has no desire for real knowledge. But he that asks what it is that endures has already passed through; he has already gone over from the time order to eternity, although he is still alive. The one inquires of things only in comparatives. The other questions eternally and if in the hour of temptation, when his honesty is tested, he asks properly, he will receive now, and in the next world he will again receive eternity's answer: Yes, it endures! Yes, it is better to go to the house of mourning than to the house of feasting, (Ecclesiastes 7:2) for there one can learn, that after a hundred years, all is forgotten. Yes, to be sure, long ago the feast and the gallant brothers were forgotten, but truly the Eternal is not forgotten, not after a thousand years.

Chapter 8: The Price of Willing Our Thing: Commitment, Loyalty, Readiness to Suffer All

B. If a Man Shall Will the Good in Truth, Then he Must be Willing to do all for the Good or be Willing to Suffer All for the Good.

My listener, before going further, if it seems right to you, we shall look at the course our talk has taken up to this point. For the talk, too, has its laborious development, and it is only when this is completed in the necessary slowness that we may come to an understanding with each other about what the talk presupposes. Only at that point can the talk, being then secure, make use of the agreeable speed that is properly the very life of Conversation. Thus, purity of heart is to will one thing, but *to will one thing could not mean to will the world's pleasure and what belongs to it,* even if a person only named one thing as his choice, *since this one thing was one only by a deception. Nor could willing one thing mean willing it in the vain sense of mere bigness* which only to a man in a state of giddiness appears to be one. FOR IN TRUTH TO WILL ONE THING, A MAN MUST WILL THE GOOD. This was the first, *the possibility of being able to will one thing.* But in order GENUINELY TO WILL ONE THING, A MAN MUST IN TRUTH WILL THE GOOD. On the other hand, as for each act of willing the Good which does not will it in truth, it must be declared to be double-mindedness. Then there was a type of double-mindedness that in a more powerful and active sort of inner coherence seemed to will the Good, but deceptively willed something else. It willed the Good *for the sake* of *reward, out of fear of punishment, or as a form of self-assertion.* But there was another kind of double-mindedness *born of weakness,* that is commonest of all among men, that versatile double-mindedness that wills the Good in a kind of sincerity, but only wills it "to a certain degree."

Now the talk may continue. If, then, a man in truth wills the Good, then HE MUST BE WILLING TO DO ALL FOR IT or HE MUST BE WILLING TO SUFFER ALL FOR IT.

Once more we understand that this classification divides mankind, or rather reminds us of a division that exists in reality: a division into the active ones and the sufferers, so that when the talk is about willing to do all, we may think about the suffering which this act may entail without calling such a man a sufferer, since he actually is an active person. But by the sufferers, we think of those to whom life itself seems to have assigned the speechless, and if you will, the useless sufferings, useless because the sufferings are not benefiting others, are helping nothing at all, but rather are a burden both to others and to the sufferers themselves.

I. ***If a man shall will the good in truth, then he must be willing to do all for the Good.***

Let us first consider: the willingness to do all for the Good. All -- yet will not this talk easily exceed all bounds, if all is named? Will it not become an impossibility to master all the differences included under the term "all" and as a result will the talk not become vague, since the Good can demand the most different things of different people? It can sometimes demand that a man leave his esteemed calling and put on lowliness, that he give away all his possessions to the poor, that he shall not even dare to bury his father.(Compare Luke 9:59.) Again it can demand of others that they shall assume the power and the dignity that are offered them, that they shall take over the working power of wealth, that they shall bury the father, and that perhaps a large part of their lives shall be consecrated to faithfulness which is to be faithful over the little to this extent, that their own life has no claims of its own, but rather is faithful to the memory of a departed one. Now let us not multiply confusion and distraction in a host of individual details. For these also remind us of the struggle of pettiness for preference, where one person thinks that by doing one thing he is doing more for the Good than another who does something else. For if both in relation to the demand do all, then they do equally much. And if neither of them does all, then they do equally little. Instead of multiplying details, let us simplify this all into its essential unity and likeness by saying that to will to do all is: *in the commitment to will to be and to remain loyal to the Good.* Because the commitment is just the committing of all, just as it is also that which is essentially one thing. In this way no tempting occasion for the mistaken quarrel of pettiness about preference need arise. Then, too, the talk can be briefer, for it is unnecessary to enumerate variety's many names and yet be in keeping with strict accuracy, since this essential brevity answers to that rich brevity which is present in life, in the act of commitment to will to be and to remain loyal to the Good. No one believes that this is a long-drawn-out affair. On the contrary, from the standpoint of eternity, if I dare say so, it is this abbreviating of all of life's fractions (for eternity's length is the true abbreviation) that frees life of all its difficulties, and it is through deciding to will to be and to remain loyal to the Good that so much time is gained. For that which absorbs men s time when they complain about the lack of time is irresoluteness, distraction, half thoughts, half resolutions, indecisiveness, great moments -- great moments. It was because of these that we said: to be and to remain loyal to, so that the commitment should not be confused with the extravagance of an expansive moment. The person, who in decisiveness wills to be and to remain loyal to the Good, can find time for all possible things. No, he cannot do that. Hut neither does he need to do that, for he wills only one thing, and just on that account he will not have to do all possible things, and so he finds ample time for the Good.

The commitment of willing to be and to remain loyal to the Good is truth's brief way of expressing: to be willing to do all. And in this expression there is apparent that leveling insight that recognizes no distinction proportionate to that actual difference of life or of human circumstances: to be an active person or to be a sufferer, because the sufferer too, can be committed to the Good. This is of importance to the thought and to the talk, so that discord shall neither exist nor be kindled; so that the talk shall not incite the active person who is able to accomplish much in the outer world to compare himself in a conceited way with the sufferer; nor provoke the heavily laden sufferer who apparently spends his time in useless suffering, despairingly to compare his uselessness, his pain, his not merely superfluous, but for others even burdensome existence, with the great accomplishments of the active ones. Alas, often enough such an unfortunate person, in addition to his heavy, innocent suffering must bear the severe judgment of the arrogant, the busy, and the stupid, who are indeed able to irritate and hurt him, but who can never understand him.

So now let us talk of doing all, and speak of the men who, in this or that way, are assigned to the external world as to a stage. It makes no difference at all, God be praised, how great or how small the task may be. In relation to the highest of all this simply does not matter when it comes to being willing to do all. Oh, how great is the mercy of the Eternal toward us! All the ruinous quarreling and comparison which swells up and injures, which sighs and envies, the Eternal does not recognize. Its claim rests equally on each, the greatest who has ever lived, and the most insignificant. Yes, the sun's rays do not shine with more equality on the peasant's hut and the ruler's palace, than the equality with which the Eternal looks down upon the highest and the lowest. Yet not equally, for if the most exalted is not willing to do all, then eternity gazes in wrath upon him. And, even though the rich man by human ingenuity should at last succeed in being able to trick the sun into shining more invitingly upon his palace than over the poor man's hut, man will never be able to trick the Good and eternity in this fashion.

The demand upon each is exactly the same: to be willing to do all. If this be fulfilled then the Good bestows its blessing equally upon each one who makes and remains loyal to his commitment.

Suppose that we should now in earthly and temporal fashion recommend the commitment. Suppose we should say, "It does not matter whether you leap into it or creep into it. You may as well risk it first as last. For although you may very well succeed for a time in dancing on roses, nevertheless the difficult time of trouble will come, and so it is always well to be prepared." Oh, let us never wish to sell what is holy, or more properly, let us never forget that in this sense eternity is not for sale, that it regards itself as too good to be sold where it might be bought by a bargainer -- a brazen one. Yes, for the same reason that a temple-robber is the most contemptible of criminals, so it is with this highly painted clever one who cunningly wills the highest thing of all without willing it in truth. The temple-robber may even succeed in plundering the sacred treasures, and may actually get them into his possession since these treasures are something external. But that clever one never succeeds in stealing the commitment or in stealing himself into the commitment. The ever-active righteousness that eternally dispenses justice is so vigilant that every criminal not only does not become dangerous to the Eternal, but in the sense of imperfection does not even actually come into existence, since it becomes a self-accusation. In relation to the Eternal, the criminal's worst act is much as if the temple-robber instead of stealing the sacred vessels went to the high temple officials and said, "I wish to steal the sacred vessels." So with the matter of stealing the commitment, it does not succeed, but instead the guilty one announces himself to the Eternal and says, "I wish to steal the commitment." For in eternity there is no sensory illusion, and so neither is there what in a moral sense is the same thing, any actual possession -- of stolen goods. Let us not, then, deceptively and uselessly recommend the coming to a decision. If someone wishes to sneak through life, let him do it. The truth might still take occasion to seize him so that he would will the decision for the sake of the Good. But let us not make him believe that by an artifice he could cunningly carry the commitment with him on his stealthy way through life.

The decision is, to be willing to do all for the Good; it is not cleverly to wish to have the advantage of the Good. Alas, there is in every man a power, a dangerous and at the same time a great power. This power is cleverness. Cleverness strives continually against the commitment. It fights for its life and its honor, for if the decision wins, then cleverness is as if put to death -- degraded, to become a despised servant whose talk is attentively listened to, but whose advice one does not stoop to follow.

Now in the inner world man uses cleverness an a ruinous way, in order to keep himself from coming to a decision. In countless ways cleverness can be so misused; but in order once again not to multiply that which is not important and thereby to divert attention from the really important, we will again simply designate this misuse by a definite expression: to seek to evade. To forsake one's post, to desert in battle is always disgraceful, but cleverness has invented an ingenious device that apparently prevents flight: it is evasion. By the help of evasion, namely, one does not come into danger, and neither does he lose his honor by running away in danger -- on the contrary one does not come into danger -- that is one advantage. And one wins great honor as being especially clever -- that is a second advantage. Only eternity, the Good, and so also the Holy Scriptures, are of another opinion about this matter of evasions and about the much-honored clever ones. For they are referred to when it speaks of, "those that draw back into perdition" (Hebrews 10:39). How strange that a man can, therefore, avoid a danger, and when he believes himself secure and saved (which one indeed should believe after he has escaped danger), just at that point he has sunk into perdition.

A clever one speaks in this way, "Afterwards it is too late. If I have already ventured too far out and been crushed, who will help me then? Then I should be a cripple for all the rest of my life, an object of mockery and a by-word among men. Who will help me then?" Who will help him then? Who other than the power in which he trusted in venturing so far out? Yet surely not as one who is stronger helps a weakling, but rather as when the unprofitable servant[23] does everything in order to do his lord's will. But now with the help of evasions the clever one talks as if the Good itself was no power, or as if its power counted for nothing, so therefore, that it could be the clever one, who (if he chose to risk it) by doing all, would help out the Good. If this is so, then it is true enough that no one exists who can help him -- in case he actually should venture out -- and that which a clever ingenious imagination invents in order to be able to forget the troublesome background of evasion above the terrifying foreground, actually comes to pass. Evasion thus accomplishes nothing.

And even if the terrible thing now happens the confident venturer is injured. Even an earthly government is I accustomed to care for its faithful servants who risk danger in loyalty to the state, then shall not God and the Good also care for their faithful servants, if only they are sincere!

And even if the terrible thing happens that when the sincere person had risked all, that it was then that the government said to him, "My friend, I cannot use you." Oh, how clear it is that the smallest crumb of grace in the service of the Good is infinitely more blessed than to be the mightiest of all outside that service. Verily, verily, it is indeed true, it is with trembling true, in relation to the ungodly, but it is also by grace happily true for the sincere, that God is not tricked by a man? Even if the sincere one comes to grief, perhaps it was just this that the government needed. Has it not often happened that the well is first covered only after the child has fallen in, while before this the most reasonable arguments and warnings had been of no avail? Now if the sincere one is willing to be the child who falls in, has his venture been wholly in vain?

Another says, "I have not the strength to risk all." Again evasion, an evasion by the aid of the word "all." For the Good is quite capable of reckoning and computing its demand in relation to the strength that this man has. And what is more, if he will venture in all sincerity, then he will certainly receive strength enough in the act of decision. But the clever one desires by the help of evasions to have strength in advance. He wishes to misuse it like the soldier who, in order to be sure of being distinguished in battle, demands his distinction in advance. And yet this picture is untrue, for it is doubtful how far the battle gives strength. But it is certain, that the confidence, wherewith he has ventured, does give superhuman strength. Yet it is also certain (oh, wonderful accuracy!) that the one who does not have trust does not receive this strength. Look, the great battleship first gets its orders when it is far out at sea, the little sloop knows all in advance. And in a spiritual sense, a person is only really out at sea who is willing w do all, irrespective of whether he is the highest or the least. The little sloop is the clever person, no matter whether he be the highest or the least.

One says, "The bit that I can do is not worth while." The clever one is polite, he understates, he says, "Do excuse me." He acts as if the Good were a distinguished man, and as if willing the Good were a distinguished act. But it is a misconception. No, here it is an evasion. The Good is not distinguished. It demands neither more nor less than all, whether that is a mere bit or not is neither here nor there. The widow's mite was all that she owned. Before God it was as great a sum as all of the world's gold in a single heap, and if one who owned all the gold in the world gave it all, he would give no more. Yes, when that public collection of money was made, it was possible that the collectors both kindly and politely might have said to the widow, "No, Mother, you keep your mite." But the Good -- how shall we express it? Its goodness is so great, that it recognizes no difference.

One man says, "I am not justified in doing that because of my wife and children." Alas, even the civil government looks after, yes . . . yet this is out of place here. But I wonder if he, as man and father, really could do anything better for wife and children than to impress upon them this trust in Providence. Here, then, it is not as in civil life that the person who risks dares hope that the state will look after his wife and children. No, spiritually understood, he has by his venture cared for them in the best possible way, for by this he has shown them that he at least has faith in Providence. Here, then, it is not as in civil life that the person who undertakes to risk can do it by caring for wife and children. For spiritually understood, the fearful one shows that he has no concern for the true welfare of wife and children.

One may say, "Experience teaches that it is best to divide one's energies in order that one can win by the one, when he loses by another. I owe it to myself, and to my future, not to place all upon a single thing." Yes, God grant that he will not restrict his pains to his future, for that is too little; but may this alone be set before his eyes, and ever called to his mind; that his future is -- an eternity.

Yet how could one ever finish talking about all the evasions? Who would undertake this fruitless work, this battle with the air! And even if someone should, even if he succeeded in enumerating them all and for an instant succeeded in holding them together so that they could not, like true runaways, slip away and assume another role while remaining in essence the same, still one evasion would always remain behind even if none ought to be there, even if by repeated inspection a commendable cleverness should be unable to discover that a single ground had been overlooked and hence that a single evasion was still possible.

So the double-minded person, seduced by cleverness, yielded to the evasions. "But this brought him nothing." Oh, let us not deceive youth, let us not sit and bargain in the outer court of the holy, nor formulate a profane introduction to the holy, as if one should in truth will the Good in order to prosper in the world. Readily grant that the clever one amounts to something, even to something great in the world. There is, however, a power that is called memory. It should be dear to all the good ones as well as to all lovers. Yes, it may even be so dear to lovers that they almost prefer this whisper of memory to the sight of each other, as when they say, "Do you remember that time, and do you remember that time?"

Now memory also visits the double-minded person. Then it says to him, "Do you remember that time? . . . You as well as I knew well enough what was there required of you, but you shrank back (to your own destruction), do you remember that! It was by this that you won a great deal of your property (to your own destruction). Do you remember that! Do you recall that time? . . . You knew as well as I what you should venture, you knew what danger it involved, do you remember, you shrank back (to your own destruction), do you remember? . . . Yet it served you well, for the badge of honor on your breast calls you back to a memory of how you shrank back to your own destruction!

"Do you remember that time . . . you knew well enough by yourself and by my solitary voice in your heart, what you should choose, but you shrank back (to your own destruction), do you remember that? It was that time when the popular favor and the exultation of the masses hailed you as the righteous one, do you remember that?" Yes, it indeed becomes your concern to remember the popular exultation and favor, for in eternity such things are not recognized. But in eternity it is not forgotten that you shrank back! For what shall it profit a man if he shall gain the whole world and lose his own soul.(Compare Mark What shall it profit him, if he shall gain the time order and all it possesses, if he breaks with the Eternal? What shall it profit him if he comes through the world under full sail aided by the favorable winds of popular exultation and admiration, if he runs aground upon eternity? What shall it profit the sick man to imagine himself, as all men do, to be well, if the physician says he is sick!

Outwardly, too, cleverness is used in a ruinous way, in the matter of the decision, that is to say, it is outwardly misused. And we are indeed speaking of the active ones, and of being willing to do all for the Good. Here cleverness may be misused in a multitude of ways. But, once more, let us not increase the distracting element. Let us, rather, simplify that which is significant, and call all these different kinds of misuse by a single name: deception. The clever one knows just how the Good must be altered a tiny particle in order to win the world's good will. He knows how much should be added to it and how much should be subtracted. He knows just what ingratiating thing should be whispered in men's ears, what should be entrusted to their hands, and how the hand should be pressed, how it should be swung away from truth's decision, how the turning should be done, and how he himself in suppleness should shift and turn --"in order that he can accomplish all the more for the Good." But the secret of deception, to which in one way or another all the expressions can be traced back, is this: that certainly it is not men that stand in need of the Good, but that it is the Good that stands in need of men. On that account it is men who must be won. For the Good is a poor beggar that is in desperate need, instead of its being men who are in need of the Good, and so much in need of it that it is the one thing necessary to them, that it must be bought at any price, that absolutely all must be given up and sold in order to buy it, but that also, the one who owns it owns all. Yet It happens that all are naturally fooled by the deception. Someone makes an attempt to fool the Good, which in all eternity inevitably fails, for that it seems to succeed for a fortnight or a lifetime is only a jest. The clever one, on the other hand, wins great distinction in the world -- and he, too, is fooled. The crowd delights itself with the flattering sweets of imagination -- and is fooled! This was deception's secret, that it is the Good that stands in need of men. The clever one's secret is, that he cannot be wholly content with the Good's poor reward, but must cast about to earn a little extra by eluding the Good a little.

Seduced by cleverness, the double-minded person yielded, "but he accomplished nothing in this world." No, let us not give a false impression; he accomplished much. A large number of friends of the Good, or of good friends rallied admiringly around him. Of course, they believed by this to attach themselves once more to the Good, but that certainly must be a deception, for the clever one himself went outside the Good. Many joined together, for they had the idea that the Good is something extraordinary, and all honor be to them and all honor be to this true idea. But they also had the idea that the Good is something so exceptionally great that many must join together in order to buy it. Yet this conception is not worthy of honor, even if it be deceptively called humility. It is an insult to the Good, which in its infinite goodness does not refuse the most insignificant, but allows him also to bid and to buy -- if he is willing to do all and so in truth to honor the Good. On the other hand, the Good rejects all stupid honor and distinction, where its greatness would be compared with an estate which the "individual" has not money enough to buy so that it is necessary to take up a collection. With the help of the masses the clever one now erected an enormous building. True enough, it was only a frame building (there were many others like it), but it looked well as long as it stood. But memory, memory that in the highest and most sober sense purifies even the coarser expressions is what in plain everyday language is called a "dunner." Now and then memory even pays a visit to the popular idol. Upon these occasions, memory murmurs softly to him, "Can you remember the deceptive turn you gave the thing, by which you won the blind masses, and by which you were able to build the tower so high?" But the popular one says, "Only keep quiet, never let anyone get to know it." "Very well," memory answers. "You know that I am no petty bickerer who is in desperation over what is owed him. Let it rest. No one shall get to know it, as long as you live, perhaps not even when you are dead and forgotten. But eternally, eternally it will continue to be remembered." Oh, what did it net the unprofitable servant, if his Master went away, if his Master traveled so far away that he should never more see him in this life, what good was this to him, if the Master that traveled away was memory with which he must be together throughout eternity! What help is it indeed to the condemned one, if the day of punishment is put off throughout his whole life; how does this help him, if indeed the judgment that was passed on him is the judgment of eternity and shall be carried out in eternity!

The clever one, therefore, accomplishes much. Let us for once think through this thought: *to accomplish something in the world.* One hears so much of both impatient and misleading talk about this. To be sure, it is well that all should wish to do something. It is indeed earnestness to desire it, but should it not also be earnestness to understand in oneself and in life precisely what is meant by saying that one man accomplishes such an exceptional amount, or that another man seems to accomplish nothing at all. Suppose the temporal order is not understood as it pictures itself, but rather as the recognizable fact that it is in reality. Suppose the temporal order was a homogeneous transparent medium of the Eternal. Then every eternal volition in a man, and every volition of the Eternal would straightway become perceptible in the temporal order, if the same kind of powers of comprehension be assumed in the temporal order: so that when the man who wills does get on in the temporal order, and is accounted to be something in the eyes of the many, the eternal volition in a man would be plainly evident, just as the quantity of a cry is obvious by the quantity of the sound in a room, just as when a stone is cast into the water its size is evident by the size of the circle it makes. If matters stood like this between the temporal order and the Eternal, so that they answer each other as the echo answers to the sound, then that which is accomplished would be a trustworthy rendering of the eternal volition in a man. By what a man had accomplished, one could immediately see how much will toward the Eternal there was in him. But in that case it could never have come to pass in the temporal order (in order to mention the highest and the most horrible, but also what is the key that explains all) that God's son, as He was revealed in human form, was crucified -- repudiated by the temporal order. For He truly willed the Eternal in the eternal sense, and yet in the temporal order He became distinguished by being repudiated, and so accomplishing but little. As it had happened to God's son, so it went with the Apostles, just as they themselves had expected, and so it has gone with so many witnesses of the Good and the true in whom this eternal will has burned fiercely.

It is obvious, then, that the temporal order cannot be the transparent medium of the Eternal. In its given reality the temporal order is in conflict with the Eternal. This makes the determination to accomplish something less plain. The more active the Eternal is toward the witness, the stronger is the cleavage. The more the striver, instead of willing the Eternal, is linked with temporal existence, the more he accomplishes in the sense of the temporal existence. So it is in many ways or in all possible ways in the temporal order. When a peculiar thinker, who just by his peculiarity is more tied up with the Eternal and less with time's moment, addresses his speech to men, he is rarely understood or listened to. When, on the other hand, a voluble follower comes to his aid in order that the peculiar one can become -- misunderstood: then it succeeds, then there are many who instantly understand it. The thinker becomes a kind of superfluous element in life, the follower an effective man who accomplishes such an extraordinary amount in the temporal order. Only upon a rare occasion does it ever happen that the Eternal and the temporal's accomplishments conform after a fashion to each other -- by accident. For let us not insult God and the God-Man by assuming that what happened to Him there was an accident, that His life expressed something accidental, perhaps something that had He lived at another time, among another people, would not have happened to Him. If, then, there is to be significance in the talk about accomplishing, a distinction must be made between the momentary and the eternal view of the thing. These are two opposed views which each man has to choose between in regard to his own striving and in regard to each contemporary striving. For to judge by the outcome (whereby an attempt is made to unite a judgment of temporal existence and of eternity into a judgment that comes after the event is past) is not humanly possible in the instant that a man himself acts, nor is it possible in the instant when others act.

By the help of a sense deception, a living generation often believes itself able to pass judgment on a past generation, because it misunderstood the Good. And it is even guilty of committing the same offense against a contemporary. And yet it is just in regard to his contemporary that a man should know whether he has the view of the moment, or the view of the Eternal. At some later date, it is no art to decorate the graves of the noble and to say, "If they had only lived now," now -- just as we are starting in to do the same thing against a contemporary. For the difficulty and the test of what dwells in the one who judges is precisely -- the contemporary. The view of the moment is the opinion which in an earthly and busy sense decides whether a man accomplishes anything or not. And in this sense, nothing in the world has ever been so completely lost as was Christianity at the time that Christ was crucified. And in the understanding of the moment, never in the world has anyone accomplished so little by the sacrifice of a consecrated life as did Jesus Christ. And yet in this same instant, eternally understood, He had accomplished all. For He did not foolishly judge by the result that was not yet there, or more rightly (for here is the conflict and battleground of the two interpretations of what is meant by "accomplishing") the result was indeed there. Question His contemporaries, if you ever meet them. Do they not say of the crucified one, "The fool, he would help others and he cannot help himself, but now the outcome also shows, so that everyone may see what he was."(Matthew 27:41-44.)Was it not said by His contemporaries, especially where the clever led the conversation, "The fool, he who had it in his power to become king if he cared to make use of his opportunity, if he had only half my cleverness, he would have been king. In the beginning I really believed that it was ingenuity, that he let these people express themselves in this fashion without wishing to give himself up to them. I believed it was a trick in order to inflame them still more. But now the result shows clearly enough what I more recently have myself been quite clear about, that he is a shallow, blind visionary!" Was it not said by many intelligent men and women, "The result shows that he has been hunting after phantasies; he should have married. In this way he would now have been a distinguished teacher in Israel."

And yet, eternally understood, the crucified one had in the same moment accomplished all! But the view of the moment and the view of eternity over the same matter have never stood in such atrocious opposition. It can never be repeated. This could happen only to Him. Yet eternally understood, He had in the same moment accomplished all, and on that account said, with eternity's wisdom, "It is finished."

For it is not after the passage of eighteen hundred years that He will now again appear, and referring to the outcome, say, "It is finished." In contrast to this, He would still not say that. Perhaps it would require many centuries before He would be able to say that in regard to temporal existence. Yet what He is still unable to say after the passage of eighteen triumphant centuries, He said in His own age, eighteen centuries ago, in the very moment when all was lost. Eternally understood, He said, "It is finished." "It is finished." He said that just when the mass of the people, and the priests, and the Roman soldiers, Herod and Pilate, and the idle ones on the street, the crowd in the gateway, and the newspaper reporters (if there were any such at that time) in short, when all the powers of the moment, however different their sentiments might have been, were agreed upon this view of the matter: that all was lost, hopelessly lost. "It is finished," He said, nailed to the cross as He was, at the very time when His Mother stood there -- as if nailed to the cross, when His disciples' eyes were as if nailed to the cross by horror at this sight. Hence Motherhood and faithfulness submitted to the moment's view of the matter, that all was lost. Oh, then let us by this most horrible thing, which once took place (and that it happened only once is not to the world's credit, but rather that the crucified one is eternally and essentially different from every other man) let us learn wisdom in the lesser relationships. Let us never deceive youth by foolish talk about the matter of accomplishing. Let us never make them busy in the service of the moment, instead of in patience willing something eternal. Let us not make them quick to judge what they perhaps do not understand, instead of willing something eternal and being content with little for themselves! Let us rightly consider that a generation is not on that account superior because it understands that a previous generation acted wrongly, if in the present moment they themselves do not understand how to discriminate between the momentary and the eternal aspect of the thing at hand.

Chapter 9: The Price of Willing One Thing: The Exposure of Evasions

But the one who in truth wills the Good, puts cleverness to an inward use: in order to prevent all evasions and thereby to help him enter into and persist in the commitment.

Cleverness is indeed a great power, yet it is treated by him as an insignificant servant, as a shrewd contemptible one. He hears the servant, to be sure, but in action he is not guided by him. He uses cleverness against himself as a spy and informer, which informs him instantly of each evasion, yes, even gives warning at any suspicion of an evasion. Now just as the thief knows the hidden way -- and goes by it, so the authorities also know it and go by it in order to detect the thief, but the knowledge as knowledge is the same in both cases.

This is the way he makes use of cleverness. I do not know whether it is true that at each man's birth two angels are born, his good and his bad angel. But this I do believe (and I will gladly listen to any objection, although I will not believe it) that at each man's birth there comes into being an eternal vocation for him, expressly for him. To be true to himself in relation to this eternal vocation is the highest thing a man can practice, and, as that most profound poet has said: "Self-love is not so vile a sin as self-neglecting."(Shakespeare in Henry V, Act 2, Scene 4.) Then there is but one fault, one offense: disloyalty to his own self or the denial of his own better self. One who is guilty of such a fault is not like a thief or a robber. The civil authority will not lie in wait for him. This fault may begin its course in complete silence so that none will be aware of it. Is it, therefore, perhaps of no account? Certainly many believe that a man can search out and grasp the Truth just as well, creatively express the Beautiful just as well, vitally perfect the Good just as well, even if, in order to win some advantage in the world, he was secretly a little unfaithful to himself, even if he did shift the boundary stones of his inner life a particle by Just a shade less scrupulousness, so that even though he had won this material advantage by doubtful means, yet he "can truly work for the Good, the Beautiful, and the True." So low an estimate of the Good and the Beautiful and the True is expressed by this as to think that it ought to be able to make use of anyone as a serviceable instrument from whom to elicit a harmonious strain, anyone -- even the one that had polluted himself!

Yes, man can deceive himself and men. But when eternity listens attentively, listens in order to discover whether the playing of the strings is pure and in time with itself -- alas, it instantly detects false tones and hesitation. It rejects such a man just as a connoisseur rejects a stringed instrument when it is damaged. Alas, it is indeed a sorry cleverness (however much it boasts of the material advantage that it won as a proof -- of its folly; however much it points to the badges of distinction and thereby again to -- the hidden dejection within), a sorry cleverness that deceives itself about what is the highest of all. The only genuine cleverness is that which helps a man in all devotedness truly to will the Good.

The one who truly wills the Good, therefore, makes use of cleverness against evasions. But by this does he not achieve something great in the world? Perhaps so, perhaps not. But one thing he does become: he becomes a friend, a lover of memory. And so when in a quiet hour, memory visits him (and already at this point how different it is from that visit when memory threateningly knocks at the door of the double-minded man!), then it says to him, "Do you remember that time, that time when the good resolution conquered within you?" And he answers, "Yes, dear one!". But then memory continues (and between lovers memory is so dear that they almost prefer to the sight of each other the whisper of memory when they say, "Can you remember that time?" and "Can you remember that time?"), memory continues, "Can you remember all the hardships and sufferings you endured for the sake of the resolution?" He answers, "No, dear one, I have forgotten that -- let it remain forgotten! But when in the toils of life and struggle, when in my troubled thoughts all is in confusion, it may seem to me as if even that was forgotten which I know I had willed in sincerity. Oh, thou hast thy very name from that act of remembering, thou messenger of the Eternal: Memory. At that hour, visit me, and bring with thee the long-desired, the strengthening meeting with thyself once more." And memory answers in parting, "I promise you that, I swear it to you by all eternity." Then they part one from another, for so it must be here in the world of time. Deeply moved, he takes one more look after memory's vanishing form as one looks after a glorified saint. Now it has gone and so has the quiet hour. It was only a quiet hour, it was not some great moment -- on that account he hoped that memory would keep its promise. He preserved in his own soul that stillness in which he met with memory when it was pleased to visit him. To him this is his reward, and to him this reward is above all others. Yes, just as a Mother, who carries her beloved child asleep at her breast along a difficult road, is not troubled about what may happen to her, but only fears that the child may be disturbed and upset, so he, too, does not fear the troubles of the world on his own account. He is only troubled lest these should upset and disturb that possibility of a visit that slumbers in his soul.

The one who in truth wills the Good also uses cleverness on the outer world. It is no disgrace to be clever; it is a good thing. It is no disgrace that the authorities are clever, that they shrewdly know how to trace the criminal's hidden trail in order to seize him and make him harmless. In so far as the good man is clever, he, too, knows, how in the very face of truth the world wishes to have the Good made agreeable, how the crowd desires to be won -- the much feared crowd, who "desire that the teacher shall tremble before his hearers and flatter them." He knows all about this -- in order not to follow it, but rather by the very opposite conduct to keep as free as possible of these deceptions, that he himself may not adopt any illicit way of deriving some advantage from the Good (earning money, distinction, and admiration) and so that he may deceive no one by a figment of the imagination. Whenever possible he will prefer to withdraw the Good from contact with the crowd. He will seek to split the crowd up in order to get hold of the individual or to get each by himself. He will be reminded of what that simple old sage remarked in ancient times, "When they meet together, and the world sets down at an assembly, or in a court of law, or a theater, or a camp, or in any other popular resort, and there is a great uproar and they praise some things which are being said or done, and blame other things, equally exaggerating both, shouting and clapping their hands, and the echo of the rocks and the place in which they are assembled redoubles the sound of the praise or blame -- at such a time will not a young man's heart, as they say, leap within him?"[27] And indeed this is exactly what is necessary in order in truth to will the Good -- that a man's heart should leap, but leap with the unspoiled quality of youth. And therefore the good man, in case he is also a clever one, will see that if anything is able to be done for the Good, then he must try to get men to be alone. The same persons, who singly, as solitary individuals are able to will the Good, are immediately seduced as soon as they associate themselves and become a crowd. On that account the good man will neither seek to secure the assistance of a crowd in order to split up the crowd, nor will he seek to have a crowd back of him, during the time that he breaks up the crowd in front of him.

But just how the good man will make use of cleverness in the outer world does not permit of being more precisely specified in general terms, for that which is necessary can be totally different with respect to each time and to the out into the desert and lived on locusts knew how, in relation to his circumstances of each time. That stern prophet(John the Baptist) who went out into the desert and lived on locusts knew how, in relation to his contemporaries, he ought to express this decisively: that it is not the truth that is in need of men, but men who are in need of the truth. Hence they must come to him, come out into the desert. Out there, there was no opportunity for them to be able to decorate the truth, to be able most graciously to do something for it; out there where the ax did not lie in the woods, but at the foot of the solitary tree, and where each tree that did not bear good fruit was bound to be chopped down. Yes, to be sure, there have been self-appointed judges since that time, who have erred and chopped away at the whole forest -- and the crowd found it most flattering. Again, there was that simple wise man, who worked for the Good under the form of a joke. He knew by his cleverness exactly what his frivolous people needed, in order that they should not simply take the earnestness of the Good in vain, and thereby be led to pay the wise man a good deal of money as a reward for having deceived them. The form of the joke prevented their misusing the Good's earnestness; the opposition of the joke, on the other hand, made their frivolity obvious: it was the judgment.

Without this cleverness, the frivolous ones would in all probability have imitated him in being earnest. Now, on the contrary, he confronted them with the choice, and see, they chose the joke. They never even noticed, that there was anything earnest in it -- because there was no earnestness in them. This was the judgment, and the judge's conduct. His art was paganism's highest ingenuity, for the Christian type has still another consideration.

Yet this, too, may not be generalized upon. It applies only to that initiated one, whose secret it is, so that by paying close attention to such an individual, one can learn to know a whole generation, concluding from him, from the form he found it necessary to clothe himself in, how the entire age must have been. But it is certain and acknowledged by all, that each one who in truth wills the Good, is not in the world in order to conjure up an appearance of the Good, thus winning approval in the eyes of the world and becoming a man who is beloved by all. He has not the task of changing the Good into a thing of the moment, into something that shall be voted upon in a noisy gathering, or something that swiftly gains some disciples who also will the Good up to a certain degree. No, he has always the task, not by word, nor by intention, but by the sincere inner concentration of his own life -- the task of making it most obvious of all that his surroundings have been set in opposition to him, not in order that he shall judge in terms of words, but in order that his life may unconditionally serve the Good in action. The task is his own obligation in the service of the Good. Judging is not his real function, not his act, but is an accompaniment whereby the surrounding world relates itself to him. Judging is not his activity, because to will the Good in truth is his activity. Yet his suffering is an act of judging, because the surrounding world becomes manifest by the manner in which it lets him suffer; and at the same time by these sufferings he is helped to test himself as to whether it actually is the Good that he wills or whether he himself is caught up in a deception.

Above all, the one, who in truth wills the Good must not be "busy." In quiet patience he must leave it to the Good itself, what reward he shall have, and what he shall accomplish. He dare not allow himself a single word of compromise, not a glance. He dare not ask the slightest relief from the world. He has only to give himself up to the Good and to that thing and to that person that might possibly be helped by him. He is no judge. On the contrary, he is just the opposite, he is the one who is judged. He effects a judgment only in the sense that the surrounding world becomes manifest by how it judges him.

But in this way does he accomplish nothing at all, since he is weighed down with men's opposition, and then gets the worst of the battle? Now in this life indeed no, and in eternity, never. In this life indeed no, for the one who sincerely trusts in God is enthusiastic. He is not like a candle-stub, whose tiny flame goes out before a wind. No, he is like a great fire; a storm cannot quench it! And the flame in his fire is like that one in Greece: water cannot put it out! And even if finally the world does make him suffer, on that account neither the Good nor he has lost -- for to be too far up in the world is most often, as in the ordeal that is called "trial by water," a sign of guilt. To be sure, since the world puts more store by the fashionable than by the truly Good, just on that account in the reckoning of the moment, he will accomplish far less by not giving in, not bargaining, not even making himself comfortable and powerful, by not willing to have profit for himself. But the remembering, the remembering! Let us indeed never forget the remembering, although a person might certainly believe that he would at least be able to forget. And shall not memory be able to remind him of that time when he sneaked away by underhanded means, in order to avoid a decision; of that time when he gave the matter another turn, in order to please men; of that time that he deserted his post, in order to let the storm pass over; of that time he knuckled under, in order to secure an easing off of his painful position; of that time he sought refuge and association with others -- perhaps, as it is called, in order to work all the more effectively for the Good's victory, that is, in order to make his own position a little less difficult than as though at the midnight hour, somewhat terror-stricken, one stood all alone "with heavily loaded weapons at his dangerous post."(Compare Rosenkranz, Erinnerungen an Karl Daub, p. 24: "So as on sentry duty, at night on a lonely post, perhaps before a powder magazine a man has thoughts that under any other circumstances would be quite impossible." Kierkegaard refers to this same passage again in Fear and Trembling, Collected Works, Vol. III, p. 100.)

Nay, what he accomplishes, and what he does not accomplish, in the sense of the moment, that is not his concern. He always accomplishes this -- that he becomes the friend and lover of memory. He accomplishes this whether he is remembered in the world or not. For this world's memory is like the moment: a series of moments. Eternity's memory, that he is certain of. When he leaves this world, he leaves nothing behind him, he takes all with him, he loses nothing, he gains all -- for "God is all to him."

Chapter 10: The Price of Willing One Thing: An Examination of the Extreme Case of an Incurable Sufferer

2. If a man in truth wills the Good then he must be willing to suffer all for the Good.

This applies to the active ones. But from the sufferer, if he shall in truth will the Good, it is demanded that he must be willing to suffer all for the Good, or, as was previously explained, for the expression is essentially the same (and therein lies precisely the equal participation of the Eternal in the differentiations of earthly life), he must be willing in his decision to be and to remain with the Good. For he may also suffer and suffer and continue to suffer without ever arriving at any decision, in the true sense, of assenting to the suffering. A man may have suffered throughout his whole life without it ever, in any true sense, being able to be said of him that he has been willing to suffer all for the Good. But in that respect the sufferer's suffering is different from the active person's suffering, for when the active one suffers, then his suffering has significance for the victory of the Good in the world. When the sufferer, on the other hand, willingly takes up his appointed sufferings, he is willing to suffer all for the Good, that is, in order that the Good may be victorious in him.

Therefore, the sufferer must be willing to suffer all. All; but now how at this point shall the talk be conducted? For alas, even now the sight and the knowledge of suffering can easily rob anyone of composure. How shall the talk be briefly formulated? For the sufferings are able to be so different, and of such long duration. Here, once again, let us not multiply distractions but rather let us simplify that which is really important. Let us center all the talk about suffering upon the wish. For the wish is the sufferer's connection with a happier temporal existence (faith and hope are related to the Eternal through the will); and at the same time the wish is the sore spot where the suffering pains, the sore spot which the suffering continually touches. Even if suffering could still be spoken of where there is no longer any wish, it is an animal-like suffering, not suffering that befits a man. It is a kind of spiritual suicide to will to put the wish to death. For we are not talking about wishes, but rather about the wish with the real emphasis of distinction, just as we also are not talking about passing sufferings, but of the real sufferer. The wish is not the cure. This happens only by the action of the Eternal. The wish is, on the contrary, the life in suffering, the health in suffering. It is the perseverance in suffering, for it is as one thinker has said, "The comfort of temporal existence is a precarious affair. It lets the wound grow together, although it is not yet healed, and yet the physician knows that the cure depends upon keeping the wound open." In the wish, the wound is kept open, in order that the Eternal may heal it. If the wound grows together, the wish is wiped out and then eternity cannot heal, then temporal existence has in truth bungled the illness.

And so let us speak of the wish and thereby of the sufferings; let us properly linger over this, convinced that one may learn more profoundly and more reliably what the highest is by considering suffering than by observing achievements, where so much that is distracting is present. There are wishes that die in being born; there are wishes that are forgotten like our yesterdays; there are wishes that one outgrows, and later can scarcely recall; there are wishes that one learns to give up, and how good it was to have given them up; there are wishes from which one dies. away, which one hides away, just as a departed one is hidden away in glorified memory. Those are the wishes to which an active person is exposed. They may be more or less dangerous diseases. Their cure may be accomplished by the extinction of the individual wish.

Yet there is also a wish that dies slowly, a wish that remains with the real sufferer even in the pain of his loss, and that only dies when he dies. For wishes concern particular objects, and a great number of objects, but the, wish applies essentially to the whole life.

Yet sad as it is with the wish, how joyful it is with hope! For there is a hope that is born and dies; a short-lived hope, that tomorrow is forgotten; a childish hope, that old age does not recognize; a hope that one dies away from. But then -- in death, in death's decision, a hope is born, that does not die in being born because it is born in death. By this hope the sufferer, under the pain of the wish, is committed to the Good. So it is with the hope in which the sufferer, as though from afar off, reaches out toward the Eternal.

With faith it is still more joyful. For there is a faith that disappoints and vanishes; a faith that is lost and is repented of; there is a faith, which, when it droops is like death. But then -- in death, in death's decision a faith is won that does not disappoint, that is not repented of, that does not die; it seizes the Eternal and holds fast to it. By this faith, under the pain of the wish, the sufferer is committed to the Good. So it is with faith in which the sufferer draws the Eternal nearer to himself.

But with love it is most joyous of all. For there is a love, that blazes up and is forgotten; there is a love that unites and divides -- a love until death. But then -- in death, in death's decision, there is born a love that does not flame up, that is not equivocal, that is not -- until death, but beyond death, a love that endures. In this love under the pain of the wish, the sufferer is committed to the Good. Oh, you sufferer, whoever you may be, will you then with doubleness of mind seek the relief that temporal existence can give, the relief that permits you to forget your suffering (yes, so you think) but rather that allows you to forget the Eternal! Will you in doubleness of mind despair, because all is lost (yes, so you think) yet with the Eternal all is to be won! Will you in doubleness of mind despair? Have you considered what it is to despair? Alas, it is to deny that God is love! Think that over properly, one who despairs abandons himself (yes, so you think); nay, he abandons God! Oh, weary not your soul with that which is passing and with momentary relief. Grieve not your spirit with forms of comfort which this world affords. Do not in suicidal fashion murder the wish; but rather win the highest by hope, by faith, by love -- as the mightiest of all are able to do: commit yourself to the Good!

Once again let us speak of the wish, and hence of sufferings. A discussion of sufferings may always be profitable if it does not confine itself to the stubbornness of the affliction but is concerned whenever possible with the edification of the sufferer. It is both permissible and an act of sympathy to dwell upon suffering in order that the sufferer may not become impatient with our superficial discussion in which he does not recognize his own suffering and in order that in such impatience he may not thrust aside all consolation and be strengthened in doublemindedness. It is indeed one thing to move out into life with the wish when that which is wished for, continued to be work and a task. It is another thing to move out into life away from that wish. Look at Abraham.(Genesis 12:1) He had to leave the home of his fathers and journey out among a strange people, where there was no reminder of that which he loved -- yes, it is true that sometimes it may be a consolation, that nothing reminds one of what he wishes to forget, but it is a bitter consolation for one who is filled with longing. Hence a man can also have a wish that for him contains all, so that in the hour of separation. when the journeying is begun, it is as if he wandered out into a strange land where nothing but the contrast with what he has lost reminds him of that which he wished for. It can be to him as if he journeyed into a strange land. even if he remains in his home, perhaps on the same spot -- through the loss of the wish, indeed, it may be as if he were among strangers, so that to suffer the loss of the wish seems to him heavier and more critical than the loss of his mind. Even if he does not leave the spot, his life moves along a laborious path away from that wish, perhaps into useless sufferings, for we are talking of the real sufferer, hence not of the ones who have the consolation that their sufferings are serving some good cause, are of benefit to others. It must have been like this: The journey to the strange country was not long; in a moment he was there, there in that strange country, where the sufferers were gathered, only not those that had stopped grieving; not those whose tears eternity cannot wipe away, for the reason that as an old religious writing so simply and so touchingly says, "how shall God be able in heaven to dry up your tears when you have not wept?"(Jose Arndt's True Christianity.)

Another comes perhaps by another way but to the same place. Silently, the guiding necessity leads him onward. Austere and earnest, not cruel, for it is never cruel, duty comes behind and brings up the rear of the company. But the path is not the path of the wish. Now he halts for a moment, even the two austere guides are touched by his suffering: look, there a side path branches off; "good-by, thou wish of my youth, thou friendly place, where I had hoped to be able to build and to dwell with my wish!" So they move on; the guiding necessity silently in advance, duty austere and silent comes behind, not cruel, for duty is never cruel. Alas, look, there a road runs off to the side that leads to the wish; "good-by, my place of work where by the full joy of work I had hoped to be able to forget the wishes I was denied in youth." So the company moved on. Yet the manner in which it happens does not matter, whether it be the spot that is altered and the sufferer remains at that same spot, or whether the sufferer changes his whereabouts and journeys away; this does not matter, if the place is the same, if they are gathered at this one place, which human language may well be tempted to call: the useless suffering that is beyond the reach of any comfort. The sufferings themselves could have different names, but let us not multiply names. Let us consider what is essential; that the real sufferer does not benefit others by his suffering, but rather is a burden upon them. If this latter is not the case, the former must then be so if the suffering is to be regarded as useless, that is, if the sufferer is in the strictest sense to be called a sufferer. In the strictest sense, and let us really be strict with ourselves in order that we may not venture to call ourselves sufferers, the first time anything goes against us; but let us be all the more tender with those who are in the strictest sense sufferers. Oh, such a sufferer, whoever you may be; if a man is come to the point in the land of his birth where every way of making a living is closed to him, then he thinks seriously of emigrating to a foreign country and there seeking his fortune. But perhaps you answer, "'What does that mean, how shall I be able to emigrate, and what good would it do me to change my location? My lot is cast, everywhere on earth it would be just the same." Of course, but let us understand one another; the journey of which we speak is not long, neither is the lot cast, unless you have already found the way out of your suffering: it is only a single step, a decisive step, and you, too, have emigrated, for the Eternal lies much nearer to you than any foreign country to the emigrant, and yet when you are there the change is infinitely greater. So then, go with God to God, continually take that one step more, that single step that even you, who cannot move a limb, are still able to take; that single step, that even the prisoner, who has lost his freedom, even the one in chains, whose feet are not free, is still able to take: and you are committed to the Good. Nobody, not even the greatest that has ever lived, can do more than you.

But bear in mind: your sufferings might well be called useless, and that we men can certainly be tempted to speak of useless suffering as beyond the reach of comfort. But this is only human speech. In the language of eternity, the suffering that helped you to reach the highest is far from useless. Alas, it is only useless and unused when you will not let yourself be helped by it up to the highest -- for perhaps you killed the wish and became spiritually like dead flesh that feels no pain, otherwise it is just at the point of the wish that the sufferer winces and that the Eternal comforts.

Let us once again speak of the wish, and hence of sufferings. It is well not to turn away from the sight of suffering too soon. Let us properly dwell upon it, being convinced that for the deadly disease of "busyness" there is no medicine so specific as the pondering of the hard path of the true sufferer and as a fellow human being sharing with him in the common lot of suffering. But alas, how often man's sympathetic sharing in the suffering of others stands in inverse ratio to the length of the suffering! For if the suffering is drawn out in length, sympathy tends to pall: as the suffering increases, the sympathy decreases. At the first appearance of suffering, men's sympathy rushes out to the victim. But when the suffering lingers on, then sympathy subsides, and, on the part of the busy individual when the first active stage of his sympathy has waned, this sympathy at times changes into a certain bitterness against the sufferer. Yes: wishes could be healed after a time, they could become a part of the past: but not the wish. There is a real distinction here, for there is a pain of the wish which sympathy can fix upon, but there is also a pain of the wish that eludes all scrutiny, that conceals itself and secretly follows through an entire life. Yes, it follows, but in the sense of privation. Yes, like a faithful companion this pain follows the sufferer throughout his whole life and keeps him company, but there is no sympathy in attendance. Now in what way ought we to speak of this wish that may possibly exist but that withdraws into concealment, and yet speak so that the sufferer will acknowledge the description, so that he will not take offense and impatiently turn away from our officious account of sufferings which we are either not capable or have not had the time to think ourselves into? Let us then, wherever possible in the description, speak with the sufferer's own tongue and leave it to God to communicate to his heart any light that he may have for him.

Let us assume that dumb animals could have thoughts and could make themselves understood to one another even though we could not make out what they said, let us take that for granted. It seems almost as if this were so. For when in summer the peasant's horse stands in the meadow and throws up his head or shakes it, surely no one can know with certainty what that means; or when two of them who throughout their lives have walked side by side pulling in the same yoke are turned out at night, when they approach one another as if in intimacy, when they almost caress each other by movements of the head; or when the free horses neigh to one another so that the woods echo, when they are gathered on the plains in a big herd as if at a public meeting -- assume then that they really could make themselves understood to one another.

But then there was one horse that was all alone. Now when this horse heard the call, when he saw that the herd was gathering in the evening, and he understood that they were about to hold a meeting, then he came running in the hope that he might learn something about life and its ways. He listened carefully to all that the elders had to say about how no horse should think himself fortunate until he is dead, how the horse of all creatures is most subject to the tragic changes of fate. And now the elder went over the many agonies: to suffer hunger and cold, to all but kill oneself through overwork, to be kicked by a cruel driver, to be abused by unskilled persons whom not a single step you take will satisfy, yet who blame and punish the horse for their own blunders, and then at last some winter, when old age has come on, to be driven out into the bare woods.

At this point the meeting broke up and that horse who had come with such eagerness went away dejected "by sorrow of the heart the spirit is broken" (Proverbs 15:13). He had understood perfectly all that had been said, but no one there had even as much as mentioned his sufferings. Yet each time he noticed the other horses hurrying off to a gathering he came running eagerly, hoping always that now it would be spoken of. And each time he listened he went away with a heavy heart. He came to understand better and better what the others were concerned about, but he came to understand himself less and less, just because it seemed as though the others excluded him, although he, too, was present.

Oh, you sufferer, whoever you may be, if your suffering was not hidden because you wished to hide it (for then you can manage; your action calls for a different comment) but if it is because of misunderstandings then you, too, have gone among men, listened carefully to their explanations, sought out their instruction, taken part in their meeting. But each time you finished the book, and each time the conversation was over, and each time the "Amen" was pronounced: then was your spirit broken because your heart grew troubled as you sighed: "Oh, that such a thing was all that I suffered from!" Oh, but you are not wholly wanting in being understood, for even if you yourself may have done nothing to deserve it, you shall be bidden to the highest thing of all, and to the Highest Himself. Nor are you wholly without human sympathy. There is a common human concern that is called edification. It is not so common as those undertakings about which the crowd shouts and clamors, for each participant is in reality alone with himself, but yet in the highest and most inclusive sense, edification is a common human concern. The edifying contemplation finds no rest until it has come to understand you. Is not one sinner who repents more important to Heaven than ninety nine righteous men(Luke 15:7.) who have no need of repentance? So it is with you if you are one who truly suffers, your edifying contemplation is more important than the actions of ninety-nine busy ones who have no need of edification. Yes, even if you did not exist, the edifying contemplation finds no rest before it has also plumbed this sorrow. For woe to the edifying talk that wishes only to chat between man and man about all the different inconveniences in life but does not dare risk touching upon the more terrible sufferings: such a talk is without frankness and can but have a bad conscience if it poses under the name of "edifying." The busy ones that neither toil nor are oppressed (Compare Matthew 11:28.) but are just busy, think that they have escaped when' they have contrived to avoid sufferings in this life; hence they do not wish to be disturbed either by hearing or thinking of that which is terrible. Yes, it is true that tibey have escaped. They have also escaped having any insight into life and have escaped into meaninglessness.

Oh, you sufferer, alone and abandoned as you are by the generation to which you belong, know that you are not abandoned by God, your creator. Everywhere you are surrounded by His understanding which offers itself to you at each moment. In it you unite your will with the Good. And the edifying contemplation is always ready to remind you of that presence; and its very existence is a source of security to the living.

As it is a comfort to seafarers to know that no matter on what strange water they may venture there are always pilots within call, so the edifying contemplation stands near the breakers and reefs of this life prepared by daily sight of terrible sufferings swiftly to render what little aid it can. Yet it cannot help in the way that a pilot helps the ship. The sufferer must help himself.

But then neither shall he owe to this or to any other man what the seafarer owes to the pilot. Indeed if this sufferer like anyone else sincerely wills the Good, then he must be ready to suffer all. Then he is committed, not in that commitment by which he is exempted from suffering, but in that by which he remains intimately bound to God, in which he wills only one thing: namely, to suffer all, to be and to remain loyally committed to the Good -- under the pain of the wish.

My listener! Perhaps you are tired of so much talk about suffering -- but an edifying talk never tires of it, no, a mother may sooner tire of nursing her sick child than the edifying talk of speaking of suffering. You are perhaps what is called a "happy one" whom talk of this kind tires. Yet surely you are not so happy as to wish to remain coldly ignorant of sufferings; on the contrary you aspire to this knowledge of suffering for your own sake in order that your education may be improved by its somber spectacle! Or perhaps you are a sufferer, who is wearied by talking of so many different kinds of suffering when yours is not even mentioned. Oh, to edify oneself in a living way with the sufferings of others is a comfort, and to dwell too exclusively on one's own suffering may easily become that doubleness of mind which thinks that there is comfort for all others but none for itself. But this is not so. For with suffering each has his own, be it great or small. But with comfort it is certainly true that there is comfort for all, and in fact the same comfort for all.

Now let us once again speak of the wish, and hence of sufferings, for the duration of the suffering makes it heavier and heavier. But its duration depends as a matter of fact upon when the suffering began. A shrewd pagan has wisely observed that a man can accustom himself to protracted sufferings. (Epicurus in Diogenes Laertus, 140.) But the question here is, whether such comfort is the right thing. For what is being considered here is not how to find the readiest and best source of comfort, but rather how to will the Good in truth, how to will to suffer all in order to be and to remain committed to the Good.

Let us speak of a whole life of sufferings or of some person whom nature, from the very outset, as we humans are tempted to say, wronged, someone who from birth was singled out by useless suffering: a burden to others; almost a burden to himself; and yes, what is worse, to be almost a born objection to the goodness of Providence. Alas, the career of many a busy man is described by and gives rise to fresh busyness. The contemplation of such an unfortunate one is an excellent antidote for busyness. For just by observing such a sufferer, one comes to know unmistakably what the highest is. But we will not speak carelessly or in passing, hastening away from the sight of this suffering, absorbed in rejoicing over our having been spared it. Neither shall we speak despondently.

To be sure it is wonderful to be a child, to fall asleep upon the mother's breast only to awaken to see the mother again; to be a child and to know only the mother and the toy! We laud the happiness of childhood. The very sight of it soothes us by its smile, so that even the one to whom fortune is granted does not forget this down through the years. But, God be praised, it is not so ordered, that this should be the highest thing of all. It may be dispensed with without losing the highest thing of all. It may be absent without having lost the highest thing of all.

And to be sure it is fine to be young, to lie sleepless with the ferment of joyful thoughts, and to fall asleep only to wake up early with the song of the birds to continue the gaiety! We laud the happiness of youth. We rejoice with the joyful ones. We wish that youth might feel grateful for its happiness, and in the future we wish that it might be thankful for that which has vanished. But, God be praised, it is not so ordered that this should be the highest thing of all. It may be dispensed with without losing the highest thing of all. It may be absent without having lost the highest thing of all.

And to be sure it is blessed to love, to be reduced to a single desire. What does it matter if all other desires are fulfilled or denied? There is but one desire, the loved one; one longing, the loved one; one possession, the loved one! We laud the happiness of love. Oh, that the fortunate one may be steadfast in the daily thankfulness of domestic life; that he may be faithful in the continuing thankfulness of remembrance. But, God be praised, it is not so ordered that this should be the highest thing of all. It may be dispensed with without losing the highest thing of all. It may be absent without having lost the highest thing of all.

But now the sufferer! Alas, there was no happy childhood for him. Of course a mother's love is faithful and tender, especially toward an ailing child. But a mother is also a human being. When he lay at his mother's breast, she did not gaze joyfully upon him. He saw that she was troubled. Sometimes when he wakened he noticed her weeping.

Even among grown-ups when they sit about depressed, let a man appear at the door, a happy, gifted one with light heart and gay spirit, and let him say, "Here am I!" and at once the merriment begins, and the clouds of care are routed. Such a gifted one is uncommon. But even the rarest genius of all, when can he bring in comparison to a child, when it makes its entrance amid the agonizing pain of the birth hour, opens the door and says, "Here am I!" Oh, the good fortune of childhood, to be so welcome!

Then he grew into a youth, but he never played with the others, and if someone asked him, "Why do you not play with the others?" he might well have replied, "How have you the heart to ask me such a question?" So he withdrew from life, yet not with the object of dying, for he was still only a youth.

Then came the season of love, but no one loved him. Of course there were a few that were friendly toward him, but it was out of compassion and sympathy. Then he became a man, but he stood apart from life. Then he died, but even here he was not spared. For the little band that made up the mourner's train all said it was a blessing that God took him away, and the priest said the same thing. Then he was dead, and then he was forgotten -- together with all of his useless sufferings. When he was born there was no gladness or rejoicing, only fearful dismay; when he died there was no grief or affliction, only a melancholy joy. In this fashion his life was passed, or, to speak more accurately, is passed, for this is not an ancient fairy tale that I am telling, of what has happened to an "individual" in bygone days. The same thing happens frequently. It lies close enough to us even though frivolity and sensuousness, worldly cleverness and godlessness wish to remain ignorant of it. It lies close enough to us even though they wish to keep away from any such unfortunate ones and to avoid all sober reminders not alone from the careless judgment of the storyteller's art, but also from the church and from the edifying insight that must certainly know that the Holy Scriptures have almost a predilection for the halt and the lame, the blind and the lepers. When the disciples began to seem "busy," Christ set a little child in their midst.(Mark 9:36) The crowd that storms and blusters in the bewildered name of the century might well tempt a serious man to set just such an unfortunate sufferer in their midst. The sight of him certainly would not detain anyone that willed anything eternal; but busyness has nothing whatever to do with the Eternal.

He, the sufferer, took part in life -- by living. But to his life one thing was unknown, a thing which in all relations of life, as in the passion of love, makes for happiness: to be able to give and to receive "like for like." This "like for like" he never received, and he himself could never give; for as a sufferer he was always an object of sympathy and compassion. No, he never got like for like, not as a child, so that if others saddened his mother he might make her happy merely by smiling as he wakened. No, he never got like for like, for he loved his playmates in a different way than they loved him. No, he never got like for like, and therefore he got no mate. All through his life he could never do anything to repay others. And even in death he did not get like for like, for he was not mourned, as he had mourned those dear to him. He died, but what did the mourners and the priest say there except, "God be praised." Do not all these things cut him off from the highest?

Oh, you sufferer, wherever you may be, wherever you hide from the sight of men in order to spare them from being reminded of the pitiable, oh, do not forget that you, too, can accomplish something. Do not let your life consume itself in a futile counting up of the worthless sufferings of the days and years. Do not forget that you can accomplish something. If some feigned sufferer wishes to throw himself upon others because of a slight adversity, this does not mean that he should be told as is sometimes done, that he can accomplish something for others. For one who is capable of accomplishing something for others is not regarded by the edifying contemplation as in the strictest sense a sufferer. Instead he would be harsh with him. Oh, you true sufferer, even though your very suffering cuts you off from any such service to others, you can still do -- the highest thing of all. You can will to suffer all and thereby be committed to the Good. Oh, blessed justice, that the true sufferer can unconditionally do the highest quite as well as fortune's favorite child! Honor and praise be to the Eternal, in whom is no shadow of turning, in whom is neither malice nor favoritism but perfect justice. By willing to suffer all you are committed to the Good, having changed your garments -- yes, as when the dead rise up and cast off their grave clothes, so you have cast off the mantle of your misery. Now you are indistinguishable from those whom you wish to be like-those that are committed to the Good. All are clothed alike, girded about the loins with truth, arrayed in the armor of righteousness and wearing the helmet of salvation!(Ephesians 6:14, 17). If it be so, and it is the hope of every good man that there is a resurrection where there shall be no difference, where the deaf man shall hear, the blind man see, where he that bore a form of misery shall be fair like all the others, then there is indeed on this side of the grave some such resurrection each time a man, by willing to do all or to suffer all, rises up by entering into the commitment, and remains bound to the Good in the commitment. The sole difference is the pain of the wish in the him into the sufferer. But at the same time this may be a help to bring him into the decision.

The sufferer must therefore be willing to suffer all. This means equally to be willing to do all: to bring it to a commitment, to be and to remain loyal to the Good in the commitment. While it is true that the pain of the wish is the sign that the suffering in a way continues; yet the healing also continues, as long as the sufferer remains firm in the commitment. But there is a force that is momentarily powerful. It is cleverness. From cleverness and from the moment, or through it and from the moment, a man's destruction is born -- if it is a fact that a man's salvation comes in the Eternal and by the Eternal. Now cleverness may be inwardly misused; for outwardly a true sufferer has little chance of misusing it. Cleverness in this inner realm is rich in evasions by which the time is put off and the decision is postponed. It will come to understand the decision only in an earthly and temporal sense. From its momentary standpoint, it has in view only a decision by which the suffering shall be brought to an end. But be assured, the Eternal does not heal in this fashion. The palsied man does not become whole, because he has been healed by the Eternal, nor the leper clean, nor the deformed made physically perfect. "But then it is a useless device, this help of the Eternal," cleverness suggests, "and what is still worse, is this decision, where the sufferer dedicates himself to his suffering, which indeed makes his condition hopeless" -- because the decision renounces the juggling hope of temporal existence. Where the Eternal does not come to heal such a sufferer, what happens, with the aid of cleverness, is about as follows: first, the sufferer lives for some years by an earthly hope; but when this is exhausted and the suffering still continues, then he becomes superstitious, his state of health alternates between drowsiness and burning excitement. As the suffering continues, there settles over him finally a dull despair, broken only rarely by an unnatural and terribly enfeebling intensity, as when the gambler hopes on and on that some day he will meet with luck. Alas, at length a man sees what cleverness and this earthly hope amount to! For to cleverness it seems so clever "that one should not foolishly give up an earthly hope for a possible mythical healing" -- in order to win the Eternal. To cleverness it seems so cunning "that one would not decide to say farewell to the earth; indeed, one can never know what possibly could happen . . . and then one would regret" -- that one had let himself be healed by the Eternal. The earthly hope and the heavenly hope grew up well together and played together in childhood like born equals, but the difference reveals itself in the decision. Yet, this hinders cleverness which steadily hinders the decision. Those who cling to life put off the time, have countless inventions whose genius is this: that one must not take life and his own sorrows too much to heart, that it was just possible, who can know that -- etc.

When the sufferer actually takes his suffering to heart, then he receives help from the Eternal toward his decision. Because to take one's suffering to heart is to be weaned from the temporal order, and from cleverness and from excuses, and from clever men and women and from anecdotes about this and that, in order to find rest in the blessed trustworthiness of the Eternal. For the sufferer, it is as if one should liken him to a sick man who turns himself from side to side, and now at last discovers the position in which there is relief -- even if the wish still pains. Even if it was only a trifle, one can never have taken something too much to heart, when in taking it so to heart he thereby wins the Eternal.

But the sufferer who does not wish to be healed by the Eternal is double-minded. The doublemindedness in him is a disease that gnaws and gnaws and eats away the noblest powers; the injury is internal and infinitely more dangerous than being deformed and palsied. This doubleminded one wishes to be healed and yet does not wish to be healed: eternally, he does not wish to be healed. But the temporal cure is uncertain, and the different stages in the scale of uncertainty are marked by increasing restlessness, in his double-mindedness. When the double-minded man comes to the final moment of his life, cleverness will still be sitting at his deathbed and explaining that one cannot know what might suddenly and unexpectedly happen. Under no circumstances should a messenger be sent after the clergyman, for cleverness is so afraid of the decision that it even regards the clergyman's coming as a tacit decision, and indeed one can never know what suddenly and unexpectedly might happen. So the double-minded one dies, and now the survivors know for certain that the deceased was not cured of his long-standing suffering by any sudden and unexpected means. Alas, the Eternal is a riddle for the one who, m the clever sense of the moment, loves the world. Over and over again he thinks, what if some temporal help should suddenly appear, then I would be trapped, I, who by commitment to the Eternal had died to the temporal. He prefers to say, one still regards the temporal as the highest, one looks upon the Eternal as a kind of desperate "last resort." Therefore, one objects to giving it the decision for as long as possible. And even if temporal help is the most absurd and unreasonable of all expectations, yet one would sooner whip up his superstitious imagination to hope for it than to lay hold on the Eternal. One is constantly afraid that he might live to regret it, and yet the Eternal, if one honestly lays hold on it, is the only thing, absolutely the only thing of which it may be said without reservation, it will never be regretted. But because of this fear that he should one day regret committing himself to the Eternal, a man deserves some day to be compelled to regret bitterly that he allowed the time to pass by.

Oh, it is indeed a shallow cleverness (no matter how much it brags or how loquacious it may be) that stupidly cheats itself out of the highest consolation, getting along with a mediocre and even less than mediocre consolation and ending in inevitable remorse. Even if the sufferer is able to use his cleverness in such a way as to give his double-mindedness a little better public appearance than is depicted here, that in no way affects the real situation. If he uses cleverness to hinder commitment to the Eternal, he is. double-minded. He is, and he remains doubleminded, even, if temporal help did come and he did revel in the cleverness by which he had managed his shrewd escape; yes, one should still believe that it was a calamity that he cleverly; managed to evade commitment to the Eternal. Commitment to the Eternal is the only true salvation. Therefore it is also double-mindedness when the sufferer uses his strength to conceal the pain instead of letting himself be healed by the Eternal. Such a sufferer is not seeking release from the suffering but only from a sympathy, in so far as this also can be an affliction. Therein lies the contradictory character of double-mindedness. For only by commitment to the Eternal may he become really free from the painfulness of sympathy, since by the commitment he really overcomes the suffering. Hence only the wish pains, while the Eternal cures.

In relation to the sufferer, all double-mindedness has its ground in and is marked by the double-minded one's unwillingness to let go of the things of this world. In the same way the double-minded talk that is from time to time addressed to the sufferer may be recognized by the fact that it puts its trust in the things of this world. It is only too often the case that the sufferer shrinks from receiving the highest comfort, and the speaker is ashamed to offer the highest consolation. Contrary to the truth, the consoling talk seeks to offer comfort by saying that the illness will soon be better -- perhaps; and begs for some little patience. It coddles the sufferer a little, and says that by Sunday all will surely be going well. Yet why give a pauper, if we may for a moment compare the sufferer with a pauper, silver or even counterfeit coin when one has a rich supply of gold to offer him? For the Eternal's comfort is pure gold. Let us remember the active one even though his suffering is always different from that of a real sufferer. We read of the Apostles,(Acts 5:40-41) that when they were scourged they went on their way rejoicing and gave thanks to God. Here there is no talk of having a little patience, and of things going well by Sunday; but here is found the Eternal's victorious comfort, and these scourged Apostles have more than conquered. So, too, shall it be with the true sufferer. For when the Eternal heals, the wish continues to pain (for the Eternal does not remove the sufferer from time), but there is no whining, no temporary distraction, no deceitful evasion. One knows well enough that when the true sufferer has whined himself through time and by all kinds of imaginings has managed to pass away the time or to kill time: still eternity stands open to him. Alas, no, the true sufferer must also answer for the manner in which he has used his time, answer for whether or not he has used the earthly misery to allow himself eternally to be healed. But cleverness asserts, "still, one should never give up hope." "You hypocrite," answers the Eternal, "why do you speak so equivocally? You know well enough that there is a hope that should be put to death; that there is a lust and a desire and a longing that should be slain. Earthly hope should be put to death, for in just this way did man first come to be saved by the true hope." Therefore, the sufferer should never be willing to "accept deliverance" (Hebrews 11:15) on this world's terms.

Chapter 11: The Price of Willing One Thing: The Sufferer's Use of Cleverness to Expose Evasion

But the sufferer who sincerely wills the Good, uses this very cleverness to cut off evasions and hence to launch himself into the commitment and to escape the disillusionments of choosing the temporal way. He does not fear the mark of the commitment that, as it were, draws the suffering over him; for he knows that this mark is the breaking through of the Eternal. He knows that in the Commitment the nerve of the temporal order is being cut, even though pain continues in the wish. There is no doubt that what often makes a sufferer impatient is that he takes upon himself in advance the suffering of a whole lifetime and now quails before what would be lighter to bear if he were to take each day's burden as it comes.

The commitment should not Concentrate sufferings in this way. For the error is just this, that in spite of all his advance acceptance of suffering, the sufferer wins nothing that is eternal but only becomes terrified in a temporal sense. Because of the uncertainty of the temporal order, it is also true that over a period of many years a sufferer may talk himself out of the original impression of the commitment. And this is a calamity. On that account the sufferer who sincerely wills the Good knows that cleverness is a treacherous friend, and that only the commitment is fully trustworthy.

The active one will do all for the Good, the sufferer will suffer all for the Good. The similarity is that they both may be and remain committed to the Good. Only the direction in which they work is different, and this difference must not be understood as making them mutually exclusive. The active one works from without in order that the Good may conquer; even his suffering has significance from its bearing upon this goal. The true sufferer does everything inwardly (by being willing to suffer all) for the Good in order that it may conquer in him. Yet the Good must have conquered and must continue to conquer in the active one's own heart, if he sincerely works for the Good outwardly. The true sufferer can always work for the Good outwardly by the power of example, and work effectually. For his life, just because so much is denied him, contains a great challenge to the many to whom much is given. His life when he is and remains committed to the Good, contains a severe judgment upon the many, who use in an inexcusable way the much that has been given them. Yes, even if the sufferer were denied this working by the power of example, even if he were cut off from all other men, he would still be sharing in mankind's great common concern. On his lonely outpost he, too, would be defending a difficult pass by saving his own soul from all of the ensnaring difficulties of suffering. Although not a single man should see him, mankind feels with him, suffers with him, and conquers with him! For everywhere that the Good truly conquers, the victory is really as great whether the Good conquers in the many by means of one, or whether it conquers in a solitary forsaken one by his own efforts; in reality the victory is equally great. Oh, praised be the blessed justice of the Eternal!

Yet one thing still remains to be discussed before leaving the matter of sufferings: Can one be said to will suffering? Is not suffering something that one must be forced into against his will? If a man can be free of it, can he then will it, and if he is bound to it, can he be said to will it? If we would answer this question, let us first of all distinguish between what it is to will in the sense of inclination, and what it is to will in the noble sense of freedom. Yes, for many men it is almost an impossibility for them to unite freedom and suffering in the same thought. Hence, when they see a man of means who could spend his time easily and comfortably, when they see him straining himself as much as a scrupulous workman, exposing himself to many sufferings, choosing the burdensome way of a higher calling: they look upon him as either a fanatic or a lunatic. They all but complain that Providence has given all of these fortunate circumstances to someone that simply does not know how to make use of them. They think in their hearts even when they do not say it aloud, even when they do not consider how tragically they are betraying their own inner life: "We should have been there in his place, we should have really known how to enjoy that life." According to this, if one can be free of suffering it is either fanaticism or insanity to will it.

But what then is courage? Is it courage to go where pleasure beckons in order to see where pleasure is? Or, in order for courage to be revealed, is it not required that there be opposition (which even language seems to indicate)(The Dutch word for "courage" is Mod and for "opposition" is Modstand,[Tr.]) as though the courageous person looks the danger in the eye, even though the danger is not what the eye wants to see? To illustrate, is it not as when the courageous knight spurs his horse forward against some terrifying object? There is no tremor of fear in his eye because courage controls even the expression of the eye. Yet the knight and the horse illustrate the structure of courage. The knight is the courageous one, the horse is skittish. The horse and its skittishness answer to that which is low in a man and its skittishness is that which courage checks. In this way, courage voluntarily wills suffering. The courageous one has a treacherous opposition within himself that is in league with the opposition without. But just on that account, he is the courageous one, because in spite of it he voluntarily wills the suffering.

On the other hand (and this is what we must primarily consider, for we are speaking of the true sufferer), the sufferer can voluntarily accept that suffering which in one sense is forced upon him, in so far as he does not have it in his power to get rid of it. Can anyone but one who is free of suffering, say, "Put me in chains, I am not afraid"? Can even a prisoner say, "Of my own free will I accept my imprisonment" -- the very imprisonment which is already his condition? Here again the opinion of most men is that such a thing is impossible, and that therefore the condition of the sufferer is one of sighing despondency. But what then is patience? (The Danish word for "patience," Taalmod, contains the Danish word for "courage," Mod, and invites the discourse which follows. (Tr.) Is patience not precisely that courage which voluntarily accepts unavoidable suffering? The unavoidable is just the thing which will shatter courage. There is a treacherous opposition in the sufferer himself that is in league with the dread of inevitability, and together they wish to crush him. But in spite of this, patience submits to suffering and by just this submission finds itself free in the midst of unavoidable suffering. Thus patience, if one may put it in this way, performs an even greater miracle than courage. Courage voluntarily chooses suffering that may be avoided; but patience achieves freedom in unavoidable suffering. By his courage, the free one voluntarily lets himself be caught, but by his patience the prisoner effects his freedom -- although not in the sense that need make the jailer anxious or fearful.

The outward impossibility of ridding oneself of suffering does not hinder the inward possibility of being able really to emancipate oneself within suffering -- of one's own free will accepting suffering, as the patient one gives his consent by willing to accept suffering. For one can be forced into the narrow prison, one can be forced into lifelong sufferings, and necessity is the tyrant; but one cannot be forced into patience. If the tyrant necessity presses upon a soul which neither possesses nor wills to possess the elasticity of freedom, then the soul becomes depressed, but it does not become patient. Patience is the counterpressure of resiliency, whereby the coerced ones are set free from restraint. Or can only the rich man be economical because he may, if he likes, be extravagant? Cannot the poor man also be economical even though he is powerless to be extravagant, even though he is forced to be -- economical? No, he cannot be forced to be economical even though he is forced to be poor. Alas, the wisdom of many men seems calculated to abolish the Good. When a person of means voluntarily chooses the hard way, then he is called strange, "he who could be so well off without working and who could indulge his every desire for comfort." And when the victim of unavoidable suffering bears it patiently, one says of him, "to his shame, he is coerced, and he is making a virtue out of a necessity." Undeniably he is making a virtue out of a necessity, that is just the secret, that is certainly a most accurate designation for what he does. He makes a virtue out of necessity. He brings a determination of freedom out of that which is determined as necessity. And it is just there that the healing power of the decision for the Eternal resides: that the sufferer may voluntarily accept the compulsory suffering. Just as it is a relief to the sufferer to open himself in confidence to a friend, so it is deliverance to the sufferer to commit himself to the Eternal even though the compulsion of necessity should press against his heart, it is deliverance to open himself to the Eternal and to consent eternally to be willing to suffer all.

For that man is captive indeed for whom a door stands open: the trapdoor of eternity! And he is indeed in bonds, who is eternally free! When Paul said, "I am a Roman citizen,"(Compare Acts 22:27-30, and 24:23.)the prefect did not dare to put him into prison, and he was placed in voluntary confinement. In like fashion when a man dares declare, "I am eternity's free citizen," necessity cannot imprison him, except in voluntary confinement.

My listeners! If you are willing, let us recall the direction that our talk has taken. If a man should will one thing, then he must will the Good, for in this way alone was it possible for him to will a single thing. If, however, it is to be genuine, he must will the Good in truth. According to whether he is an active one or a sufferer he must be willing either to do all for the Good, or he must be willing to suffer all for the Good. He must be willing either to do all for the Good, or to be and to remain committed to the Good. But cleverness may be misused internally, to seek evasions; and misused externally in deception. The good man, on the contrary, uses cleverness to cut off all evasions and thereby to launch out and to remain constant -- in the commitment. He also uses cleverness to prevent such external deception. He must be willing to suffer all for the Good, or to be and to remain committed to the Good. And the talk went on to describe the true sufferer's condition, because by looking at sufferings one may really learn what the highest is. Once again in regard to suffering, cleverness may be misused internally to seek ways of escape, but the Good man makes use of just this very cleverness against ways of escape, in order that he may be and remain committed to the Good, by being willing to suffer all, by accepting the enforced necessity of suffering.

But purity of heart is to will one thing. It is this thesis that has been the object of the talk which we have linked to the apostolic words: "Draw nigh to God and he will draw nigh to you, cleanse your hands, ye sinners, and purify your hearts, ye double-minded!" For commitment to the Good is a whole-souled decision, and a man cannot by the craft and the flattery of his tongue lay hold of God while his heart is far away. No, for since God is spirit and truth, a man can only draw near to Him by sincerity, by willing to be holy, as He is holy:(Compare I Peter 1-16.) by purity of heart. Purity of heart: it is a figure of speech that compares the heart to the sea, and why just to this? Simply for the reason that the depth of the sea determines its purity, and its purity determines its transparency. Since the sea is pure only when it is deep, and is transparent only when it is pure, as soon as it is impure it is no longer deep but only surface water, and as soon as it is only surface water it is not transparent. When, on the contrary, it is deeply and transparently pure, then it is all of one consistency, no matter how long one looks at it; then its purity is this constancy in depth and transparency. On this account we compare the heart with the sea, because the purity of the sea lies in its constancy of depth and transparency. No storm may perturb it; no sudden gust of wind may stir its surface, no drowsy fog may sprawl out over it; no doubtful movement may stir within it; no swift-moving cloud may darken it: rather it must lie calm, transparent to its depths. And today if you should see it so, you would be drawn upwards by contemplating the purity of the sea. If you saw it every day, then you would declare that it is forever pure -- like the heart of that man who wills but one thing. As the sea, when it lies calm and deeply transparent, yearns for heaven, so may the pure heart, when it is calm and deeply transparent, yearn for the Good. As the sea is made pure by yearning for heaven alone; so may the heart become pure by yearning only for the Good. As the sea mirrors the elevation of heaven in its pure depths, so may the heart when it is calm and deeply transparent mirror the divine elevation of the Good in its pure depths. If the least thing comes in between, between the heavens and the sea, between the heart and the Good, then it would be sheer impatience to covet the reflection. For if the sea is impure, it cannot give a pure reflection of the heavens.

Chapter 12: What Then Must I Do? The Listener's Role in a Devotional Address

My listener! This talk was brought forth upon the occasion of the office of Confession. If after the opening references to this occasion no more has been said of it, yet it has never been forgotten in the talk. For what has been given is most intimately connected with what is appropriate to an address of invitation to such an occasion. From its single point of departure - *to will one thing,* the talk has moved out in different directions, ever returning, however, to this point of departure. It has at the same time scanned the earth, making note of human differences. From time to time it has depicted the individual error and the state of soul of one who has lost his way. This has been done on a magnified scale, so that man may the better become aware of, and look out for, what, in the trivial circumstances of daily life so rarely appears unmixed that it is much harder to detect than are these instances that are "writ large." As it has proceeded, the talk, holding tenaciously to the demand -- *to will one thing* -- has taught how to recognize many errors, disappointments, deceptions, and self-deceptions. It has striven to track down double-mindedness into its hidden ways, and to ferret out its secret. By striving at every possible point to make itself intelligible, the talk has sought to bring these things within the reach of each listener. But the intelligibility of the talk, and the listener's understanding of it, are still not the talk's true aim. This by no means gives the meditation its proper emphasis. For in order to achieve its proper emphasis the task must unequivocally demand something of the listener. It must demand not merely what has previously been requested, that the reader should share in the work with the speaker -- now the talk must unconditionally demand the reader's own decisive activity, and all depends upon this.

So, my listener, turn your attention now to the occasion, while consciousness of sin sharpens the need until it becomes the one thing necessary; while the earnestness of this holy place strengthens the will in holy determination, while the all-knowing One's presence makes selfdeception impossible, consider your own life! The talk, which is without authority, will not have the presumption to pass judgment upon you. By vigorously pondering the occasion you will stand before a higher judge, where no man dares judge another since he himself is one of the accused. The talk does not address itself to you as if to a particularly designated person, for it does not know who you are. But if you weigh the occasion vigorously, then it will be to you, whoever you may be, it will be as if it spoke precisely to you. This is not due to any merit in the talk. It is the product of your own activity that for your own sake the talk is helpful to you; and it will be because of your own activity that you will be the one to whom the intimate "thou" is spoken. This is your own activity, it really is. Alas, above all let us not be drawn away from the decision by any attention to the speaker and the artistry of the talk. If this happens, then busyness and double-mindedness are again to blame that the emphasis in the composition is wrongly placed. In this case the devotional speaker is admired for his art, his eloquence, while that decision of which each man is capable, and that which it may be well to note, is the highest thing of all, is completely ignored. In a devotional sense, to be eloquent is a mere frill in the same way that to be beautiful is a happy privilege, but is still a non-essential frill. In a devotional sense, earnestness: to listen in order to act, this is the highest thing of all, and, God be praised, every man is capable of it if he so wills. Yet busyness places its most weighty emphasis upon the frills, the capacity to please, and looks upon earnestness as nothing at all. In a contemptuous and frivolous fashion, busyness thinks that to be eloquent is the highest thing of all and that the task of the listener is to pass judgment on whether the speaker has this gift.

In order that no irregularity may be admitted or no double-mindedness left unmentioned, let me then at this point, where the demand is being made for a person's own activity, briefly illustrate the relation between the speaker and the listener in a devotional address. Let me in order once again to take up arms against double-mindedness, make this illustration by borrowing a picture from worldly art. And do not let the two senses in which this may be taken disturb you or give you grounds for accusing the address of impropriety. For if you have dared to attend an exhibition of worldly art, then by doing this, you yourself must have come to understand what is meant by spiritual. Therefore you must have considered the spiritual with the worldly art even though it was the means of your first distinct recognition of the difference between the two. If you did not, discord and double-mindedness are in your own heart, so that you live for periods of time on the worldly plane with only an occasional thought of the spiritual. It is so on the stage, as you know well enough, that someone sits and prompts by whispers; he is the inconspicuous one, he is, and wishes to be overlooked. But then there is another, he strides out prominently, he draws every eye to himself. For that reason he has been given his name, that is: actor.(The Danish word for "actor," *Skuespiller*, means literally *show* or *display – player*. [Tr.]) He impersonates a distinct individual. In the skillful sense of this illusory art, each word becomes true when embodied in him, true through him -- and yet he is told what he shall say by the hidden one that sits and whispers. No one is so foolish as to regard the prompter as more important than the actor.

Now forget this light talk about art. Alas, in regard to things spiritual, the foolishness of many is this, that they in the secular sense look upon the speaker as an actor, and the listeners as theatergoers who are to pass judgment upon the artist. But the speaker is not the actor -- not in the remotest sense. No, the speaker is the prompter. There are no mere theatergoers present, for each listener will be looking into his own heart. The stage is eternity, and the listener, if he is the true listener (and if he is not, he is at fault) stands before God during the talk. The prompter whispers to the actor what he is to say, but the actor's repetition of it is the main concern -- is the solemn charm of the art. The speaker whispers the word to the listeners. But the main concern is earnestness: that the listeners by themselves, with themselves, and to themselves, in the silence before God, may speak with the help of this address.

The address is not given for the speaker's sake, in order that men may praise or blame him. The listener's repetition of it is what is aimed at. If the speaker has the responsibility for what he whispers, then the listener has an equally great responsibility not to fall short in his task. In the theater, the play is staged before an audience who are called theatergoers; but at the devotional address, God himself is present. In the most earnest sense, God is the critical theatergoer, who looks on to see how the lines are spoken and how they are listened to: hence here the customary audience is wanting. The speaker is then the prompter, and the listener stands openly before God. The listener, if I may say so, is the actor, who in all truth acts before God.

Oh, let us never forget this, let us not reduce the spiritual to the worldly. Even though we may earnestly think of the spiritual and the worldly together, let us forever distinguish between them. As soon as the spiritual is looked upon in worldly fashion (an observation for which one has the same foolishness to thank as that which would look upon the prompter in a play as more important than the actor) then the speaker becomes an actor and the listeners become critical theatergoers. In the same way, from the secular point of view, the devotional address is simply held for a group of attenders and God is no more present than he is in the theater. God's presence is the decisive thing that changes all. As soon as God is present, each man in the presence of God has the task of paying attention to himself. The speaker must see that during the address he pays attention to himself, to what he says; the listener, that during the address he pays attention to himself, to how he listens, and whether during the address he, in his inner self, secretly talks with God. If this were not done, then the listeners would be presuming to share God's task with him, God and the listeners together would watch the speaker and pass judgment upon him. So it is with the true relationship of speaker and listener in a devotional address.

Or to put it in another way, it is as if a subordinate functionary of the church, who is without authority should read aloud the prescribed prayer. Properly speaking, it is not the church functionary who prays. The one who prays is the listener who sits in the church and opens himself to God while he listens to the reading of the prayer. Yet the listener does not speak, his voice is not heard, nor does he pray softly to himself; but silently and with his heart he is praying in the presence of God by means of the audible voice of the one who reads out the prayer, and whispers to him what he shall say. Yet this is not earnestness: that one man shall tell another or dictate to another what he shall say. But this *is* earnestness: that the other man now should tell it to God speaking for himself. Now we have come to a clear understanding about this, and the demand will only be repeated in order that the speaker may focus his mind actively upon the occasion of the address.

The talk asks you, then, or you ask yourself by means of the talk, *what kind of life do you live, do you will only one thing, and what is this one thing?* The talk does not expect that you will name off any goal that only pretends to be one thing. For it does not intend to address itself to anyone with whom it would not be able to deal seriously, for the reason that such a man has cut himself off from any earnest consideration of the occasion of the address. There is still another reason: a man can, to be sure, have an extremely different, yes, have a precisely opposite opinion from ours, and one can nevertheless deal earnestly with him if one assumes that finally there may be a point of agreement, a unity in some universal human sense, call it what you will. But if he is mad, then one cannot deal with him, for he shies away from just that final point, in which one at last may hope to find agreement with him. One can dispute with a man, dispute to the furthest limit, as long as one assumes, that in the end there is a point in common, an agreement in some universal human sense: in self-respect. But when, in his worldly strivings he sets out like a madman in a desperate attempt to despise himself, and in the face of this is brazen about it and lauds himself for his infamy, then one can undertake no disputing with him. For like a madman, and even more terribly, he shies away from this final thing (self-respect) in which one might at last hope to find agreement with him.

The talk assumes, then, that you will the Good and asks you now, *what kind of life you live, whether or not you truthfully will only one thing.* It does not ask inquisitively about your calling in life, about the number of workers you employ, or about how many you have under you in your office, or if you happen to be in the service of the state. No, the talk is not inquisitive. It asks you above all else, it asks you first and foremost, whether you really live in such a way that you are capable of answering that question, in such a way that the question truthfully exists for you. Because in order to be able earnestly to answer that serious question, a man must already have made a choice in life, he must have chosen the invisible, chosen that which is within. He must have lived so that he has hours and times in which he collects his mind, so that his life can win the transparency that is a condition for being able to put the question to himself and for being able to answer it -- if, of course, it is legitimate to demand that a man shall know whereof he speaks. To put such a question to the man that is so busy in his earthly work, and outside of this in joining the crowd in its noisemaking, would be folly that would lead only to fresh folly -- through the answer.

Chapter 13: What Then Must I Do? Live as an "Individual"

The talk asks you, then, *whether you live in such a way that you are conscious of being an individual."* The question is not of the inquisitive sort, as if one asked about that "individua1" in some special sense, about the one whom admiration and envy unite in pointing out. No, it is the serious question, of what each man really is according to his eternal vocation, so that he himself shall be conscious that he is following it; and what is even more serious, to ask it as if he were considering his life before God. This consciousness is the fundamental condition for truthfully willing only one thing. For he who is not himself a unity is never really anything wholly and decisively; he only exists in an external sense -- as long as he lives as a numeral within the crowd, a fraction within the earthly conglomeration. Alas, how indeed should such a one decides to busy himself with the thought: truthfully to will only one thing!

Indeed, it is precisely this consciousness that must be asked for. Just as if the talk could not ask in generalities, but rather asks you as an individual. Or, better still, my listener, if you would ask yourself, whether you have this consciousness, whether you are actively contemplating the occasion of this talk. For in the outside world, the crowd is busy making a noise. The one makes a noise because he heads the crowd, the many because they are members of the crowd. But the all-knowing One, who in spite of anyone is able to observe it all, does not desire the crowd. He desires the individual; He will deal only with the individual, quite unconcerned as to whether the individual be of high or low station, whether he be distinguished or wretched.

Each man himself, as an individual, should render his account to God. No third person dares venture to intrude upon this accounting between God and the individual. Yet the talk, by putting its question, dares and ought to dare, to remind man, in a way never to be forgotten, that the most ruinous evasion of all is to be hidden in the crowd in an attempt to escape God's supervision of him as an individual, in an attempt to get away from hearing God's voice as an individual. Long ago, Adam attempted this same thing when his evil conscience led him to imagine that he could hide himself among the trees. It may even be easier and more convenient, and more cowardly to hide oneself among the crowd in the hope that God should not be able to recognize one from the other. But in eternity each shall render account as an individual. That is, eternity will demand of him that he shall have lived as an individual.

Eternity will draw out before his consciousness, all that he has done as an individual, he who had forgotten himself in noisy self-conceit. In eternity, he shall be brought to account strictly as an individual, he who intended to be in the crowd where there should be no such strict reckoning. Each one shall render account to God as an individual. The King shall render account as an individual; and the most wretched beggar, as an individual. No one may pride himself at being more than an individual, and no one despondently think that he is not an individual, perhaps because here in earth's busyness he had not as much as a name, but was named after a number.

For, after all, what is eternity's accounting other than that the voice of conscience is forever installed with its eternal right to be the exclusive voice? What is it other than that throughout eternity an infinite stillness reigns wherein the conscience may talk with the individual about what he, as an individual, of what he has done of Good or of evil, and about the fact that during his life he did not wish to be an individual? What is it other than that within eternity there is infinite space so that each person, as an individual, is apart with his conscience? For in eternity there is no mob pressure, no crowd, no hiding place in the crowd, as little as there are riots or street fights! Here in the temporal order conscience is prepared to make each person into an individual. But here in the temporal order, in the unrest, in the noise, in the pressure of the mob, in the crowd, in the primeval forest of evasion, alas, it is true, the calamity still happens, that someone completely stifles the voice of his conscience -- his conscience, for he can never rid himself of it. It continues to belong to him, or more accurately, he continues to belong to it. Yet we are not now talking about this calamity, for even among the better persons, it happens all too readily that the voice of conscience becomes merely one voice among many. Then it follows so easily that the isolated voice of conscience (as generally happens to a solitary one) becomes overruled -- by the majority. But in eternity, conscience is the only voice that is heard. It must be heard by the individual, for the individual has become the eternal echo of this voice. It must be heard. There is no place to flee from it. For in the infinite there is no place, the individual is himself the place. It must be heard. In vain the individual looks about for the crowd. Alas, it is as if there were a world between him and the nearest individual, whose conscience is also speaking to him about what *he* as an individual has spoken, and done, and thought of good and of evil.

Do you now live so that you are conscious of yourself as an individual; that in each of your relations in which you come into touch with the outside world, you are conscious of yourself, and that at the same time you are related to yourself as an individual? Even in these relations which we men so beautifully style the most intimate of all, do you remember that you have a still more intimate relation, namely, that in which you as an individual. are related to yourself before God? If you are bound to another human being by the holy bond of matrimony do you consider in this intimate relation that still more intimate relation in which you as an individual are related to yourself before God? The talk does not ask you whether you now love your wife: it hopes so; nor whether she is the apple of your eye and the desire of your heart: it wishes you this. It does not ask what you have done to make your wife happy, about how you both have arranged your household life, about what good advice you have been able to get from others, or what harmful influence others have had upon you. It does not ask whether your marital life is more commendable than that of many others, or whether it perhaps might be looked upon by some as a worthy example. No, the talk asks about none of these things. It asks you neither in congratulation, nor inquisitively, nor watchfully, nor apologetically, nor comparatively. It asks you only about the ultimate thing: whether you yourself are conscious of that most intimate relation to yourself as an individual. You do not carry the responsibility for your wife, nor for other men, nor by any comparative standard with other men, but only as an individual, before God, where it is not asked whether your marriage was in accordance with others, with the common practice, or better than others, but where you as an individual will be asked only whether it was in accordance with your responsibility as an individual. For common practice changes, and all comparison goes lame, or is only half truth. But eternity's practice, which never goes out of fashion, is, that you are the individual, that you yourself in the intimate relation of marriage should have been conscious of this.

In truth, it is not divorce that eternity is aiming at, neither is it divorce, that eternity does away with the difference between man and woman. Your wife will have no occasion to grieve because you are pondering this, your most intimate relation to God. And should she be so foolish as to desire for herself only that which is earthly or even foolish enough to desire as well to draw you down to the earthly: yet a woman's folly shall certainly not be able to change the law of eternity. In eternity it will not be asked whether your wife seduced you (eternity will talk with her about that), but simply as an individual you will be asked whether you allowed yourself to be seduced. If your marriage is so blessed that you see a family growing up around you, may you be conscious that while you have an intimate relation to your children you have a still more intimate relation to yourself as an individual. You share the responsibility with your wife, and hence eternity will also ask her as an individual about her share of the responsibility. For in eternity there is not a single complication that is able to make the accounting difficult and evasion easy. Eternity does not ask concerning how far you brought up your children in the way that you saw others do it. It simply asks you as an individual, how you brought up your children. It does not talk with you in the manner that you would talk with a friend in confidence. For alas, even this confidence can all too easily accustom you to evasions. For even the most trustworthy friend still speaks as a third person. And by much of such confidence, one easily gets used to speaking of himself as if he were a third person. But in eternity, you are the individual, and conscience when it talks with you is no third person, any more than you are a third person when you talk with conscience. For you and conscience are one. It knows all that you know, and it knows that you know it. With respect to your children's upbringing you can weigh various matters with your wife, or your friends. But how you act and the responsibility for it is finally wholly and solely yours as an individual. And if you fail to act, hiding from yourself and from others behind a screen of deliberation, you bring down the responsibility solely upon yourself as an individual.

Yes, in the temporal order where in all directions both this and that are asked about in the manifold complex complications of their reciprocal action, there one may rightly enough believe that it was a fantasy of the imagination, a chimera, that each one among these countless millions of people should be convinced accurately down to the least trifle of what his life consisted. But in eternity this is possible, because each becomes an individual. And this applies to every relation of your life.

If you do not live in some out-of-the-way place in the world, if you live in a populous city, and you direct your attention outwards, sympathetically engrossing yourself in the people and in what is going on, do you remember each time you throw yourself in this way into the world around you, that in this relation, you relate yourself to yourself as an individual with eternal responsibility? Or do you press yourself into the crowd, where the one excuses himself with the others, where at one moment there are, so to speak, many, and where in the next moment, each time that the talk touches upon responsibility, there is no one? Do you judge like the crowd, in its capacity as a crowd? You are not obliged to have an opinion about what you do not understand. No, on the contrary, you are eternally excused from that. But you are eternally responsible as an individual to render an account for your opinion, and for your judgment. And in eternity, you will not be asked inquisitively and professionally, as though by a newspaper reporter, whether there were many that had the same -- wrong opinion. You will be asked only whether you have held it, whether you have spoiled your soul by joining in this frivolous and thoughtless judging, because the others, because the many judged thoughtlessly. You will be asked only whether you may not have ruined the best within you by joining the crowd in its defiance, thinking that you were many and therefore you had the prerogative, because you were many, that is, because you were many who were wrong. In eternity it will be asked whether you may not have damaged a good thing, in order that you also might judge with them that did not know how to judge, but who possessed the crowd's strength, which in the temporal sense is significant but to which eternity is wholly indifferent.

You see, in the temporal order, a man counts and says: "One more or less, it makes no difference" -- and he applies this even to himself! In the temporal order a man counts and says: "One over against a hundred, after all what can come of that?" So he grows cowardly in the face of -- number. And numbers are usually false. Truth is content to be a unity. But a man wins something by this cowardly indulgence. He does not win a bed in a hospital. No, but he wins the amazing thing of becoming the strongest of all, because the crowd is always the strongest. Eternity, on the other hand, never counts. The individual is always only one and conscience in its meticulous way concerns itself with the individual. In eternity you will look in vain for the crowd. You will listen in vain to find whether you cannot hear where the noise and the gathering is, so that you may run to it. In eternity you, too, will be forsaken by the crowd. And this is terrifying. Yet in the temporal order to be forsaken by the crowd, provided that the Eternal comforts, may be something blessed, and the pain of it, a mere jest. What then in eternity will conscience demand of you by the consciousness that you are an individual? It will teach you that if you judge (for in very many cases it will restrain you from judging), you must bear the responsibility for your judgment. It will teach you that you should examine what you understand and what you do not understand as if you stood trembling in the presence of a departed one; it wishes to frighten you from resorting to the brilliant flights into wretchedness to which you are often subject. For many fools do not make a wise man, and the crowd is doubtful recommendation for a cause. Yes, the larger the crowd, the more probable that that which it praises is folly, and the more improbable that it is truth, and the most improbable of all that it is any eternal truth. For in eternity crowds simply do not exist. The truth is not such that it at once pleases the frivolous crowd -- and at bottom it never does; to such a multitude the truth must appear as simply absurd. But the man who, conscious of himself as an individual, judges with eternal responsibility, he is slow to pass judgment upon the unusual. For it is possible that it is falsehood and deceit and illusion and vanity. But it is also possible that it is true. He remembers the word of the simple sage of ancient times: "This, that a man's eye cannot see by the light by which the majority see could be because he is used to darkness; but it could also be because he is used to a still clearer light, and when this is so, it is no laughing matter."(Socrates in Plato's *Republic* VII. 518 A.)

No, it is no laughing matter, but it is laughable, or it is pitiable, that the frivolous ones laugh at a man because he is wiser or better than they. For even laughter calls for a reasonable ground, and when this is absent, the laughter becomes the very thing that is laughable. But here in the temporal order, in the midst of earth's appalling prodigality with human beings, here number tempts. It tempts a man to count, to count himself in with the crowd. Here, by the use of round numbers, everything can be manipulated with ease. Yes, here in the temporal order it is possible that no individual can ever succeed, even if it were true that he sincerely willed the Good, in dispersing the crowd. But eternity can do it. Eternity seizes each one by the strong arm of conscience, holding him as an individual. Eternity sets him apart with his conscience. Woe unto him, if he is left to this judge alone! For in that case eternity will set him apart with his conscience in that place where there is pressure, to be sure, but not as in the temporal order where the pressure is the excuse, yes, the victory. No, eternity places him where to be under pressure is to be alone, stripped of every excuse; to be alone and to be lost. The royal psalm singer says that: while the heathen clamor, God sits in his heaven and laughs at them.(Psalms 2:4) I dare not believe this. It would seem to be preferable to say that: while the crowd clamors and shouts and triumphs and celebrates; while one individual after another hastens to the place of tumult, where it is good to be if one is in search of oblivion and indulgence from that which is eternal; while at the same time the crowd shouts mockingly at God, "Yes, now see whether you can get hold of us"; yet since it is difficult in the rush of the crowd to distinguish the individual, difficult to see the single tree when one is looking at the wood, the sober countenance of eternity quietly waits. And if all the generations that have lived on earth rose up and gathered themselves in a single crowd in order to loose a storm against eternity, in order to coerce eternity by their colossal majority: eternity would scatter them as easily as the firmness of an immovable rock would scatter frothy scum; as easily as the wind when it rushes forward scatters chaff. Just as easily, but not in the same way. For the wind scatters the chaff, but then turns around and drifts it together again. Eternity scatters the crowd by giving each an infinite weight, by making him heavy -- as an individual. For what in eternity is the highest blessing is also the deepest seriousness. What, there, is the most blessed comfort, is also the most appalling responsibility.

In eternity there are chambers enough so that each may be placed alone in one. For wherever conscience is present, and it is and shall be present in each person, there exists in eternity a lonely prison, or the blessed chamber of salvation. On that account this consciousness of being an individual is the primary consciousness in a man, which is his eternal consciousness. But that man is slow to pass judgment who bears in mind, that he is an individual, and that the final and highest responsibility for the judgment rests solely upon him. For even the most trusted friend in passing judgment as an impartial observer must necessarily leave out what is crucial. To be the party directly concerned, the one to whom conscience in this affair speaks the intimate "thou," is another matter, for conscience only speaks this intimate "thou" to your friend in regard to the manner in which he is to give counsel. Such a thoughtful one does not willingly pass judgment on many things, and just this helps him to will only one thing. He thinks it is not altogether an advantage to live in a populous city where because of the swiftness of the means of communication almost everyone can easily have a hasty and superficial judgment about everything possible. On the contrary, he looks upon this easiness as a temptation and a snare and he learns earnestness in order as an individual to be concerned about his eternal responsibility.

"Even a fool might be a wise man if he could keep silent," says the proverb.(The Latin proverb "Tu si tacuisses, philosophus mansisses." See Boethius Consolatio philos. II. 17.) And this is so, not merely because then he would not betray his foolishness, but also because this self-control would help him to become conscious of himself as an individual, and would prevent him from adopting the crowd's opinion. Or if he had an opinion of his own, it would prevent him from hastening to get the crowd to adopt it. The one who is conscious of himself as an individual has his vision trained to look upon everything as inverted. His sense becomes familiar with eternity's true thought: that everything in this life appears in inverted form. The purely momentary, in the next moment, to say nothing of eternity, becomes nonsense and vanity: the fiery moment of lust (and what is so strong for the moment as lust!) is loathsome in memory; the fiery moment of anger, revenge, and passion whose gratification seems an irresistible impulse is horrible to remember. For the angry one, the vengeful one, the passionate one, thinks in the moment of passion that he revenges himself. But in the moment of remembrance, when the act of revenge comes back to him, he loathes himself, for he sees that precisely in that moment of revenge he lost himself. The purely momentary seems to be profitable. Yet in the next moment its deception becomes apparent and, eternally understood, calls for repentance. So it is with all things of the moment, and hence with the crowd's opinion or with membership in the crowd in so far as this opinion and this membership is a thing of the moment.

My listeners, do you at present live in such a way that you are yourself clearly and eternally conscious of being an individual? This was the question the address was to ask, or rather that you are to ask yourself, if you actively consider this occasion. The talk should not tell you only that which will disturb you, even though many are of the conviction that a man ought ever to live in such an aroused state of consciousness. Nor is it concerned how many or how few hold that conviction. The speaker will not attempt to win you to this conviction, even if he does as a rule hold it himself. He does not wish to force it upon you any more than you would desire to force it upon him if you were of this conviction. For the exalted earnestness of the Eternal wishes neither the commendation of the majority nor the commendation of eloquence. One thing alone the talk does not dare to promise you -- nor does it wish to insult you. It does not dare to promise you earthly gain if you enter upon and in dedication persevere in this conviction. On the contrary, if persevered in, it will make your life more taxing, and frequently perhaps wearisome. If persevered in, it may make you the target of others' ridicule, not to mention even greater sacrifices that perseverance might choose to require of you. Of course, the ridicule does not distract you if you continue to persist in your conviction. Ridicule will even be a help to you, in the sense that it is a further proof to you that you are on the right path. For the judgment of the crowd has its significance. One should not remain proudly ignorant of it, no, one should be attentive to it. If after this he sees to it that he does the opposite from the judgment of the crowd, then he, for the most part, does the right thing. Or if at the outset a man does the opposite, and he is then so fortunate as to have the judgment of the crowd express itself to the contrary, then he can be fairly certain that he has laid hold of the right thing. Then he has not only himself inwardly weighed and tested the conviction properly, but he has also the advantage of having it tested a second time by the help of ridicule. Ridicule may wound his feelings but just by that wound it shows that he is on the right path -- the path of honor and of victory, like a warrior's wound, when it is on the breast where both the wound and the badge of honor are to be borne.

You have surely noticed among schoolboys, that the one that is regarded by all as the boldest is the one who has no fear of his father, who dares to say to the others, "Do you think I am afraid of him?" On the other hand, if they sense that one of their number is actually and literally afraid of his father, they will readily ridicule him a little. Alas, in men's fear-ridden rushing together into a crowd (for why indeed does a man rush into a crowd except because he is afraid!) there, too, it is a mark of boldness not to be afraid, not even of God. And if someone notes that there is an individual outside the crowd who is really and truly afraid -- not of the crowd, but of God, he is sure to be the target of some ridicule. The ridicule is usually glossed over somewhat and it is said: a man should *love* God.

Yes, to be sure, God knows that man's highest consolation is that God is love and that man is permitted to love Him. But let us not become too forward, and foolishly, yes, blasphemously, dismiss the tradition of our fathers, established by God Himself: that really and truly a man should fear God. This fear is known to the man who is himself conscious of being an individual, and thereby is conscious of his eternal responsibility before God. For he knows, that even if he could with the help of evasions and excuses, get on well in this life, and even if he could by this shady path have gained the whole world, yet there is still a place in the next world where there is no more evasion than there is shade in the scorching desert.

The talk will not go into this further. It will only ask you again and again, do you now live so that you are conscious of being an individual and thereby that you are conscious of your eternal responsibility before God? Do you live in such a way that this consciousness is able to secure the time and quiet and liberty of action to penetrate every relation of your life? This does not demand that you withdraw from life, from an honorable calling, from a happy domestic life. On the contrary, it is precisely that consciousness which will sustain and clarify and illuminate what you are to do in the relations of life. You should not withdraw and sit brooding over your eternal accounting. To do this is to deserve something further to account for. You will more and more readily find time to perform your duty and your task, while concern over your eternal responsibility will hinder you from being "busy" and busily having a hand in everything possible -- an activity that can best be called: time-wasting.

Chapter 14: What Then Must I Do? Occupation and Vocation: Means and End

This was the principal question. For as only one thing is necessary, and as the theme of the talk is the willing of only one thing: hence the consciousness before God of one's eternal responsibility to be an individual is that one thing necessary. The talk now asks further, "*What is your occupation in life?*" The talk does not ask inquisitively about whether it is great or mean, whether you are a king or only a laborer. It does not ask, after the fashion of business, whether you earn a great deal of money or are building up great prestige for yourself. The crowd inquires and talks of these things. But whether your occupation is great or mean, is it of such a kind that you dare think of it together with the responsibility of eternity? Is it of such a kind that you dare to acknowledge it at this moment or at any time? Suppose that something terrible happened; suppose that the city in which you live suddenly perished like those cities in the far south, and everything came to rest, each one standing in his once-chosen occupation. But suppose this happened without the excuse of "being in practical harmony with the commonly accepted customs of his age," the excuse pronounced by a later generation, in order to shield you from disgrace! Or what is still more serious, suppose one of the most eminent dead, one whose memory the masses keep green, as is their custom, by noisy festivities and by shouting; suppose such a one should come to you. Suppose he visited you and that you there before him, before his piercing gaze, dared continue in your present occupation! Are you not used to thoughts of this kind? It is in just such a way that the transfigured one might well wish to serve after death: by visiting the individual. For it must certainly fill them with disgust if, in their blessed dwelling place, they should become aware that a frivolous crowd treats the transfigured dead as only a living fool could wish to be treated: paying them honor by noisemaking and hand-clapping. Do not think, that the transfigured one has become an aristocrat. On the contrary, he has become even more humble, more humanly sympathetic with each man. Hence when, like a superior official, he travels on his visits to individuals, he will not reject the meanest occupation, if it is truly honorable. Oh, in eternity where he dwells, all trivial differences are forgotten. But the transfigured one, like eternity, does not desire the crowd. He desires the individual. On that account, if you should ever be almost ashamed of your mean occupation, because, among the world's distinctions, it is so mean, the transfigured one's visit to you as an individual will give you the courage of frankness. The transfigured one's visit to you as an individual will give you that courage of frankness -- but what am I speaking of -- and if you actively consider the occasion of this talk, then you will stand as an individual before a still more exalted one who, none the less, thinks still more humanly -- about the meanness of the occupation, but also infinitely more purely about which occupation is truly honorable.

In your occupation, what is your attitude of mind? And how do you carry out your occupation? Have you made up your own mind that your occupation is your real calling so that you do not have to make explanation hinge on the result, maintaining that it was not your real calling if the results are not favorable, if your efforts do not succeed? Alas, such fickleness weakens a man immeasurably. Therefore persevere. By God's help and by your own faithfulness something good will come from the unpromising beginning. For there are beginnings everywhere, and there are good beginnings, where you begin with God; and no day is the wrong one to begin upon -- not even an unpromising one, if you begin with God. Or have you let yourself be deceived into regarding something as your calling because it turned out well, because it brought immediate success, perhaps even remarkable success? Alas, it is actually said in the world, often enough even by those who think they speak piously: "The proof that a man's occupation is the right one is that he is able to practice it." As if, because a man *could* so harden his heart that he could placidly practice all manner of cruelty, then this was what he ought to do. As if, because this brazen one could find the most hideous atrocity in his heart, and was able to carry it out, then this was the thing he ought to do. No, an unfavorable result can no more disprove the faithful man's conviction of what his calling should be, than a favorable result can of itself prove that he is in his proper calling.

Are you of one mind about the manner in which you will carry out your occupation, or is your mind continually divided because you wish to be in harmony with the crowd? Do you stand firmly behind your offer, not obstinately, not sullenly, but eternally concerned; do you continue unchanged to bid for the same thing and continue in your wish to buy the same thing even though the terms have been altered in a number of respects? Do you think that the Good is no different from gold, that it can be bought too dearly? Is there any profit you could not do without for the sake of the Good, any distinction you could not give up, any relation you could not renounce? Is there any stamp of approval from above that is any more important than this to you or perhaps some approbation from below? If you think that the Good must be bought at any price, then will you become envious when you see others buying for a lower price, that which you had to buy so dearly -- but which, and do not forget this, is worth any price? If your endeavor succeeds, are you then conscious that you are an unprofitable servant; so that the reward does not affect you, as though you became more useful because you got a reward; and adversity does not affect you, since it merely expresses, what you shamefacedly will admit -- that you have no right to claim anything? Hide nothing away suspiciously in your soul as though you still wished that it had happened differently, so that you might be able to pounce upon the reward as if it were prey, might be able to assume credit for it, might be able to point to it; as though you wished that adversity did not exist because it constrains the selfish thing in you that, even though repressed, foolishly makes you imagine that if you had luck with you, then you might do something for the Good, something that was worth talking about. Never forget that the devout wise man wishes no stroke of adversity to be taken away when it comes his way, because he cannot know whether or not it may be good for him. Never forget that the devout wise man wins his most beautiful of all victories, when the powerful one who had persecuted him wishes, so to speak, to release him, and the wise man replies: "I cannot unconditionally wish to be released, for I cannot know for certain that the persecution might not be good for me." Do you do good only out of fear of punishment, so that you scowl, even when you will the Good, so that in your dreams at night, you wish away the punishment and to that extent also the Good, and in your dreams by day imagine that one can with a slavish mind serve the Good? Oh, the Good is no difficult master, that wills one thing today, and another tomorrow. The Good always wishes one and the same thing. But it reckons with exactness and can be that which demands sincerity and can see whether it is present!

And now the means that you use. What means do you use in order to carry out your occupation? Are the means as important to you as the end, wholly as important? Otherwise it is impossible for you to will only one thing, for in that case the irresponsible, the frivolous, the self-seeking, and the heterogeneous means would flow in between in confusing and corrupting fashion. Eternally speaking, there is only one means and there is only one end: the means and the end are one and the same thing. There is only one end: the genuine Good; and only one means: this, to be willing only to use those means which genuinely are good -- but the genuine Good is precisely the end. In time and on earth one distinguishes between the two and considers that the end is more important than the means. One thinks that the end is the main thing and demands of one who is striving that he reach the end. He need not be so particular about the means. Yet this is not so, and to gain an end in this fashion is an unholy act of impatience. In the judgment of eternity the relation between the end and the means is rather the reverse of this.

If a man sets himself a goal for his endeavor here in this life, and he fails to reach it, then, in the judgment of eternity, it is quite possible that he may be blameless. Yes, he may even be worthy of praise. He might have been prevented by death, or by an adversity that is beyond his control: in which case he is entirely without blame. He might even have been prevented from reaching the goal just by being unwilling to use any other means than those which the judgment of eternity permits. In which case by his very renunciation of the impatience of passion and the inventions of cleverness, he is even worthy of praise. He is not, therefore, eternally responsible for whether he reaches his goal within this world of time. But without exception, he is eternally responsible for the kind of means he uses. And when he will only use or only uses those means which are genuinely good, then, in the judgment of eternity, he is at the goal. If reaching the goal should be the excuse and the defense for the use of illicit or questionable means -- alas, suppose he should die tomorrow. Then the clever one would be caught in his own folly. He had used illicit means, and he died before reaching the goal. For reaching the goal comes at the conclusion; but using the means comes at the beginning. Reaching the goal is like hitting the mark with his shot; but using the means is like taking aim. And certainly the aim is a more reliable indication of the marksman's goal than the spot the shot strikes. For it is possible for a shot to hit the mark by accident. The marksman may also be blameless if the shell does not go off. But no irregularities of the aim are permissible. To the temporal and earthly passion the end is unconditionally more important than the means. On that very account, it is the passionate one's torment, which if carried to its height must indeed make him sleepless and then insane, namely, that he has no control over time, and that he continually arrives too late, even if it was by merely half an hour. And what is still worse, since earthly passion is the rule, it can truthfully be said, that it is not wisdom which saves the worst ones from going insane, but indolence. On the other hand, the blessed comfort of the Eternal is like a refreshing sleep, is like "the cold of snow in the time of harvest" (Proverbs 25:13.) to the one who wills the Eternal. He whose means are invariably just as important as the end, never comes too late. Eternity is not curious and impatient as to what the outcome in this world of time will be. It is just because of this that the means are without exception as important as the end. To earthly and worldly passion, this observation must seem shocking and paralyzing. To it conscience must seem the most paralyzing thing of all. For conscience is indeed "a blushing innocent spirit that sets up a tumult in a man's breast and fills him with difficulties" just because to conscience the means are without exception as important as the end.

Therefore, my listeners, in the carrying out of your occupation, which we have assumed to be something good and honorable, are the means without exception as important to you as the end? Or have your thoughts become giddy until the greatness of the goal made you look upon illicit means as of negligible importance? Alas, this state of giddiness is to be found least of all in eternity, for eternity is clear and transparent! Do you think that the greatness of an achievement makes it unnecessary for it to ask about a trivial wrong, that is, do you think that a wrong might exist which would be something of no significance, although as an obligation it is infinitely more important than the greatest achievement! Do you think that it is immaterial the way in which a masterpiece is produced? Well, perhaps that might hold for a masterpiece. But do you think that the master dares to be unconcerned about whether he piously consecrates his powers in holy service, or whether by despair in the midst of glittering sins he simply produces -- a masterpiece?

And if the thought does not make you giddy, if you are sober and alert, are you particular in every respect in your use of the means? If a youth (and he is also a blushing and innocent spirit) should turn to you, do you dare without exception to let him know all? In your whole conduct is there not something, yes, how shall I express it, I could describe it at length but I would rather put it briefly in this fashion: is there not something, of which you could be fairly certain that the older people and those of your own age would almost admire for its cleverness and ingenuity if you told them of it, but which, strangely enough, a youth would blush over (not over your being so clever, but over your not being big enough to despise acting so cleverly)? Perhaps it is by flattery that you had won over this person and that, by concealing something, won this or that advantage, by a little untruth made a glittering trade, by a false union promoted your cause. Perhaps you had won the victory by allying yourself with admiration based upon a misunderstanding, had won riches and power by clever scheming to enter into the smartest combination. In your whole conduct, open and secret, is there not something that you would not for any price consent to let a youth discover (and it is beautiful that you love the youth so much and wish to guard his purity!)? Is there not something -- against yourself -- that you can still be willing to admit yourself to be guilty of? Something that you would not for any price confide to a youth? Yet, as I have told you, if you actively consider the occasion of this talk, then you stand before a higher judge, who judges infinitely more purely than the purest innocence of youth; a judge, that you will not out of indulgence let into the secret of your guilt, for He already knows you.

And what is your attitude toward others? Are you at one with all -- by willing only one thing? Or do you contentiously belong to a party, or is your hand raised against every man and every man's hand raised against you? Do you wish for all others what you wish for yourself, or do you desire the highest thing of all for you and yours, or do you desire that that which you and yours desire shall be the highest thing of all? Do you do unto others what you will that they should do unto you -- by willing only one thing? For this will is the eternal order that governs all things, that brings you into union with the dead, and with the men whom you never see, with foreign people whose language and customs you do not know, with all men upon the whole earth, who are related to each other by blood and eternally related to the Divine by eternity's task of willing only one thing. Do you wish, that there should be another law for you and yours than for the others? Do you wish to find your consolation in something other than that in which each man without exception may and shall find consolation?

Suppose that sometime a king and a beggar and a man like yourself should come to you. In their presence would you dare frankly to confess that that which you desire in the world, in which you sought your consolation, certain that the king in his majesty would not despise you even though you were a man of inferior rank; certain that the beggar would not go away envious that he could not have the same consolation; certain that the man like yourself would be pleased by your frankness? Alas, there is something in the world called clannishness. It is a dangerous thing because all clannishness is divisive. It is divisive when clannishness shuts out the common citizen, and when it shuts out the nobleborn, and when it shuts out the civil servant. It is divisive when it shuts out the king, and when it shuts out the beggar, and when it shuts out the wise man, and when it shuts out the simple soul. For all clannishness is the enemy of universal humanity. But to will only one thing, genuinely to will the Good, as an individual, to will to hold fast to God, which things each person without exception is capable of doing, this is what unites. And if you sat in a lonely prison far from all men, or if you were placed out upon a desert island with only animals for company, if you genuinely will the Good, if you hold fast to God, then you are in unity with all men. And if the terrible thing happened (for religious edification should not, like a woman's finery be intended for a splendid moment) that you were buried alive, if, as you awakened in the coffin you seized upon your accustomed consolation, then even in this lonely torment, you would be in unity with all men. Is this your present attitude? Have you no special privilege, no special talent, none of life's special favors that, either separately or in company with some others, vanity has led you to take, so that you could console yourself by means of it, and that makes you dare not tell the uninitiated the source of your consolation? Thus you give alms to the poor man so that he can console himself, but treacherously you have a further consolation for yourself. To be sure, you give a consolation for poverty, but you console yourself by the fact that your wealth assures you against ever becoming poor. You help to set the simple ones right, but treacherously you have a further consolation for yourself; your talent is so outstanding, that it could never happen that when you awakened tomorrow you were the stupidest person in all the land. You wish to instruct the youth, but you do not have the heart to take him into your confidence, because you have a secret of your own, because you are a traitor who deceived youth as to what was the highest thing of all by your secret, and deceived yourself as to what was the highest thing of all -- by your secret!

And now a question concerning the sufferer. It is not a question of the state of his health. No, the talk is not sympathetic in this respect. Oh, but if you actively consider the occasion of this talk, then by being in the presence of God you would raise yourself above human sympathy. Then you would no longer pine wretchedly for sympathy. For although it happens all too seldom, if this could properly be proved to you, as you may well wish that it might, then with cheerful frankness you could give thanks for it. You would not give thanks bent over like a beggar -- God would prevent that. And if sympathy is denied you, if a man is afraid, and in a selfish and cowardly manner avoids, yes, almost loathes you because he does not dare to think of your suffering, then you should be able to do without sympathy. You should not feel bitter over this lack of sympathy -- God will take care of that. The talk asks you then, or you ask yourselves by means of the talk, whether you now live in such a way that you truthfully will only one thing. It is not the intention of the talk to presume to judge of this, far from it. The talk judges no one. Even the Holy Scriptures have an especially tender love for the unfortunate ones. Indeed it is particularly appropriate for a devotional meditation to concern itself principally with the sufferer, just as one in the world addresses the powerful man, the distinguished man. The talk does not ask inquisitively and busily about the name of your particular suffering, about how many years it has continued, about what the doctor or the pastor thinks, how much earthly hope they give you. Alas, out of vanity, sufferings, too, can in this fashion be taken as a mark of distinction that draws the attention of others to oneself.

So on that account, see that you question yourself by means of the talk. If the sufferer talks to himself in private, asks himself which kind of life he leads, whether he truthfully wills only one thing: then he is not tempted to relate in detail what he himself knows best of all, he is not tempted to compare. For all comparison injures. Yes, it is evil. Do you at present genuinely will only one thing? You know that if the only reason you will but one thing is that by this, and by this alone, you will be set free from suffering, then you do not genuinely will but one thing. But even if you could so dull yourself that the wish would die out, so that you could sever the wish's painful tie with that happier sense of being a man, of loving to live, of loving to be a happy one, still you would fail to will only one thing. What at present is your condition in suffering? The doctor and the pastor ask about your health, but eternity makes *you* responsible for your condition. Is it so that it does not frivolously or superstitiously fluctuate in a fever of impatience? Is it so that it is not a dismally sluggish painlessness? Or is it so that you are willing to suffer all and let the Eternal comfort you? As time goes by, how does your condition change? Did you begin well perhaps but become more and more impatient? Or perhaps you were impatient at the beginning, but learned patience from what you suffered? Alas, perhaps year after year your suffering remained unchanged, and if it did change, then its description would be a matter for the doctor or the pastor. Alas, perhaps the unaltered monotony of the suffering seems to you like a creeping death. But while the doctor and the pastor and your friend know of no change to speak of, yet the talk asks you whether under the pressure of the unchanged monotony an infinite change is taking place. Not a change in the suffering (for even if it is changed, it can only be a finite change), but in you, an infinite change in you from good to better. If the talk were to characterize your altered condition through the years, would it dare use the words of the Apostle and say of your life of unaltered suffering: "Suffering taught him patience, patience taught him experience, experience taught him hope?"(Romans 5:3-4.) Would the talk dare say at your grave: "He won that hope that shall never be put to shame"? At your grave, instead of mumbling a prayer of thanks that the sufferer is dead as was described earlier, would the talk dare freely and wholeheartedly to say, as though at a hero's grave, "The content of his life was suffering, yet his life has put many to shame"? For in eternity there will be as little asked about your suffering as about the king's purple, precisely as little. In eternity you as an individual will only be asked about your faith and about your faithfulness. There will be absolutely no asking about whether you were entrusted with much or little, whether you were given many talents of silver to work with or whether you were given a hundred-pound weight to carry. But you will be asked only about your faith and about your faithfulness. In the world of time one asks in other terms. Here one inquires especially about how high a command a man has, and when it is a very high one, then one forgets in one's worldly astonishment to ask after his faithfulness. But if it is very little, then one prefers to hear nothing at all about him, neither about his burden nor his faithfulness. Eternity asks solely about faithfulness, and with equal earnestness it asks this of the king and of the most wretched of all sufferers. It is no excuse to be entrusted with little, nor is it any answer to the question that asks exclusively about faithfulness, the question, which in the eternal mercy knows that sufferings can tempt a man, but knows, too, that they can be a guide. For "sorrow is better than laughter; for by the sadness of the countenance, the heart is made better" (Ecclesiastes 7:3). This is the change that eternity asks about, not about the unchangeableness of the suffering. This is what eternity asks; and if you yourself actively consider the occasion of this talk, then you will ask yourself about this matter. If the change has not taken place, then this question of whether it has truthfully been done will indeed be helpful to you in bringing about the change. For human sympathy, no matter how painstakingly it inquires about you, cannot by all its questioning alter the fixed character of the suffering. Eternity's question, if you put it truthfully to yourself before God, contains the possibility of change. But I am talking almost as if I meant to edify you. Yet out of respect for you, the talk would be embarrassed to press this question upon you. You yourself know best of all, that if you put this question, then you must render an account of whether you are living in this way at present.

Chapter 15: Conclusion: Man and the Eternal

This was the issue of the talk. But now if the individual, yes, if you, my listener, and I must admit to ourselves that we were far from living in this way, far from that purity of heart which truthfully wills but one thing; must admit to ourselves that the questions demanded an answer, and yet in another sense, in order to avoid any deception, did not require an answer, in that they were, if anything, charges against ourselves which in spite of the form of the question changed themselves into an accusation: then should the individual, and you, my listener, and I join together in saying, "Indeed our life is like that of most others"? How, then, shall we begin over again, at this time, and once more speak of the evasion which consists of being among the many? For where there are many, there is externality, and comparison, and indulgence, and excuse and evasion. Shall we, even after we have come to understand the calamity of this evasion, in the end take refuge in it? Shall we console ourselves with a common plight? Alas, even in the world of time, a common plight is a doubtful consolation; and in eternity there is no common plight. In eternity, the individual, yes, you, my listener, and I as individuals will each be asked solely about himself as an individual, and about the individual details in his life. If in this talk I have spoken poorly, then you will not be asked about that, my listener; nor will any man from whom I may have learned. For if he has stated it falsely, then he will be questioned about that and I will be made to answer for having learned from another what was false. Nor will any with whom I have had an acquaintance be made to answer. For if his acquaintance was corrupting, then he will be questioned about that, but I shall be made to answer for having sought out or not having avoided his acquaintance, and for letting myself become corrupted. No, if I have spoken poorly and just in so far as I have spoken poorly, then without any excuse whatsoever I, as an individual, will be questioned about that. For in eternity there is not the remotest thought of any common plight. In eternity, the individual, yes, you, my listener, and I as individuals will each be asked solely about himself as an individual and about the individual details in his life.

If it should so happen that in this talk, I have spoken the truth, then I shall be questioned no further about this matter. There will be no questioning as to whether I have won men (quite on the contrary, it might well be asked whether I had any notion of having by my own efforts done the least thing toward winning them); no questioning as to whether, by the talk I have gained some earthly advantage (quite on the contrary, it might well be asked whether I had any notion of having myself done the least thing toward gaining it); no questioning about what results I have produced, or whether I may have produced no results at all, or whether loss and the sport that others made of me were the only results I have produced. No, eternity will release me from one and all of such foolish questions.

In the world of time a man can be confused, for he does not know which is which: which question is the serious one and which the silly one, especially since the silly one is heard a thousand times to the serious question's once. Eternity, on the other hand, can admirably distinguish between them; yet it is obvious that the thing does not become easier on that account. The seriousness of the plight is only intensified. For in eternity there is not the remotest thought of any common plight. In eternity, the individual, yes, you, my listener, and I as individuals will each be asked solely about himself as an individual, and about the individual details in his life. If it should happen that a true reflection of life is contained in this talk, if it is so that the ability and the occasion is vouchsafed me which enabled me to set it forth; yet it may also have happened, we can suppose such a case, that the circumstances under which it had to be spoken did not seem favorable. If this were so, then eternity would not inquisitively enter into any long-drawn-out discourse about circumstances. Had I remained silent, eternity would hold me as an individual to account. For in the world of time, when the task is to be clever for one's own advantage, when worldly cleverness judges and criticizes, then unfavorable circumstances are not only a ground for silence, but silence becomes admired as cleverness; while favorable circumstances are an invitation for all to join in the conversation. On the other hand, in the eternal order, if the circumstances are difficult the obligation to speak is doubled. The difficulty is precisely an invitation. Eternally, the individual will only be asked whether he knew that they were unfavorable, and whether in this event he dared remain silent and therefore by his silence, yes, to use the proverb, by his consent, he had as an individual contributed to a condition where the circumstances became still more unfavorable for the truth. Eternally, circumstances will provide neither hiding place nor evasion for him, for he will be asked as an individual, and the difficulty of the circumstances will stand against him as a double accusation. As for remaining silent, it is not as with sleeping that he who sleeps does not sin. For in the world the individual has brought the most atrocious guilt upon himself -- through remaining silent. The fault was not that he did not manage to get the circumstances changed. The fault was that he was silent not out of discretion, which is silent when it is proper to be silent, but out of cleverness, which is silent because it is the most prudent to be so.

But what, then, shall we do, if the questions sound like accusations? Above all else, each one will himself become an individual with his responsibility to God. Each one will himself be subject to the stern judgment of this individuality. Is this not the purpose of the office of Confession? For just as little as in that silent churchyard the multitude of dead make up a society," so little does the multitude of those coming to confess make up a society -- for not even the king goes to confession alone in order to escape the common company of others. Those who are coming to confess do not belong together in a society. Each one is an individual before God. Man and wife may go to confession in beautiful fellowship with each other, but they may not confess together. The one who confesses is not in company, he is as an individual, alone before God. And if, as an individual he admits to himself that the questions, which by the help of an insignificant one's whisper he puts to himself, are accusations, then he confesses. For one does not confess merits and achievements, he confesses sins. When one confesses, he sees at once that he has no merits. He sees that merits and achievements are fantasies and sense deceptions that are at home where one moves about in the crowd and engages others in conversation. He sees that it is just on this account that the one who never himself becomes an individual is easily tempted to consider himself a most meritorious man. But the purpose of the office of Confession is certainly not to make a man conscious of himself as an individual at the moment of its celebration, and then for the rest of the time to allow him to live outside this consciousness. On the contrary, in the moment of confession itself he should give account as to how he has lived as an individual. If the same consciousness were not demanded of him for daily use, then the demand of the office of Confession is a self-contradiction. It is as if one now and then demanded of a humble man that he should render account to himself and to God of how he had lived as a king -- he that had never been a king. And so it is to ask of a man that he shall render account of his life as an individual when one allows him to lead his life outside this consciousness.

My listener! Do you remember now, how this talk began? Let me call it back to your remembrance. It is true that the temporal order has its time; but the Eternal shall always have time. If this should not happen within a man's life, then the Eternal comes again under another name, and once again shall always have time. This is repentance. And since at present no man's life is lived in perfection, but each one in frailty, so Providence has given man two companions for his journey, the one calls him forward, the other calls him back. But the call of repentance is always at the eleventh hour. Therefore confession is always at the eleventh hour, but not in the sense of being precipitate. For confession is a holy act, which calls for a collected mind. A collected mind is a mind that has collected itself from every distraction, from every relation, in order to center itself upon this relation to itself as an individual who is responsible to God. It is a mind that has collected itself from every distraction, and therefore also from all comparison. For comparison may either tempt a man to an earthly and fortuitous despondency because the one who compares must admit to himself that he is behind many others, or it may tempt him to pride because, humanly speaking, he seems to be ahead of many others.

A new expression of the true extremity of the eleventh hour comes when the penitent has withdrawn himself from every relation in order to center himself upon his relation to himself as an individual. By this he becomes responsible for every relation in which he ordinarily stands, and he is outside of any comparison.

The more use one makes of comparison, the more it seems that there is still plenty of time. The more a man makes use of comparison, the more indolent and the more wretched his life becomes. But when all comparison is relinquished forever then a man confesses as an individual before God -- and he is outside any comparison, just as the demand which purity of heart lays upon him is outside of comparison. Purity of heart is what God requires of him and the penitent demands it of himself before God. Yes, it is just on this account that he confesses his sins. And heavy as the way and the hour of the confession may be, yet the penitent wins the Eternal. He is strengthened in the consciousness that he is an individual, and in the task of truthfully willing only one thing. This consciousness is the strait gate sand the narrow way. For it is not this narrow way that the many take, following one after another. No, this straitness means rather that each must himself become an individual, that through this needle's eyes he must press forward to the narrow way where no comparison cools, but yet where no comparison kills with its insidious cooling. The broad way, on the other hand, is broad because so many travel upon it. The crowd's way is always broad. There the poisonous ornamental flower of excuses is found in bloom. The inviting hiding places of evasion are there. There comparison wafts its cooling breath of air. This way leadeth not unto life.

Only the individual can truthfully will the Good, and even though the penitent toils heavily not merely in the eleventh hour of confession, with all the questions standing as accusations of himself, but also in their daily use in repentance, yet the way is the right one. For he is in touch with the demand that calls for purity of heart by willing only one thing.

If you, my listener, unquestionably know much more concerning the office of Confession than has been set forth here; if you know the next thing that follows upon the confession of sins, still this extended talk has not been in vain if it has made you pause, made you pause before something that you already know well, you, who know so much more. But do not forget, that the most terrible thing of all is to "live on, deceived, not by what one might expect to be deceived (alas, and on that account horribly deceived) but deceived by too much knowledge." Consider that in these times it is a particularly great temptation for speakers to leave the individual as quickly as possible in order to get as much as possible said, so that nobody might suspect that the speaker did not know what every man in a Christian country knows. Alas, only God knows how the individual, knows it. But what does it profit a man if he goes further and further and it must be said of him: he never stops going further; when it also must be said of him: there was nothing that made him pause? For pausing is not a sluggish repose. Pausing is also movement. It is the inward movement of the heart. To pause is to deepen oneself in inwardness. But merely going further is to go straight in the direction of superficiality. By that way one does not come to will only one thing. Only if at some time he decisively stopped going further and then again came to a pause, as he went further, only then could he will only one thing. For purity of heart was to will one thing.

Father in Heaven! What is a man without Thee! What is all that he knows, vast accumulation though it be, but a chipped fragment if he does not know Thee! What is all his striving, could it even encompass the world, but a half-finished work if he does not know Thee: Thee the One, who art one thing and who art all! So may Thou give to the intellect, wisdom to comprehend that one thing; to the heart, sincerity to receive this understanding; to the will, purity that wills only one thing. In prosperity may Thou grant perseverance to will one thing; amid distractions, collectedness to will one thing; in suffering, patience to will one thing. Oh, Thou that giveth both the beginning and the completion, may Thou early, at the dawn of day, give to the young man the resolution to will one thing. As the day wanes, may Thou give to the old man a renewed remembrance of his first resolution, that the first may be like the last, the last like the first, in possession of a life that has willed only one thing. Alas, but this has indeed not come to pass. Something has come in between. The separation of sin lies in between. Each day, and day after day something is being placed in between: delay, blockage, interruption, delusion, corruption. So in this time of repentance may Thou give the courage once again to will one thing. True, it is an interruption of our daily tasks; we do lay down our work as though it were a day of rest, when the penitent (and *it* is only in a time of repentance that the heavy-laden worker may be quiet in the confession of sin) is alone before Thee in self-accusation. This is indeed an interruption. But it is an interruption that searches back into its very beginnings that it might bind up anew that which sin has separated, that in its grief it might atone for lost time, that in its anxiety it might bring to completion that which lies before it. Oh, Thou that givest both the beginning and the completion, give Thou victory in the day of need so that what neither a man's burning wish nor his determined resolution may attain to, may be granted unto him in the sorrowing of repentance: to will only one thing.

9 789358 480511

Printed at Repro India Ltd.